THE Quarterlifer's Companion

THE Quarterlifer's Companion

HOW TO GET ON THE RIGHT CAREER PATH, CONTROL YOUR FINANCES, AND FIND THE SUPPORT NETWORK YOU NEED TO THRIVE

Abby Wilner and Catherine Stocker

McGraw-Hill

New York | Chicago | San Francisco | Lisbon
London | Madrid | Mexico City | Milan | New Delhi
San Juan | Seoul | Singapore | Sydney | Toronto

The McGraw-Hill Companies

1 2 3 4 5 6 7 8 9 0 DOC/DOC 0 9 8 7 6 5

ISBN 0-07-145015-7

McGraw-Hill books are available at special quantity discounts to use as premiums and sales promotions, or for use in corporate training programs. For more information, please write to the Director of Special Sales, Professional Publishing, McGraw-Hill, Two Penn Plaza, New York, NY 10121-2298. Or contact your local bookstore.

This book is printed on recycled, acid-free paper containing a minimum of 50% recycled, de-inked fiber.

Library of Congress Cataloging-in-Publication Data

Wilner, Abby.

The quarterlifer's companion : how to get on the right career path, control your finances, and find the support network you need to thrive / Abby Wilner and Catherine Stocker.

p. cm.

Includes bibliographical references and index.

ISBN 0-07-145015-7 (alk. paper)

1. Young adults—United States—Life skills guides. 2. College graduates—United States—Life skills guides. I. Stocker, Catherine. II. Title.

HQ799.7.W56 2005

646.7'0084'2—dc22

2005010696

To my one and only Ben,
the ultimate life companion.—AW

To Rick, for all of your
constant support.—CW

CONTENTS

ACKNOWLEDGMENTS

We would like to thank:

Dan Mandel, our hero, for putting up a good fight.

Mary Glenn and Melissa Scuereb at McGraw-Hill for believing in our quarterlife mission, and Jane Palmieri and Barbara Coates for all your hard work and patience.

Our husbands, for letting us spend more time with each other than with them when we were under deadline.

Our parents, for making our QLCs possible.

Our siblings and friends, for always keeping us real.

Our star moderators, for keeping a watchful eye.

The quarterlife community, for its input and support.

Our panel of experts, for donating its wisdom.

Each other, for making this dream a reality.

Abby would especially like to thank Ben, Esther, Elliot, Ellona and Gus; Tammy and Will; Robin and Dan; Dave Singleton; Jen ZuWalick; Phil Kaplan;

JBL Associates; Paul Hettich; Courtney Macavinta and the Chicks who Click; Julie Murphree; Elizabeth DuPont Spencer; Ed Pennington; Andrea Bonior; Alexandra Levit; Amy Joyce; Jon Horowitz; Cathy Alter; Marty Bryant; Madeline Dolente; Honore Ervin; Harlan Cohen; Melissa Fireman; Donna Fisher; Wendie White; and Blake Newman.

Cathy would especially like to thank Rick, Jack, Mom and Dad; Tom and Brian; Colette and Elizabeth; Pat, Tom, David, Meg, and Meggan; The Jack Brigade: Kathi, Terry, Priscilla, and Delia Aguilar; all of our friends who provided so much help, input, and encouragement; Tom Gardner; Donna Fisher; Tom Morgano; Stuart Schearer; Margarita Rozenfeld; Sean Covey; Patricia Rose; Melissa Fireman; Amy Joyce; Josh Aiello; Jason Wilmett; Jon Horowitz; the Hatch columnists; Brad Tuttle; Laurel Donnellan; and Christina Saraceno.

INTRODUCTION

State of the Twentysomething Union

Quarterlife Crisis: The Unique Challenges of Life in Your Twenties identified and explored the phenomenonof the quarterlife crisis (QLC): the significant and often turbulent transition to adulthood that many twentysomethings experience. The book was based on interviews with recent graduates who were experiencing difficulty transitioning to the real world and shared their anecdotes about their quarterlife crises. They also shared some of the wisdom acquired from experiencing and solving their QLC-related dilemmas.

We learned from feedback about the book and its Web site (www.quarterlifecrisis.com) that anxiety and depression are fairly common among twentysomethings and that, for many, this is the first time in their lives they are experiencing these symptoms. They are not used to feeling lost. They are not used to feeling in need of an instruction manual. But mostly, they think they are alone in feeling this way.

Clearly, they are not alone. *Quarterlife Crisis* and the personal stories found there received an overwhelming response. The Web site receives thousands of hits per day from those seeking guidance and advice from fellow twentysomethings and, perhaps most importantly, we continue to receive positive feedback from our readers.

The Demand for More

After two years of talking and listening to twentysomethings, we realized that recognizing and explaining the quarterlife crisis was just our first step in helping twentysomethings. Now that people know about the quarterlife crisis, they want to know what they can do to move through and beyond it. The following quotes are representative of the comments and questions that we receive every day:

> "I was wondering if the authors plan to write a follow up book or even make some suggestions for further reading on how to be better prepared in the real world." —Brooke, Austin, TX

> "Thank you immeasurably for bringing this phenomenon to people's attention. I truly believe you've uncovered something very real, and I hope it can help others as much as it has me."—Renee S., New York, NY

Why We Need This Book

Every day, we receive e-mails from readers and Web site visitors like those above, asking us for affordable solutions. We never intended to offer solutions in the first book; we were simply acknowledging and describing the problem. Readers are thankful to know that the quarterlife crisis is indeed a common phenomenon. But now that we have had a chance to interact with twentysomethings, explore their symptoms, and test solutions, it is time to offer twentysomethings a comprehensive and accessible guidebook to their quarterlife crisis. We'd like to help twentysomethings eat their greens—and make some too!

WHAT'S NEW?

Since the first book, we have experienced the burst of the dot-com bubble, September 11, the war on terrorism, and scandals that rocked the public's faith in corporate America. No longer are recent graduates being wooed with $100,000 starting salaries and stock option packages. In fact, recent graduates are settling for much less glamorous job offers and living at home for a longer period of time before moving out on their own. In general our society has seen a lack of loyalty. Employers don't invest in employees anymore through mentorship programs, and whether that's a cause or result of job-hopping, paying your dues and climbing the corporate ladder have become the exception rather than the rule. Graduates are more in debt, owing money for student loans and maxed-out credit cards. Because the economy soured, twentysomethings took the first jobs that they could get and did not have the luxury of figuring out what jobs were really right for them. As a result, even more twentysomethings are in jobs that make them miserable. Although the economy seems to be shaping up, this major life transition has always been and will remain a significant one for as long as people make the move from school to work.

Twentysomethings are in need of practical answers not only to their career questions, but also to their questions about debt, loans, credit, insurance, and rent.

According to Robert Dupont, coauthor of *The Anxiety Cure*, the twenties are the most common onset age for many psychological disorders, such as anxiety, depression, addiction, and obsessive-compulsiveness. Twentysomethings often feel alone, hopeless, helpless, and overwhelmed. They experience constant change and a lack of stability as they go through this major life transition. Here are just some of the reasons why.

- **Job-Hopping**. The average person now goes through eight jobs before the age of 32 (Bureau of Labor Statistics).
- **Loans.** The average student owes $15,000 after graduation (U.S. Department of Education, National Center for Education). According to our research, 74 percent are in debt and most owe over $10,000 in either loans or credit card debt, or both.
- **Competition.** There are more college graduates than ever today, and it is tough to find a job that is fulfilling and also pays the rent. It doesn't help that the job search process has become less personal and communicative as a result of posting and searching for jobs online.
- **New Job Options.** Most graduates feel unprepared to choose from the multitude of new job options such as those in technology. Students are no longer traveling down the clear-cut career path that our parents' generation did.
- **Rent.** Housing costs, especially in big cities, are growing to outrageous levels. In 2000, 17.8 million adults aged 18 to 34 were living at home—twice as many than 30 years earlier (U.S. Census).
- **Health Care.** Many twentysomethings are uninsured because they are unemployed, in between jobs, temping or working part-time, or simply did not inquire as to whether they'd be covered at their job interviews. According to our health insurance survey conducted in 2003, which received over 2,500 responses, 35 percent are not insured through an employer.
- **Education**. In addition to housing and health care, education costs are growing at higher rates than other sectors and increasing faster than income, especially in urban areas. Not only are recent grads in debt because of undergraduate

loans, but many are unable to further their careers by attending graduate school without the guarantee that a higher-paying job will make up for that cost.

- **The Media.** While we don't expect entertainment to portray "real" life, twentysomethings see very few examples of what their lives are like—sometimes really lonely and sometimes seemingly insignificant. Reality TV doesn't help. Now that twentysomethings go from entry level to executive suite in a TV series time span, quarterlifers feel even more like losers if they are still plugging away at the bottom of the corporate ladder.
- **Delayed Marriage and Family Life.** The average age to get married is now 27; people are more cautious and looking for more fulfillment because of the high divorce rate we witnessed as kids. Unmarried cohabitation rose from just over 500,000 in 1970 to over 5 million in 2000 (U.S. Census).
- **The Stigma.** Because the quarterlife crisis has never been acknowledged before, and prior generations did not experience their twenties in the same way, people think that there is something wrong with them if their twenties are not completely easy and carefree. The twenties are fun, yes, but people need to realize it is okay to experience anxiety, and even depression.

Now we'll review the basics for you, in case you skipped the first book, or just need a refresher.

WHAT IS A QUARTERLIFE CRISIS?

Essentially, the quarterlife crisis is a state of confusion and uncertainty that accompanies the transition to adulthood.

According to William Bridges' perennial bestseller, *Transitions*, a transition is defined as:

1. An ending, followed by
2. A period of confusion and distress, leading to
3. A new beginning

For the recent graduate, the ending is life as a student or a dependent. The period of confusion and distress comprises quarterlife challenges such as finding a job, a place to live, and a new social life. And the new beginning is your newly established identity as an adult.

When the freshly minted recent grad is not prepared to face real-world challenges following school, the resulting insecurity, instability, and volatility can develop negatively into a state of anxiety or depression. Particularly when twentysomethings keep these feelings inside, and thus do not realize the universality of their experiences, does the stress become even harder to manage.

In school, whether high school or college, you knew "the game." You knew how to succeed and what to do next. But it is almost impossible to know what you will enjoy or succeed at in the real world without trying things out first. In school you feel that you know and can trust those around you, while in the real world, it is not as easy or safe to meet new people. In school, you are used to being on seasonal breaks more often than not, while in the working world you are lucky to start out with two weeks of vacation a year. In college in particular, you have an abundance of unstructured time with an average of three hours of class a day. It is easy to find time for personal errands and social activities when you are not sitting in an office for at least eight hours a day. However, once they enter the real world, recent graduates are overwhelmed by additional financial responsibilities and less time for socializing. And while in school, you can usually count on family to provide you with health insurance and meals and to fill out your tax returns. Once you are an adult, you are expected to figure things out on your own, since most schools are resistant to providing any practical, life-skills education.

The factors that lead to the quarterlife crisis are not going away. In fact, they are increasing—and people are paying attention. The term *quarterlife crisis*, originally coined by Abby Wilner after she graduated from college in 1997, continues to appear in feature articles around the globe and now appears in several dictionaries.

Since the release of the book *Quarterlife Crisis* in 2001, a crop of new literature for twentysomethings in transition has entered the market. The term *quarterlife crisis* has appeared in movie and book reviews to describe characters and in a well-known song by John Mayer. It's even the title of a one-man show in Australia. Clearly, the quarterlife crisis is here to stay.

To help you better understand your own feelings and whether or not a quarterlife crisis is happening to you or to a friend or colleague, the following examples may help.

QUARTERLIFE TYPOLOGY

The classic quarterlifer is out of or unhappy at work, may be living with his or her parents, and goes on one miserable date after another. Generally it takes two or three jobs to find a good fit. There are some variations, however, on the typical QLC experience:

- **Delayed quarterlifer—Had a career mapped out upon graduation with a plan to retire by 40. The delayed quarterlifer does not question his or her identity or career choices until several years later than the classic quarterlifer.**
- **Postponing quarterlifer—Heads immediately back to school, decides the real world isn't for him, yet. The postponing quarterlifer can be hit by a quarterlife crisis when he discovers that graduate school does not solve all of his problems.**

- Reawakening quarterlifer—Reassesses values and life choices. The reawakening quarterlifer may decide to start teaching or leave a lucrative consulting job to join the Peace Corps.
- Overachieving quarterlifer—Works 80-hour weeks or dives right into family life; burnt out by 30 and may join the delayed quarterlifer in reassessing career options later.
- Dropout quarterlifer—Won't leave campus, won't get a nine-to-five job, bartends at the local hangout to relive his glory days and still goes out drinking every night. Just like the postponing quarterlifer, the dropout quarterlifer is only delaying his quarterlife crisis.
- Risk-taking quarterlifer—Takes the unexpected road and backpacks around the globe or takes a cool job working on a movie set; has an enviable social life living in a group house in the edgy yet up-and-coming part of town. The risk-taking quarterlifer worries that sooner or later she will have to give it all up and is trying to fit in the dream while she can.

No matter what your situation, we aim to make you the:

- Relaxed quarterlifer—Expecting difficulties, enjoying the exploration.

When you come across a particularly challenging situation and consider the various options, just think to yourself: *What would the relaxed QLCer do?*

QUARTERLIFE CRISIS STAGES

The quarterlife crisis varies by life stage. Immediately following graduation from high school or college, the typical recent graduate panics and thinks about short-term goals, whereas a young professional who is a few years out of school might be thinking more long term.

- **Stage I—Real World Rehearsal.** During Stage I, approximately ages 18–22 (depending on whether you transition from high school or college to the real world) there is no sense of urgency to take lifetime decisions seriously. At this point, you still have the excuse that you are a recent graduate.
- **Stage II—Exploration and Discovery.** By this period, during ages 23–26, you feel more pressure to find both a career and a relationship to settle down with for the rest of your life.
- **Stage III—Inside Out.** You are finding your role in the big picture, usually ages 27–32. At this point, you may question choices you've made. You are thinking more about how you will contribute to society.

BASIC SURVIVAL STRATEGIES

Although we get to more specific problems and corresponding solutions later on, the most important thing to keep in mind when dealing with a QLC is to realize that it is normal to experience symptoms such as anxiety or even depression. It is okay if your twenties are not completely easy and carefree. Although you might hear otherwise from friends of your parents, who may have experienced an easy transition to adulthood, times have changed. We are dealing with midlife issues earlier now in order to avoid problems later on. This is a healthy and inevitable process, and we want to alleviate the stigma that something is wrong with you if you are depressed before reaching midlife. We encourage twentysomethings to talk about their experiences, if not with friends, than anonymously on message boards or in support groups.

Thoughts, Observations, and New Theories

One thing we did not discuss in the previous book, *Quarterlife Crisis*, is what will happen to today's quarterlifers once they reach midlife. It is our theory—and our hope—that the quarterlife crisis will essentially replace the midlife crisis for the current generation of twentysomethings. We are doing all our exploration and experimentation now rather than later in life. It is taking so long for twentysomethings today to become settled and to become independent adults, that we actually look forward to the stability—with the mortgage, the kids, and the minivan—of midlife.

In fact, the AARP itself—powerful advocacy group and provider of solutions to midlife problems—found in a recent article by Carin Rubenstein that your fifties are not a time of crisis, but in fact one of tranquility in comparison with the traumatic twenties, which they refer to as "the begin-life crisis."

As stated in that article, we may have something to look forward to:

> There seems to be no midlife crisis. Despite the dread with which many of us approach our fiftieth birthday, the roughest emotional times of our lives are usually behind us. Midlife can be a time of relative personal tranquility, happiness and self-confidence, a time when boomers begin taking stock of their lives and feeling grateful for what they have.

"Midlife expert" Alice Rossi, Ph.D., added,

> There is no midlife crisis. . . . Much more critical and traumatic events occur in early adulthood than in midlife. It's during their twenties and thirties that Americans are searching for the right partner, a suitable career and a sense of identity. The peak in depression and anxiety occurs in early adulthood, not in midlife.

Results of an AARP survey conducted in 2001 (cited in the same article) showed that:

> Americans under the age of 35 experience negative feelings more often than older Americans. A majority of boomers often feel happy, capable and competent, truly alive and peaceful.

RECENT RESEARCH

Erik Erikson, the father of psychosocial development who coined the phrase "identity crisis," was the first to recognize a development stage of young adulthood, as occurring between 19 and 40 years of age. It is only very recently that psychologists have begun to hone in on the twentysomething years, adapting variations of Erikson's theory of young adulthood to modern times.

Various psychologists and commentators have coined different terms to describe quarterlifers:

As *USA Today* reported in 2004, in an article titled "It's Time to Grow Up—Later: The Gap between Adolescence and Adulthood Gets Longer" by Sharon Jayson, this transition to adulthood has only recently been acknowledged. The article cites James Cote, a Canadian sociologist, who has termed the phase "youthhood," and Terri Apter, a social psychologist at Cambridge, who refers to today's twentysomethings as "thresholders."

Newsweek featured a cover story, titled "Bringing Up Adultolescents" by Julie Weiss, on what it termed "adultolescents" who live with their parents after college for longer than ever before.

Twentysomething, Inc., a market research firm, found that 65 percent of 2004 college seniors, now referred to as "boomerang kids," expected to live at home following graduation. According to the 2003 Census, more than 50 percent of those aged 18–24 were living at home.

Common Purpose, a research firm in the United Kingdom (www.commonpurpose.org.uk), surveyed 1,000 people aged 25–35 in 2004 and found that 8 in 10 believe there is a quarterlife crisis. Only 35 percent think they will find a career with purpose, although 87 percent want one. Six out of 10 are looking for a new job, and 68 percent don't plan to be with the same employer in four years.

A study by the Chicago National Opinion Research Center, "Coming of Age in the 21st Century," found that Americans don't believe adulthood begins until age 26. College-educated Americans believe it starts even later, at 28 or 29.

Psychologist Jeffrey Arnett of the University of Maryland has used the term "emerging adulthood" to describe this period following adolescence and lasting into the late twenties. Arnett describes emerging adulthood as a period when we are "no longer adolescents but have not yet attained full adult status."

The three markers that Arnett found to be the most reliable indicators for reaching adulthood were accepting responsibility, making decisions, and financial independence. He also found "qualities of character" to be important factors.

Arnett notes that "the transition to adulthood is characterized not by a single event but by an extended process of preparation for the challenges and responsibilities of adult life." It's a time of finding our roles, particularly in modern American society, when twentysomethings have "little in the way of definite social or family roles, and their work roles tend to be highly tentative and changeable."

A study by Frank Furstenberg and the Macarthur Foundation's Transition to Adulthood's arm found that 31 percent of men and 46 percent of women had reached adulthood benchmarks such as moving from home and financial stability in 2000, compared with 65 percent of men and 77 percent of women in 1960. The study also concluded that marriage and parenthood are no longer essential markers for adulthood.

Furstenberg noted that the "primary reason for prolonged early adulthood is that it now takes much longer to secure a full-time job that pays enough to support a family," partly because of a decline in government assistance for education and housing.

Now that more and more people are studying and writing about the quarterlife crisis, one question that has emerged is, "What role do and should colleges and universities play in preparing soon-to-be graduates for the life after graduation?"

According to Paul Hettich and Camille Helkowski in *Connect College to Career: A Student's Guide to Work and Life Transitions*, "The nature of work in the American economy has changed so drastically during recent decades that traditional assumptions relating college to career have been challenged."

Bill Coplin, author of *10 Things Employers Want You to Learn in College*, stated in a *Chronicle of Higher Education* editorial titled "Lost in the Life of the Mind":

> I had been a victim of a gigantic conspiracy on the part of colleges that was unwittingly supported by the rest of society in the name of the American dream, unfettered social mobility. I took the bait that college would lead to a high-paying and rewarding job. Once there, the switch was on. . . . According to employers, college students are not prepared for the work force because they lack the skills and character needed to succeed. Our best and brightest students might take statistics in college and score A's on the tests that measure their ability to solve some abstract problem about white and black Ping-Pong balls, but cannot figure out how to set up a bar graph to display real-world data. They learn calculus, but they can't make budget projections. They learn shortcuts to jump the academic hurdles with a minimum of effort, but not much about honesty and work ethic.

Coplin suggests that colleges adapt their curriculums to be more practical and offer to educate students with skills that employers say they are looking for, such as communications:

> Liberal-arts professors will have to accept the implicit social contract with their students. They need to treat undergraduates as clients who learn not only from what is said, assigned and tested, but also from the professor's own behavior. For their part, students must recognize professors' expertise in their subjects, but also their importance as professional-skills coaches. That means seeking constructive criticism rather than worrying only about grades, and working hard to master the material rather than cramming before tests.

Some universities have begun offering Senior Year Experience seminars, which developed out of the University of South Carolina's National Resource Center for the First-Year Experience and Students in Transition. Belmont University in Nashville, Tennessee, and Barat College in Chicago are among the few institutions attempting to make liberal arts more practical and relevant to real-world experience. Like Freshman Year Experience seminars, which help students transition into college, senior seminars teach those skills missing from a college education to help soon-to-be-graduates navigate postgraduate transitional challenges, such as finances and interpersonal work skills.

Some colleges are even creating courses that teach students about couples and relationships. According to an article titled "Relationships 101: Is a Classroom the Place to Learn about Love? Some College and High School Students Are Finding Out" by Rebecca Winters in *Time* magazine, "Young love has always been traumatic. But the anxious, euphoric stage these programs address used to be a lot shorter."

We think that it is important to continue asking questions and researching the quarterlife crisis to determine how we can best help recent grads adapt to the "real world." Now that the phenomenon has been recognized, we can better discuss how to help twentysomethings live a productive and fulfilled transition to adulthood.

How to Use This Book

This book is different from the first quarterlife crisis book not only in content, but also in format. Today's quarterlifers grew up around technology and are characterized by short attention spans. Therefore, our aim was to make this book more of an interactive guide, with the text broken up by exercises, charts, and checklists. The book is not necessarily meant to be read in one sitting, but rather can act as a quick reference for everyday as well as longer-term dilemmas, from finding a job to meeting new people. It's for all those twentysomethings who say, "Thank you for explaining the quarterlife crisis; now what do I do about it?"

The Quarterlifer's Companion: Get on the Right Career Path, Control Your Finances, and Find the Support Network You Need to Thrive is the answer to that question, as well as other questions that we often hear, such as:

- How do I figure out what I want to do with my life?
- How do I translate my passion into a real job that pays the bills?
- How do I deal with my changing relationships with my friends and my family?
- How do I meet people now that I am not in school?

People grapple with these questions throughout their adult lives, but quarterlifers are dealing with these questions for the first time. They do not have the resources to hire expensive life coaches or career counselors, many of whom are accustomed to counseling older midlifers rather than quarterlifers.

And, when people graduate from college, they lose access to career centers and professional counselors who can help explain their depression or anxiety, and they are suddenly faced with numerous decisions about insurance, health care, and finances. There is also a need to address the emotional challenges of being twentysomething, which can be just as—if not more—significant than difficulties with finances and careers. We are not just including a list of how-to instructions, but rather, we recognize that uncertainty about career and finances can lead to extreme emotional anxiety. Our goal is to prevent as much quarterlife angst as possible—but we also want to teach twentysomethings how to deal with these symptoms in case they occur, and how to do so without interrupting success in other parts of life.

The Quarterlifer's Companion, a hybrid between a workbook, self-help book, and resource guide, will help you with the big picture questions as well as with the day-to-day details. (Please note that throughout the remainder of this book we will refer to the quarterlife crisis as QLC, our readers as QLCers, and this book as QLCompanion.)

We designed this book to offer three kinds of help:

1. **Help from Other QLCers.** We have included personal experiences and stories from other quarterlifers so that you can gain some insights into what strategies work for other twentysomethings. We also asked the approximately 10,000 registered users of www.quarterlifecrisis.com to complete new surveys about life, work, and play in 2004. Over 1,200 responded. We've included the results from these questionnaires in each chapter so that you can see how you compare to other quarterlifers.

2. **Help from the Experts.** We had the good fortune to interview experts from a variety of fields, including career, finances, and social life. We asked them the same questions that twentysomethings ask on the message boards and at our workshops—and all of the stuff that we wish we had known ourselves. We include a resource list of other publications and Web sites at the end of each chapter for you to refer to for further information regarding your area of concern.

3. **Help from Yourselves.** In every chapter, we have included exercises that you can do by yourself or with friends. They

are fun and easy and give you the opportunity to take time out of your hectic schedule to get organized and think about some big questions.

The book is organized by life topic in a similar way to quarterlifecrisis.com. Quarterlifecrisis.com was originally launched as a companion site to the first *Quarterlife Crisis* book, and now provides resources and a supportive community to twentysomethings from around the globe. Each of these life topics—life, work, play, and self—contains several subsections. Life covers money issues, searching for a place to live, dealing with roommates, and managing time. Work deals with finding a job, making it through the workday, and moving on to bigger and better things. Play helps you with meeting people, maintaining friendships, and building relationships. Self covers all those things about you and your personal development as an adult—health, nutrition, fitness, managing stress and anxiety, and becoming involved as a member of the community outside of work.

Don't think that you need to absorb all of the information in this book in one sitting. Don't put pressure on yourself to fix everything in your life at once. We hope that you will use this book as a reference guide and come back and redo the exercises as needed. You may need some of this information now and some of it later—it is meant to be a "companion" to help you out in times of need.

You can also become involved outside the book:

➤ Join the quarterlifecrisis.com online community by participating in the message boards.

➤ Grassroots efforts—spread the word, help set up a seminar or workshop in your area.

➤ Host a workshop or a QLC party. We think that the ideas and exercises in the book can be used in groups as well as by individuals.

We would like you, our reader, to become involved with one another as a community through support groups, workshops, and conferences. In addition to the benefits to be found in the materials included in this workbook, peer support is frequently lacking and is vital at this time in one's life. Quarterlifecrisis.com provides information on becoming involved and is constantly updated with advice and guidance from experts as well as your peers. We encourage you to visit the site and provide us with your feedback. Our members often express their appreciation that someone is finally asking them how they feel as a twentysomething. It is we who are appreciative that they are willing to share their time and experiences with us.

Remember as you read on that it is up to you to take control of your twenties. We hope that the tools we have provided will help you overcome unfamiliar challenges, establish yourself as a successful, independent adult, and even . . . have fun!

PART 1

Life

YOU'VE PROBABLY SPENT SOME TIME in dorm hallways or classrooms exploring the meaning of life. By the time you graduate, you have written some really smart papers about big questions. You have solved your share of thorny problem sets. You're feeling prepared for anything real life has to throw your way. Anything, that is, except for all of the little things—the little life details—that are now your responsibility. You may have majored in corporate finance, but few colleges will teach you how to manage your own finances. You may have aced all of your psych classes, but you didn't learn how to navigate moving back in with your parents and what that would do to your relationship.

In this section on life, which covers money, insurance, habitat, and time, we offer advice on the everyday, practical matters that quarterlifers tell us they wish they had learned about in college.

CHAPTER 1

Money

Many graduates leave school with the idealistic and romantic goal of making the world a better place and finding a job they love to do. However, it doesn't take long for most of us to realize that there really is something to the size of a paycheck. In grade school and high school, the allowance or money we earned from part-time jobs was likely to be extra spending money for clothes, music, or movies. In college, we spent the money that we earned on beer, clothes, our cell phones, or Spring Break. Some of us lived in dorms where we did not have to worry about paying the rent, phone, or utilities every month. Many of us were on meal plans so we never thought about grocery shopping. And we were still eligible for our parents' insurance plans.

College offers a fake sense of financial security. Because someone else is usually footing the bill, whether it is your parents, a scholarship, or Stafford loans, for four (or more) years, you may not have to worry about paying the utility bill or negotiating a rental contract. College also leads to a false sense of independence. Ironically, you can feel more financially independent in school when someone else is paying for everything than you do when you have graduated and may need to borrow money from your parents.

When we get our first job, the salary that sounded pretty good suddenly pulls a quick disappearing act. After taxes, Social Security, health care, and possibly a 401(k) contribution, the size of the paycheck you bring home every month may be less than twice that of your monthly rent. After factoring in bills and existing loans or debt, there may be nothing left over to buy a new suit for your first official business meeting.

In this chapter, we are going to share some ways that you can get organized and hang onto more of the money that you are making. Our exercises will help you think about how you are spending and saving your money. Once we help you figure out how to save some money, our investing section will help you figure out what to do with it; our section on debt will help you maintain healthy credit; and our section on insurance will help you protect your financial future.

Expenses Overload

> "I didn't realize all my savings would be sucked up so fast by moving out of my parents' home. I also thought it would be easy to keep saving—it's different when you have more bills and expenses than you did when you lived at home or when you were in college. If I lived solely off of my income, it would take me a year to save up for new clothes or a car repair. I know credit cards are evil, but I would be naked if I didn't have them to buy new work clothes!"—Jen312

You can't do anything about the fact that you have a lot of new expenses when you start living on your own. What you can do is make sure that you pay attention to these new expenses and do the best you can to hang on to what money is left over.

PAY ATTENTION TO ALL OF THOSE BILLS

Start by going through your mail and paying attention to all of those bills. You can save some money by taking the following simple steps:

- When you get your mail, immediately look through all of it, even though 90 percent of it is going to be junk mail. Pull your bills out and pay them immediately. These days, you can set up most bills to be paid automatically out of your checking account, so consider setting this up and you won't have to stress about paying your bills on time each month. You can also pay most bills over the phone without incurring any additional charges, so pick up the phone when the bill comes in the door.
- The late fees on your utilities may seem like small charges, but they add up. Pay your bills on time. More importantly, you don't want to come home after a long day at work to find that you have no gas or phone service. Not only will you be taking cold showers (and in hot water with your roommates), you may be charged expensive reconnect fees and be forced to put a security deposit down with the utility before they will reconnect. Finally, you don't want to end up being reported to a credit agency because of an overdue utility or phone bill.
- Do your utility bills seem high to you? Don't be afraid to ask around and compare. If your water bill seems really high compared to what your friends pay, and you know that you are not taking hour-long showers every morning, there could be a mistake on your bill or a leak in your pipes. If your electricity bill is high, let it be a reminder to you to turn off the lights when you leave for the day.

- Now that everyone has a cell phone, are you paying for services (such as long-distance plans) on your home phone that you do not need?
- Banks are probably not going to be tripping over themselves for your business when you are just starting out, so just look around and find a no-frills checking and savings account.
- Understand your banking fees. Make sure you know what the monthly service charge is and whether there is a charge for in-person banking. If you don't write a lot of checks (which you can avoid by setting up automatic payment) it may be cheaper to find a plan that charges you by the check instead of by the month. Also look out for fees associated with ATM withdrawals or cash back from debit cards. Choose a bank and a plan that best fits your lifestyle—which bank's ATMs are most convenient to you, and how much do they charge to use other banks' ATMs? Finally, be careful that you understand what the monthly minimum balance is—the amount that you *have* to keep in the account to avoid getting penalized. It may be better to pay a monthly service fee rather than stress out about your balance each week.

CREDIT CARD COMPARISON

Credit cards come in all sorts of shapes and sizes. Make sure you understand what each of your credit cards is costing you. Look for more advice about maintaining good credit in the section on debt later in this chapter.

Here are some common credit definitions courtesy of In-Charge Institute of America.

- **Card Type.** Standard issue financial institution and bank credit cards are most common. Credit unions are another good source and will often offer equivalent rates. If you don't qualify for an ordinary credit card, investigate secured credit cards that use a savings account as collateral.

- **Annual Percentage Rate (APR).** As a recent graduate, your interest rates will probably range between 10 percent and 18 percent. This is higher than the rates an established borrower would receive but better than the rate for people with poor credit histories. Read the APR offer closely for the terms of the introductory rate. The lower the rate, the less your credit spending will cost. Tom Gardner of The Motley Fool recommends calling your credit card company if your rate is around 18 percent, which is too high, and asking for a lower rate. The rate should be closer to 10 percent. If the company doesn't comply, threaten to take your business elsewhere; if they still refuse, trade down to a better card.
- **Annual Fees.** Most standard credit cards don't come with annual fees. Some premium or reward cards, such as airline mileage cards, charge annual fees. Look at the small print disclosure to see if your card has a hidden annual fee. Also keep an eye out for excessive late fees, transaction fees, and over-limit fees.
- **Grace Period.** The grace period on a credit card is the amount of time between when you make a purchase and when interest is applied to the purchase. For many cards, the interest-free grace period is about 25 days. Cards with small or nonexistent grace periods will cost you more.
- **Credit Limit.** Your credit limit is the amount that you are allowed to "borrow" with the credit. Ideally, you should never approach your credit limit, especially on more than one card. Finding a card with a higher limit is not necessarily better. A card with a lower limit can instill some discipline in your spending. You probably want enough of a limit so that you can buy a plane ticket in an emergency, for example, but not enough that you are tempted to finance a five-day cruise on your credit card.

- **Rewards.** There are also perks that often come with credit cards, such as mileage or cash rewards. These can be a good deal but do read the fine print. There are often several restrictions, and the number of points or percentage that you receive on purchases as quoted in the offer is often the maximum possible, after you've already spent a required amount.

Saving Up

When we asked QLCers if they were saving money, 80 percent responded that they were saving something and 20 percent said that they weren't saving at all (see Figure 1.1). The reasons given for not saving are shown in Figure 1.2.

- Seventy-four percent of those who don't save don't have enough money to save.
- Eighteen percent don't understand their options.
- Eight percent said that they don't have time to arrange their saving plans.

With all of the new expenses they have, and all of the old debt, it is hard for most QLCers to think about saving a lot of money each month (see Figure 1.3).

HANGING ON TO THE LITTLE THAT YOU HAVE

We asked Tom Gardner, cofounder of The Motley Fool and its Web site, www.Fool.com, and co-host of *The Motley Fool Radio Show* on National Public Radio (NPR), what he would say to twentysomethings who live paycheck to paycheck and can't even think about putting away any money. His reply? "They're screwed." He was kidding of course. You may feel as if you are screwed, but really you are not alone.

For those of you who are living paycheck to paycheck, or would like to be saving more than you are, Gardner recommends the following:

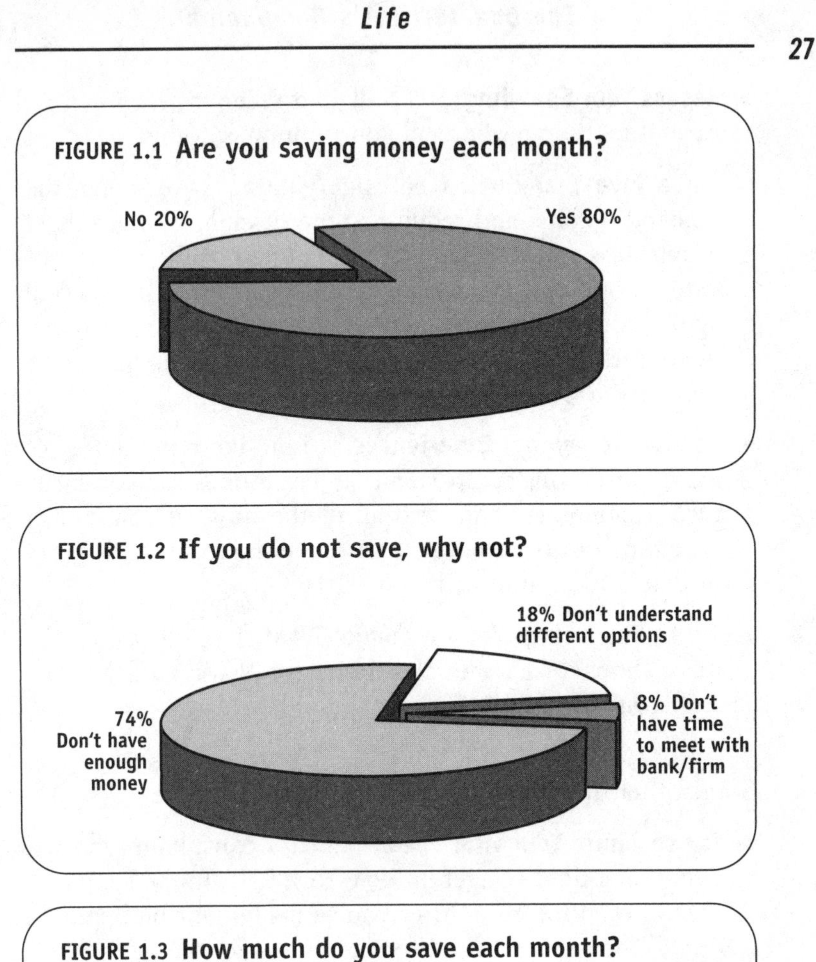

FIGURE 1.1 Are you saving money each month?

FIGURE 1.2 If you do not save, why not?

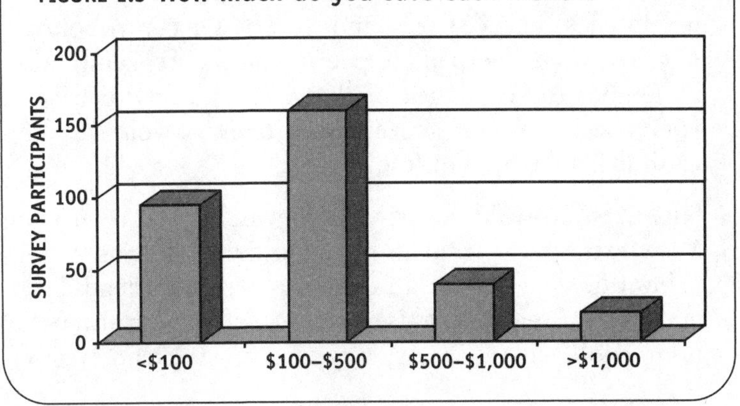

FIGURE 1.3 How much do you save each month?

- **Assess Your Spending.** Keep all your receipts for a week and carefully observe where all your money is going.
- **Set a Five-Year Goal.** Challenge yourself with a plan that demands capital and requires some discipline to get there. Maybe it is a down payment on a condo or tuition for graduate school, or a set amount you want invested by a certain age. While it is definitely important to plan for your retirement, setting a shorter-term goal will provide an immediate incentive to start saving money now.
- **Spend Money on Experiences.** Limit your purchases on materialistic objects, particularly large ones such as furniture. Remember that, with all of the moving you end up doing in your twenties, you are just going to have to lug all of that stuff around with you.
- **Try to Sell Things You No Longer Want.** Use eBay, consignment shops, or garage sales to get rid of some of the extra stuff you have acquired.

Some other tips from QLCers:

- **Try to Limit Your ATM Fees.** Genie, a consultant who was living on a tight budget in New York City, found a strategy that worked for her: "After you've made your budget, take out all the cash you need for the week each Monday. You'll pay lots less in ATM fees, and gain better control of how much you actually spend (especially on the weekend). Also, remember to keep track of these withdrawals to balance your checkbook—or at least keep track of your account. Cash machines are not free money!"
- **Side Gigs.** To avoid excessive ATM withdrawals, try making a few extra bucks through noncommittal side gigs such as babysitting or yard work. Let your family and friends know you are available for nights or weekends. You can always say no to a job, and it's an easy way to cover weekend or shop-

ping expenses. This is also a great way to translate your passions or hobbies into a job, since that job may not exist as a full-time position. For example, if you are an accomplished guitar player but can't make it big, give guitar lessons. If you like to be creative and make pottery or jewelry, try selling to friends or at a flea market.

TAKE CONTROL

It can feel really scary the first time you make a huge purchase. Gardner says, "I tell people when you go buy a car, take people with you, bring one friend who is in control of the calculator, and one friend who knows all of the information about competing cars. Put yourself in control of these situations."

THE 30-DAY "SURVIVOR" SPENDING CHALLENGE

Does the following confession from our message boards sound familiar?

> "This is a horrible confession, but I have never had a savings account in my life. I simply have a checking account that gets drawn down precisely the day before the new paycheck goes in. It is so bad. No matter how much money I earn, I always manage to spend it all."—Gluegun

A lot of QLCers are living paycheck to paycheck, so here is a 30-day spending challenge as explained by Tom Gardner. For 30 days, live as inexpensively as you can. Think of it as a spending diet. Tell all of your friends and family so they do not tempt you with delicious spending opportunities or even minor financial indulgences. And try not to feel deprived; think of it as a challenging game.

➤ Gather your friends and tackle the spending challenge as a group. You will have a built-in support group, and you won't feel left out of social activities. Get out on the town, without entering paid establishments. "A lot of people will find a lot of joy just exploring their cities," suggests Gardner.

- Take turns planning social activities, and make a contest over who can come up with the coolest, low-budget entertainment options.
- Try potluck dinners. You don't have to give up entertaining your friends just because you are tightening your belt. When everyone pitches in on dinner, it saves money and does not require a lot of work.
- Volunteer together.
- Set goals and reward yourself. If you stick to your lunch budget for the week, reward yourself with a meal out that weekend. If your group meets its goal, treat yourself to a fun excursion.

Some common fund suckers to think about as you attempt your 30-day spending challenge:

- Coffee is great, but two delicious lattes a day can add up to $250 per month. If you are feeling a budget crunch, perhaps take a caffeine vacation for a month.
- When you are in a hurry, it seems so easy to get into a cab—but even a few cab rides can add up to $50 or $100 per month. (Don't skimp if you have been drinking, however. The cost of a cab is far cheaper than the cost of drinking and driving.)
- Of course, the big fund sucker is eating out. And who can blame us? The last thing you feel like doing when you get home from work is cooking a meal. But try adding up what you spend in a month on eating and drinking out and you may be shocked into cracking open that yet-untouched cookbook. If you still need to eat out, you can save some money

(and some calories) by skipping the appetizers, desserts, and extra drinks.

- Late penalties on your utility and credit card bills are unnecessary and avoidable.
- Cigarettes. At $5 to $6 a pack, a pack a day habit adds up to almost $2,000 per year. Not to mention the toll on your health.

Take the Challenge

SUPERFLUOUS ITEM	ESTIMATED MONTHLY COST	ACTUAL MONTHLY COST
Try to go a month without:		
1 Starbucks latte a day	$ 120	_____
Appetizers or dessert with dinner	$ 50	_____
That extra drink, especially if it's top rail	$ 35	_____
Bottled water (instead of tap water filter)	$ 25	_____
Eating lunch out	$ 72	_____
Taxis (instead of public transportation)	$ 40	_____
Premium cable	$ 30	_____
Make sure you survive without:		
Late fees	$ 25	_____
Cigarettes	$ 35	_____
Lottery tickets	$ 30	_____
Parking tickets	$ 50	_____
Subtotal:	**$ 512**	_____
What else can you survive without?		
[Other]	_____	_____
[Other]	_____	_____
Total Savings:	_____	_____

Financial Personality Quiz: Which Spending Type Are You?

Think about what factors motivate your spending by taking our financial personality quiz. Examining your attitudes about money will help you make some conscious decisions about what kind of saver and spender you want to be.

- **Living the Lie.** If you have been really successful in school, the one who always got good grades or got elected or made the team, it can be hard to not earn the highest paycheck when you start working, even if you really love your job. You want people to think that you are still the successful one. So you go into debt in order to maintain your identity.
- **The Poor Friend.** Do you find yourself in the unenviable position of being the "poor friend" in your group of friends? Maybe you decided to teach for America while your best three friends went to work for Bank of America. Or maybe you went to graduate school and your friends went right into the workforce. You can end up going into a lot of debt by trying to keep up.
- **Frugal to a Fault.** Being responsible with your finances is a good thing, don't get us wrong, but don't go overboard. Frugal to a fault never goes out, does not travel, and never treats herself because she is so scared about not having money. And while it is definitely good to have money in the bank, don't forget to have a little fun and enjoy your twenties, too. This is a great time of your life to do some traveling. Also, maintaining your friendships is crucial to your happiness, and it will cost you some money to go out, socialize, or take a trip.
- **The Rebel.** A lot of our spending and saving habits are influenced by our parents. Some of us do exactly what

they did, and some of us do the opposite. Maybe your parents were really frugal and so you are a free spender, never worrying about paying your bills. Or maybe your parents got into some financial trouble and you've become extremely frugal. Either way, knowing what motivates your behavior will help you correct it.

➤ **Tightrope Walker.** You live paycheck to paycheck, with no wiggle room in your budget at the end of the month. You are the spender who has just enough money to pay for one last pizza the day before payday. You don't go into a lot of debt but you have nothing in the bank either.

Starting a Stash: Investing

By now, you've at least thought about your spending habits and may have written down your financial goals. You have become the champion of frugal. You have paid off your credit card debt. You have paid your bills. You have some money in the bank. Now that you have saved some money, what do you do with it?

A. Stuff it under the mattress.

B. Put it in your savings account.

C. Invest it in a mutual fund.

D. Invest it in your friend's hot new dot-com.

The safest, most tempting answer is B, as the results from our survey confirm. A lot of quarterlifers are intimidated by the world of investing and simply invest their money in savings accounts (see Figure 1.4).

However, while low interest rates are good for home buyers and car buyers, they are not great for savings accounts. Even if your

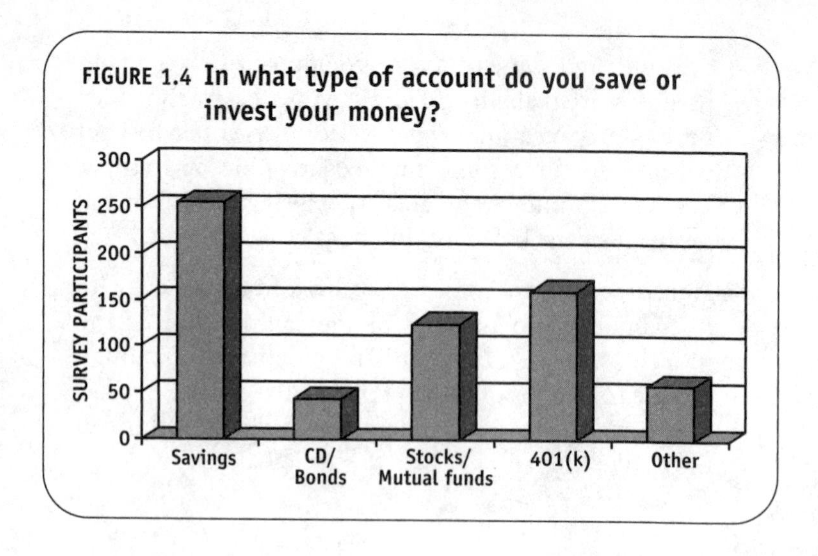

FIGURE 1.4 In what type of account do you save or invest your money?

savings account gave you 2 percent interest, it would take 36 years to double your money. If you were getting a 10 percent return on your money, it would only take 7 years to double your money.

LONG-TERM PLANNING BEGINS NOW

If investing still seems like a daunting task, listen up (unless you need to recover from debt, in which case do that first): The 21-year-old who contributes his or her maximum allowable Individual Retirement Account (IRA) amount each year for 15 years ends up with *twice* as much in savings as the 35-year-old who also makes the maximum allowable contribution each year for 30 years. (This example, which is from the *Smith Barney Accumulator*, assumes an 8 percent annual rate of return). The person who started saving at 21 ends up with $1,329,298—even if he or she stops saving at 36. And the person who started saving at 35 ends up with $642,596 at the age of 65—even after making contributions for twice as long! How does this happen? By the wonder of compounding and tax deferring. The point of this illustration is to not get depressed if you have not been saving, but rather that saving even a little now can make a big difference later.

If you are *still* not convinced, another reason to invest your money now—although it may be hard to think about retirement so early—is that we cannot necessarily depend on those contributions our paychecks are making to the government, also known as Social Security, to take care of us when we need them.

"The most common mistake is that people don't plan," says Donna Fisher, senior vice president of investments at Smith Barney. Most of us don't have access to a financial planner who can help guide our investment strategy, but we have included some great resources available both on the Web and in bookstores at the end of the chapter.

If you want to, consult with a financial planner, don't feel shy, especially if your financial situation has changed and you have a small lump sum of money [for example, a small inheritance or a 401(k) plan you are rolling over to a new job], but do go to someone licensed, someone reputable, and preferably someone who has been personally referred to you. The brokerage firms might seem foreboding and only accessible to young heirs and heiresses who need a fashionable Swiss bank account and access to the latest hip IPO to match this year's hottest runway fashions. And, of course, what kind of financial advisors wouldn't want a client roster full of the very rich? But just because you aren't earning six figures does not mean that you have to keep your money in a piggy bank.

Whether you consult with a planner or are doing your own research and investing, there a few decisions you have to make. Everyone has his or her own "risk and reward" profile. Some people don't want to worry at all about what is happening to their money and put it into a really safe place like a savings account or CD. You have to pay for this security, though. The return, or the amount your investment grows, will be lower. Some people are willing to invest in something riskier, like a mutual fund or a particular stock. These investments are not guaranteed to increase in value, but the growth is generally higher as a way to compensate you, the investor, for the risk you took. When you hear the phrase "risk and return," it refers to the idea that the less risky an investment is, the less the potential return. And, conversely, the riskier the investment is, the higher the potential return (*potential* being an important word to remember).

SO WHAT SHOULD YOU DO? HOW MUCH RISK SHOULD YOU TAKE?

This is the hard part because that is up to you. You have to figure out what your "risk profile" is. How comfortable are you with risk? Would you rather put your money in a CD or a government bond and not worry about it? Are you more comfortable with risk and willing to invest your money in stocks or mutual funds?

The other important consideration is when will you need the money? Are you saving up for a trip that you want to take next year? If so, you want that money to be safer and less vulnerable to a sudden dip in the market. If you are saving for the long term, if this is money you are putting aside for retirement, you won't have to worry so much about the intermittent ups and downs in the market.

If you prefer not to consult with a financial planner, or don't have a lot of money saved yet, it does not mean that you have to wait before investing your money. Gardner suggests taking the following first steps:

1. Buy a mutual fund. Gardner suggests going to Vanguard.com and buying a general index fund. Mutual funds enable you to own a variety of financial instruments. Simply open a fund account and deposit money, just as you would into a checking or savings account. You don't get charged when you deposit money so you can continually add a little at a time without penalties.

2. For the more enterprising person, the person who has done their homework, Gardner suggests using www.sharebuilder.com, a Web site that offers portfolio building at a discount.

For those of you confused by the alphabet soup of 401(k)s and IRAs, Donna L. Fisher, senior vice president of investments at Smith Barney, answers some common questions about 401(k) and IRA plans:

Q. What is a 401(k)?

A. A 401(k) plan allows you to deposit a percentage of each paycheck into an account that you can access after the age of 59 1/2. Technically, you can access the money before you turn 59 1/2 under certain circumstances, but depending on those circumstances, you may have to pay a penalty. The 401(k) plan is one of the most important benefits you can get on the job (if you are lucky enough to be in a job that provides benefits) because, unlike other types of investment accounts, the money you put into it is not taxed. Sometimes your employer will match your contributions, which we describe in detail below.

Q. I'm 25, why should I worry about retirement now?

A. Even if Social Security funds exist by the time we retire, they shouldn't be the sole source of support after retirement. Investing small amounts now will save a lot of worry down the road (when you need to pay for Metamucil and jet set to Boca Raton, Florida).

Q. Is a 401(k) the same as a retirement account?

A. Many companies today offer a 401(k) plan instead of a retirement plan. One important difference between a 401(k) plan and a traditional retirement or pension plan is that you, the individual, are in charge of directing the plan.

Q. Is it better to invest your money in the company's 401(k) plan or your own account?

A. The money you put into your 401(k) is *pretax*. So, if you set aside the same amount to, let's say, put into a CD or a savings account, you would pay taxes on that money before you could save or invest it. It may not seem like a big difference, but by putting the money into your 401(k) tax free, that small difference compounded over time adds up. The other very important benefit of a 401(k) plan is that many employers will *match* up to a certain percentage of your contribution. This is free money. (Well, not free. Presumably, you do some work for these benefits.) But this is as close to free money as you are going to find aside from the occasionally lucky bottle top. If it's possible to still live comfortably within your means, you should set aside the full contribution that your company will match.

Q. What does it mean to be vested?

A. When you are vested in your 401(k) plan, the contribution that the company made into your 401(k) goes with you if you leave the company. At some companies, you may be "vested" automatically. Other companies may vest you on a sliding scale, giving you 20 percent the first year, up to 40 percent the second, and so on. They do this to create an incentive for you to stick it out at their company.

Q. If I am lucky enough to have a 401(k) plan, what am I supposed to do with it?

A. You will have to choose how to allocate the money in your 401(k) account. In general, you will choose among a wide variety of mutual funds and your own company's stock, and you will decide how much of your 401(k) gets allocated to each fund. By law and regulation, your employer has to give you all of the information about the options you have for making investments with your 401(k) account. You will get such a plethora of information about each mutual fund that you may not even understand, for example, whether the fund invests in small companies, big companies, foreign companies, government bonds, corporate bonds, etc. This may be the point where you say, "Help!"

Q. Who can help me allocate my 401(k) funds?

A. You may want to seek the help of a professional financial advisor to help you allocate your 401(k), but you may also be able to find the help you need through your own company. Some larger companies have 800 numbers to call or intranets that offer information. Ultimately, however, it will be up to you to educate yourself because you cannot rely on your company to take care of you and your 401(k). Ask your benefits officer what resources are available that might help you choose between funds. Whether or not you seek advice from a professional, here are a few basic guidelines:

➤ Don't assume that a $100 contribution actually costs you $100 out of your pocket. Remember, your contribution into your 401(k) is not taxed when you put it in. If you *don't* make a contribution, you will get taxed on that income. It may be that the amount you put into the 401(k) does not feel that different from the amount that you had to pay taxes on because you didn't put it into a 401(k). Wouldn't you rather pay yourself than Uncle Sam? The benefits person at your company should be able to help you figure out what the contribution really does to your wallet.

➤ In general, do not put more than 25 percent of your contribution into your own company's stock. You may really believe in your company. And that's great. But, if things go downhill at your company, you don't want to find yourself in the position of getting laid off while simultaneously watching the value of your stock-heavy 401(k) plan slip into the abyss.

➤ Just remember the eggs in the basket rule. Don't put them all in the same one, no matter how pretty the basket looks. Diversifying your 401(k) keeps your money safer because no investment, no mutual fund, is fool proof. So spreading your savings around keeps it safer.

- Set aside a comfortable amount for your 401(k) each month. You may get really excited about your 401(k), especially if your company matches it, and you may stretch too far when deciding how much to allocate every month. You don't want to allocate so much that it gets painful and you stop doing it altogether.

IMPORTANT QUESTIONS TO ASK ABOUT YOUR BENEFITS:

Is there a 401(k) plan?

Does the company make matching contributions?

How long does it take for my 401(k) plan to be fully vested?

- A lot of plans will allow you to borrow against your 401(k) for a first home or for educational expenses, so don't assume that the account is only useful to you at retirement.

THE 401 PARENT PLAN

If you don't get a 410(k) through your job, think about hitting up the 401 Parent Plan! Gardner suggests looking for collaborators in your savings venture. You may not be lucky enough to work for a company that matches your 401(k) contribution but you could ask your parents to match a certain percentage of your savings—even as a birthday or holiday present. It feels a lot less painful to put that $100 in the bank if you know that it will automatically double.

IRAs

If your company does not have a 401(k), you can still set up your own IRA (Individual Retirement Account). Just as with a 401(k), you still get to defer paying taxes on your contribution into your IRA. There are two different kinds of IRAs:

- **Traditional IRA.** Depending on your income, your contributions into a traditional IRA are tax-deductible; the money grows over time and then you pay taxes when you take the money out.

- **Roth IRA.** Again, depending on your income, you can set up a Roth IRA. For a Roth, your contribution is after taxes, but then the money grows tax free and you don't have to pay taxes when you take the money out at retirement.

Debt—Payback Time

Our survey results on debt are perhaps the most alarming of our findings:

- The majority of recent grads graduate in debt, and over half of the respondents owe more than $10,000 (see Figures 1.5 and 1.6).
- Thirty-two percent of survey respondents said, "I have to postpone my plans" because of my debt.
- Twelve percent said, "I feel as if I'll never be able to pursue my goals because of debt."

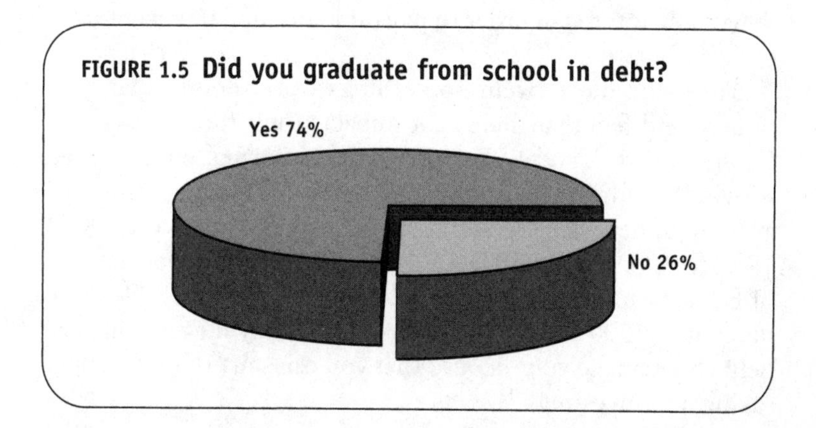

FIGURE 1.5 Did you graduate from school in debt?

FIGURE 1.6 What was your amount of debt upon graduation?

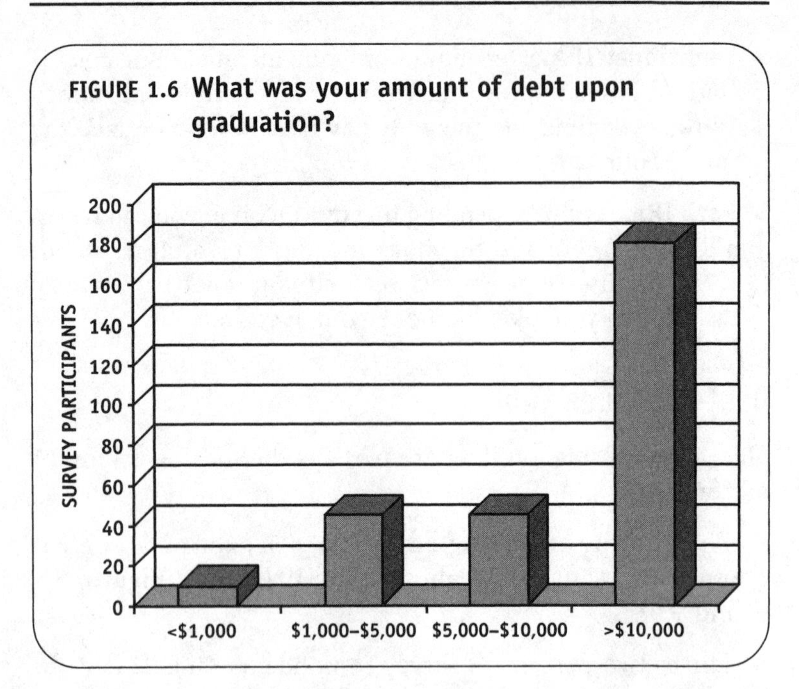

A study by the Collegiate Funding Services in 2003 confirmed our findings: "more college grads are putting their dream jobs on hold to take higher-paying jobs that would help them pay off their student loans." They found that over 30 percent of recent grads took their second-choice job rather than the one they really wanted in order to pay off loans, up 20 percent from the year before.

More and more twentysomethings worry about their level of debt and feel that their debt impacts their future plans (see Figures 1.7, 1.8, and 1.9). According to information from loan provider Nellie Mae, as cited by *Young Money* magazine, the average undergraduate debt rose 66 percent from $11,400 in 1997 to $18,900 in 2003. And, according to the Department of Education, borrowers are up from 46 percent in 1990 to 70 percent in 2000. That's the reality. The following sections will help you manage your debt so that you can start thinking about saving and investing.

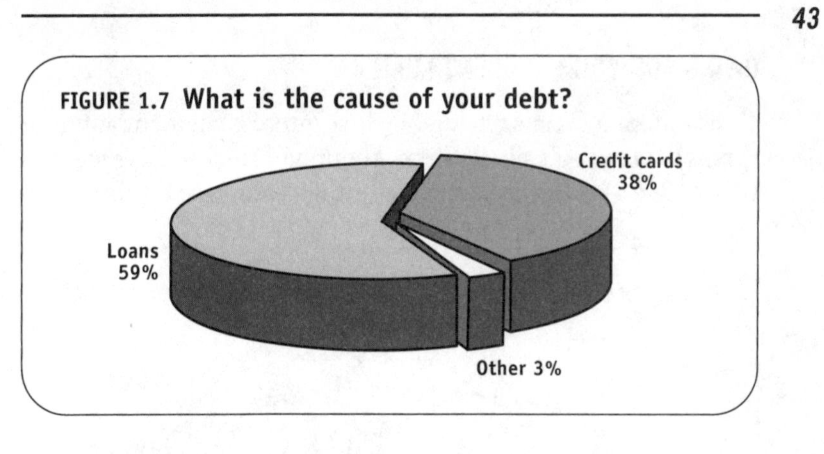

FIGURE 1.7 What is the cause of your debt?

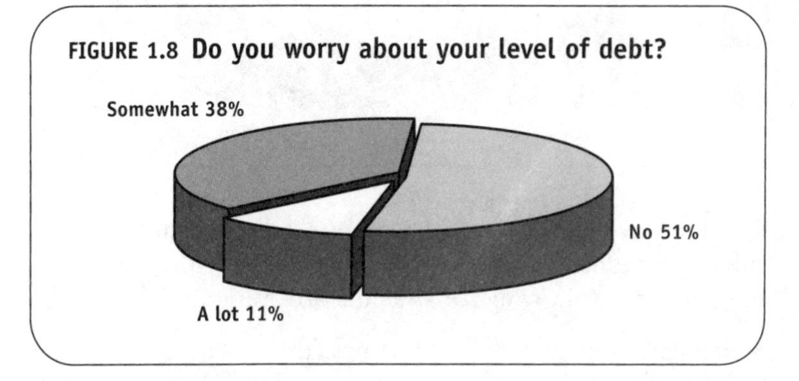

FIGURE 1.8 Do you worry about your level of debt?

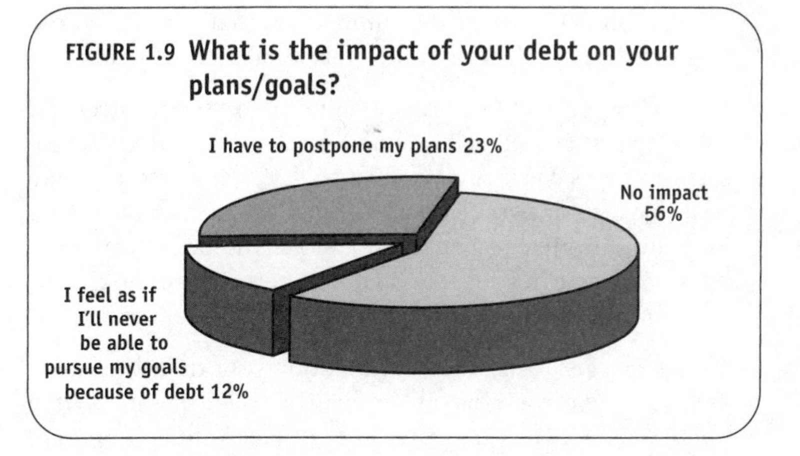

FIGURE 1.9 What is the impact of your debt on your plans/goals?

OWING FOR YOUR STUDENT LOANS

Consolidating means paying one low-interest payment a month versus paying multiple lenders. About half the QLCers we surveyed have a consolidation plan for their debt (see Figure 1.10).

FIGURE 1.10 **Do you have a plan to consolidate your debt?**

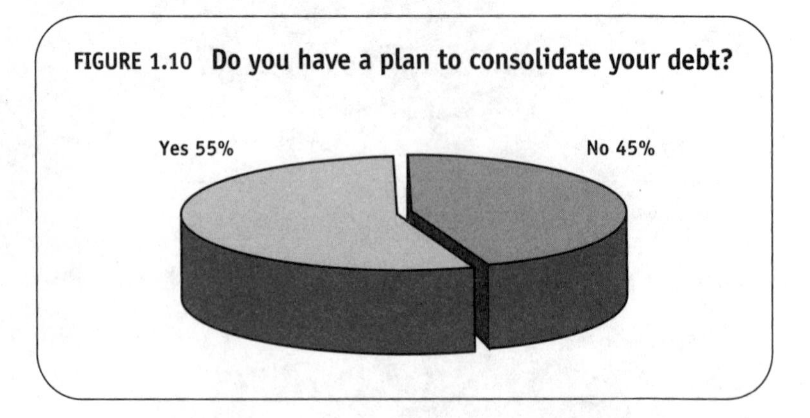

John Lee, vice president of Student Marketmeasure and consultant in higher education policies such as financial aid, recommends the following for students drowning in debt:

- Review your government loans, then consolidate them ASAP to lock in currently low interest rates. You can stretch the payments out over 10 or more years, but remember, the longer the payback period, the more total interest you'll pay.
- For the most reliable information on loan payment, check out the Department of Education's student financial assistance section on its Web site. Commercial lenders such as Sallie Mae have information on managing finances after school. Stay away from unsolicited e-mails—if the offer seems too good to be true, it probably is. Talk to current loan holders to find out if they are satisfied with a prospective lender.
- Consider your loans when formulating your monthly budgets. Since you can consolidate loans at a lower rate, worry about paying off higher-rate cards and loans first. You don't

need to worry about debt as much if it's at a low fixed rate—in fact, you can still set aside an amount of money to save each month.

- You may get a discount on interest if you're reliable; check with the lender. If you pay early or on time, you will be eligible for benefits such as auto withdrawal and reduced rates. You may also be eligible for tax relief for some interest on the loan.
- If you're single and your income is less than $55,000, or $130,000 when married, you can receive a full or partial tax deduction of the interest you pay on your loans.
- Aim to pay off loans by the time you start saving for your kids' education. So, if you plan to have a baby by thirty, plan to pay your loans off by then. College tuition is going up 5 percent a year, and at that rate will double in 15 years to around $30,000 a year for public universities.
- Make sure that if you move, you get in touch with the bank and continue to repay the loan. Don't wait for the bank to contact you. You will default and the loans will never go away. In particular, if you've lived in a group house, no one will know how to get in touch with you and you'll end up with bad credit and unable to make big purchases, such as a car.
- Think carefully about consolidating with someone else, you will be responsible for even a dead spouse's loan debt.

OWING ON YOUR CREDIT CARDS

It can seem a lot easier just to bury your head in the sand and ignore your mounting pile of credit card debt, because after all:

- You *are* going to win the lottery. You feel it. You are really sure this time.
- Some relative you never knew you had is going to leave you everything.

- You are going to meet the person of your dreams *and* he or she is going to be filthy rich!
- In your spare time, as soon as you get around to it, you are going to bang out the next Harry Potter-esque book.

But just in case your dream doesn't come true . . . it's better to face reality, no matter how ugly it may be. If you do feel as if you are getting into trouble, confront it. Call your creditors and talk to them so that they know that you are trying. Most creditors will work with you to come up with a payment plan.

AVOIDING CREDIT CARD DEBT

John Lee recommends the following:

- Carefully evaluate credit card offers and long-term rates. Find out what happens after incentives. Frequent flier perks are often more than offset by fees, and you'd be better off with a low-rate card. Don't be tempted by perks that are often no more valuable than "a prize in the Cracker Jack box."
- Try to pay off credit cards each month. Never make a payment longer than you'll use an item. For example, it's fine to take three years to pay debt on a car or furniture that you'll use for more than three years, but dinners and concert tickets are for short-term consumption and therefore should be paid off in the short term.
- Don't have too many cards in your name; you could be at risk for a poor credit rating. Only keep cards you'll actually use. Your credit is rated down by the number of cards you hold, because if your income is low, it looks like you're at high risk. You're also at risk for identity theft when you have many open accounts.
- If you get a store card, close the account after you stop using it.

- Pay attention to your purchase reasoning—are you being swayed by emotional factors or pressure? Twentysomethings tend to make aspirational purchases for image or status, and credit cards make it easy to overbuy.
- Don't use your credit card after four drinks, especially if it's 1 a.m. and you're watching an infomercial.

Owing Mom and Dad

> "I thought that I would make enough to handle the debt I had accrued. According to my professors, the education we were receiving would more than compensate for the expense. Alas, no. I am in debt and am toiling at a job that I could have received without a college degree. The job pays barely enough to cover the student loans, and I am still eating the ramen noodles that I thought were part of 'paying my dues.'"—Iwanttoscream

You have a diploma in hand. You are ready to take the world by storm. You are on your own. But first . . . you need to borrow some money from Mom and Dad. There is nothing like calling home for money that makes you feel more like a high schooler begging for money for a movie and a pizza every weekend. Not being financially independent can add to all of the feelings of the quarterlife crisis: feeling like you are posing as an adult by putting a false face forward that you can afford an adult lifestyle.

According to our survey results, 41 percent of quarterlifers occasionally borrow money from their parents. Most borrow on rare occasions—for big-ticket items or in case of emergency—and most do not borrow from any sources other than their parents (see Figure 1.11).

> "I did have to borrow money from my parents when I bought my first apartment. I wasn't embarrassed to ask

my parents (I think they offered and I said okay—otherwise I would not have been able to come up with a down payment). My parents were thrilled to be able to help me with the down payment because they knew buying the apartment was a great investment, and they knew I would eventually pay them back. So it was a 'win—win' situation."—Marie, a university program administrator

FIGURE 1.11 Do you borrow money from your parents?

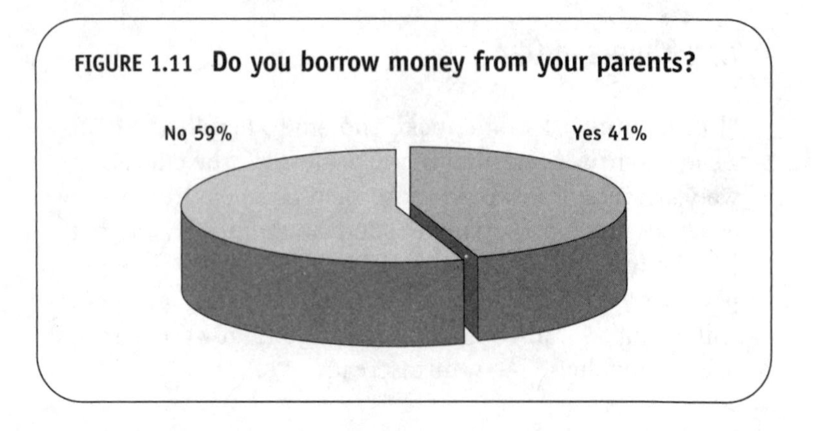

If you do borrow money from your parents or another family member, make sure that everyone understands what the terms of the loan are. Do you need to repay the money by a certain point? Is the loan designated for a specific purpose? You probably won't have to pay interest on the loan but are there other strings attached? Make sure that you communicate in very precise terms what your and your parents' expectations are.

YOUR CREDIT HEALTH

According to Daniel Jimenez, managing editor of *Young Money* magazine:

> Your credit score is the single most important factor determining whether you'll get approved for a mortgage, car loan, credit card, and insurance. And, even if you do

get approved, your score will determine what the interest rate will be. There are several factors that make up your credit score: credit history, payment history, bankruptcies, debts, the number of times you have requested credit, and the type of credit you are applying for.

You can take a look at your financial record by getting your credit score along with a copy of your credit report. Your credit report has all the juicy details that creditors are sharing with each other about you. What bills have you been late on? How free and loose are you with credit cards? Are you a good risk, someone who can be trusted with other people's money? You can order your credit report online and receive it instantly from www.Equifax.com, www.TrueCredit.com, and Experian's www.CreditExpert.com. Be sure you choose the option that gives your credit score too. More than likely, this will cost you about $15. Shop around for the best deal. Your credit score may be slightly different at each, but until you know there's a problem, one credit report should do.

WHEN YOU GET IN TROUBLE

If you are getting unpleasant calls about past due bills from your creditors or their collection agencies, the worst thing that you can do is ignore them. In fact, the best thing that you can do to head off those calls is to be up front when you cannot pay a bill. Call *before* those bills come past due, explain that you are unable to pay, and try to come up with a payment plan that you can handle. If you stay in contact, your creditors will at least know that you are trying and that you are not going to skip out on your obligations.

CREDIT COUNSELORS

If you find that you are really in over your head and need the help of a professional credit counselor, be careful that you don't get taken advantage of.

Daniel Jimenez warns that the first thing you will find when you search for a counselor is that not all credit counseling agencies are created equal. In fact, as detailed in an April 2003 report by the Consumer Federation of America and the National Consumer Law Center, there are some agencies that end up doing more harm than good. The old adage is true: If it seems too good to be true, *it probably is*.

At a minimum, you should look for a nonprofit, experienced credit counselor who can provide personalized service coupled with sound financial education to ensure a long-term solution to debt.

Jimenez recommends asking the following questions before choosing a credit counseling agency:

- What industry association do they belong to?
- Are they accredited, and if so by whom?
- Are they certified, and if so by whom?
- Are they licensed in your state?
- What type of ongoing educational services will you receive?
- How long will they hold your money before paying your creditors? Ask if your money will be held in a separate trust account. This will ensure that the agency can't use your money for anything other than paying your creditors.

Also, do some research to find out what to expect in the counseling process:

- Check their record with the local Better Business Bureau.
- Ask about all of the fees or contributions you will be expected to pay.
- Make sure the counselor will not receive a bonus for enrolling you in a program.

- If you enroll in a debt management plan, then make sure you will be out of debt within five years.
- Ask for a copy of any contract so you can review it before you sign it.

QUICK TIPS FROM INCHARGE DEBT SOLUTIONS

Debt can add up in a hurry when you're just making the minimum monthly payment. It would take you 16 years and 7 months and cost a total of $9,698.46 to pay a $5,000 debt at 18 percent interest if you were making the 3 percent monthly minimum payment.

Credit counseling agencies typically suggest that you contact a credit counselor if you have over $2,000 in credit card debt and/or are having trouble making your monthly payments on a regular basis.

TAXES

Paying taxes is a good sign. It actually means that you are making enough money that the government thinks you should give some of it to them. If you are like most typical twentysomethings, your job is taking out your taxes with each paycheck. (If you notice that your job is withholding no taxes from your salary, talk to someone about this. Sure, it means that your monthly salary is higher, but it won't be pleasant to have to come up with a big pile of dough come April 15.)

People get really nervous about doing their taxes, but for most of us who don't own a lot yet, it is pretty easy. Here's a brief rundown of the process, but keep in mind that everyone's tax return is going to be different and you may need to seek out a professional tax return preparer if your situation is complicated.

1. Hang on to your pay stubs each month. Also, keep records on charitable donations you make. If you have student loans, you will get a statement from your lenders indicating how much interest you paid on your loans that year.
2. After January 1, you will get a copy of your W-2 from your employer. You get a copy for yourself, a copy for filing your federal taxes, and a copy for filing your state taxes.
3. Make sure the numbers on your pay stubs add up to the numbers on your W-2.
4. When it actually comes time to fill out your tax return, you can go to www.irs.gov to determine:
   - Which form you need and download it.
   - Whether you are itemizing or taking the standard deduction.
   - Whether to fill them out and send them in electronically. You will have to read through some forms, but the Web site is surprisingly easy to use.
   - Who pays up. You can receive your refund electronically. Or, if you owe the government money, you can send that in electronically as well.

Another option is to use software such as TurboTax or Quicken to help you answer the questions on your form.

It gets more complicated, and you may want to seek professional guidance if you:

- Just bought a house
- Own a house and rent out a room or rooms
- Have a lot of medical expenses

Also, if you work for yourself, the tax rules are different and will vary by state. Be very careful that you know how many times you need to file and how much tax and Social Security you should be paying.

BASIC BUDGETING

Now that you have brushed up on your saving and investing skills, it's time to create a monthly budget. A lot of people know that they should write their budgets down and just don't get around to it. Start by saving all of your receipts for a month. At the end of the month, dump them out of whatever drawer or bag you have been keeping them in and start dividing them up into little piles.

Assign a category to each pile of receipts:

- Groceries
- Clothes, shoes, and accessories
- Toiletries
- Personal services (i.e., dry cleaning, haircuts)
- Transportation (including car maintenance)
- Home furnishings/décor
- Happy hours and eating out
- Entertainment (i.e., clubs, concerts, and sporting events)
- CDs and books
- Electronics
- Travel
- Gifts
- Other

Now go through your bills:

- Rent/Mortgage
- Car payment
- Student loan payments
- Insurance:
    - Car
    - Rental
    - Health
    - Life

Utilities:
- Phone
- Cell phone
- Gas
- Water
- Electric
- Cable
- Internet

Other

Total Monthly Expenses (add receipts and bills):

Monthly Income (What you bring home—after taxes, Social Security, and maybe a 401(k) contribution):

Monthly Savings (Subtract monthly expenses from income):

Now that you see what you have been spending, it is time to think about what you *want* to be spending. If you would like to be spending less and saving more, it might be a good time to start your 30-day spending challenge.

Resources

INVESTING

www.Fool.com

www.YoungMoney.com

Rich Dad, Poor Dad by Robert T. Kiyosaki and Sharon L. Lechter

Smart Women Finish Rich by David Bach

The Motley Fool Investment Guide: How the Fool Beats Wall Street's Wise Men and How You Can Too by David and Tom Gardner

The Motley Fool's You Have More Than You Think: The Foolish Guide to Personal Finance by David and Tom Gardner

CREDIT/DEBT

www.CardRatings.com
www.CreditExpert.com
www.Incharge.org
www.TrueCredit.com

LOAN CONSOLIDATION

www.SallieMae.com
www.Studentaid.ed.gov

TAXES

www.irs.gov
www.turbotax.com

CHAPTER 2

Insurance

One acronym we did not cover in the previous chapter is the ever-daunting, but ultimately necessary, HMO (Health Maintenance Organization). Insurance, like bill paying or investing, is perhaps a responsibility we've never given much thought to, as it's always been covered for us. And, just as you may not yet think that it's time to consider retirement accounts, you may also feel that you don't need to bother with doctors, other than the occasional checkup. However, just because you feel healthy does not mean that you won't get sick or have an accident. And health insurance aside, which is absolutely unquestionably a lifesaver, it may also be time to shop around for a car, travel, life, or renters insurance plan. Everything is vulnerable, from your car to your body to your apartment, and inevitably, something will stop working if you are not protected by good insurance. We explain the nitty-gritty about insurance in this chapter.

Health Insurance

In 2002, we conducted a health insurance survey on www.quarterlifecrisis.com. As shown in Figure 2.1, 17 percent of the respondents were not covered. The number one reason why

FIGURE 2.1 **Do you have health insurance?**

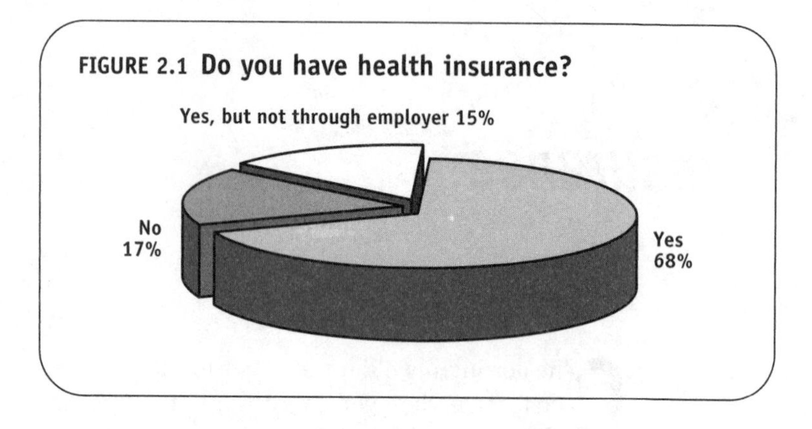

FIGURE 2.2 **What are the reasons you don't have health insurance?**

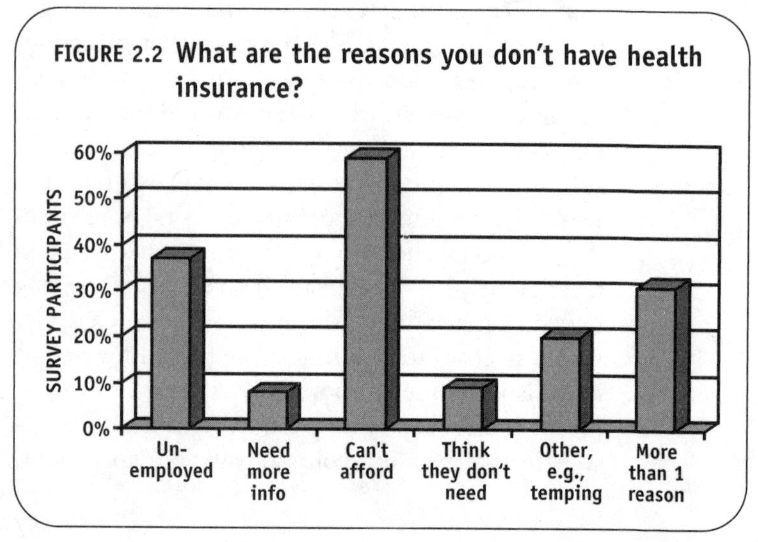

survey respondents said they did not have health insurance was that they could not afford it (see Figure 2.2). We think that you can't afford to *not* have health insurance. In this chapter, we discuss not only why health coverage is so important, but we provide some advice and resources for finding and evaluating health insurance coverage. For those of you who are covered, we provide some advice for how to navigate your current plan.

We conducted the online health insurance survey because one of the most frequent topics of concern for the thousands of twentysomethings who contact us is learning about and securing health insurance coverage. And they have every reason to be worried. One twentysomething's story was featured in the March 17, 2003, *Wall Street Journal* article "Full Price: A Young Woman, an Appendectomy, and a $19,000 Debt—Ms. Nix Confronts Harsh Fact of Health-Care Economics: Uninsured Are Billed More—Moving In with Mom at Age 25."

Reporter Lucette Lagnado interviewed uninsured 25-year-old Rebekah Nix, whose health-care bills forced her to move back in with her mother and, to top it off, declare bankruptcy at the age of 25.

The problem is that many twentysomethings feel invincible—no one who is young and healthy ever thinks that they are going to get sick or seriously hurt. And it is often not until your middle to late twenties that physical ailments begin to sneak up on you and require medical attention. Therefore many of us do not even think to ask about benefits such as health insurance when we interview for jobs early on. Or we may be between jobs and don't know where or how to look into an individual plan—or whether it's worth the expense while we are unemployed.

Stuart Schear, who developed www.covertheuninsured.com to increase awareness of the nation's uninsured, agrees that "It's definitely a huge problem." And that may be putting it mildly:

- Eight million people between the ages of 18 and 24 were uninsured last year. This number accounts for 27 percent of the total number of people in that age range, says Schear, based on data collected by the Robert Wood Johnson Foundation.

- As was reported in the *Wall Street Journal* article, 22 percent of the 42 million uninsured Americans are between the ages of 25 and 34.
- One of the two leading causes of people declaring personal bankruptcy is unpaid medical bills.
- And here's a real kick in the pants. The uninsured twentysomething making $19,000 a year filing and faxing things—when he does have to go the hospital—pays *more* for the same care than an insurance company would have to pay to cover those costs. Why? Because the insurance company can promise a lot more business to that hospital than you can (well, we would hope so) so it can negotiate for discounts. *So*, not only will you have to pay out of pocket for your care, but you will have to pay the full price. Sorry, no discounts for you.

A lot of twentysomethings just risk it and hope that nothing bad happens. But Schear warns, "It's true, [your twenties are] not the highest risk age but [the uninsured] can suffer terrible health consequences when they become ill." Uninsured people tend to put off care until they have no choice, and by then, they are really sick and consequently the bill is higher.

Even if you are young and healthy, it does not mean that you won't get hurt in an accident. Do you really want to forgo that biathlon you've always wanted to do or miss your friends' annual paintball tournament because you can't afford to get hurt?

So, now that we have convinced you (we have, right? Just remember: illness, bankruptcy, and having to move back in with your parents) that it is really important to have health insurance, how do you get it?

You can't wait for someone else to fix the problem. Everyone hears politicians volleying ideas back and forth about health insurance reform. And there are a lot of smart people at think tanks who are trying to fix the big picture problem. And maybe they will solve the problem, eventually. But in the meantime, it would be nice if you could play in the company softball game without worrying about breaking your leg and ending up having to sell your car (and then getting to work on a broken leg).

We're not going to sugarcoat it. It's not easy and it's not cheap. But you need to try to do anything you can do to get some kind of coverage.

- If you are choosing between jobs, and one job offers health benefits and the other job does not, seriously consider the job that offers benefits. Do not just look at your salary; you have to look at the whole package.
- If you really want the job that does not offer benefits, try to negotiate for them. Offer to pay for part of your insurance premium out of your salary.
- If you are in a job already and do not have health benefits, again, find out if you can buy into them. Even if you have to pay the total premium, the cost will be cheaper, and the benefits and service better, than if you have to go out and find an individual policy on your own.
- Schear reminds us "there is strength in numbers." It's pretty simple. Big groups can get better rates and better service, which means you should try to affiliate with any group that you can find that has access to health insurance coverage.
    - Does your alumni association offer access to any temporary or individual health insurance plans?
    - Is there a professional organization that you can join? Or a union? For example, the Freelancers Association in New York City offers access to health insurance coverage.
- Health insurance is important enough to (gulp) ask your parents for some help. If they can help out, it would be better for them to help with an insurance premium now than have to help you with the medical bills later.

Most recent grads who are unemployed but no longer eligible to be covered by their parents' plan simply take the risk of being uninsured. If you find yourself without a job, or without a spouse (which is another way to get insurance), you can try short-term or standard individual policies. Short-term, or bridge, plans are inexpensive, but they may have high deductibles and co-payments and may not cover preexisting conditions. This can be a good option if you don't expect to have major claims or out-of-pocket expenses, but want to prevent shelling out tens of thousands of dollars in case of an accident. Short-term plans are also a good fit if you know you have a job lined up for later, but just have a couple of months to wait. Otherwise, you should go with a standard policy, which is more expensive but provides more extensive coverage. Try a site like www.ehealthinsurance.com or www.insure.com to compare plans.

If you cannot access a group plan through your job or some other organization, you can buy a temporary health insurance policy or an individual health insurance policy. You are really going to have to do some research to make sure that you don't get ripped off.

Make sure to ask:

- What kind of plan is it? Do you have to see certain doctors or can you see doctors that you pick? If you are part of an HMO and there is a network of doctors from which to choose, can you still see other doctors, or "out of network," if you want to? And what is the cost out of your pocket if you do?
- Do you need a referral (or permission) to see a doctor who is not your primary care provider? For example, if you think that you may have aggravated an old football injury, do you need to go to your primary care doctor before seeing your orthopedist?
- What services are 100 percent covered by your plan? Most HMOs, in an effort to keep you healthy, completely cover preventive care checkups and flu shots. (Take advantage of these free services.)

- The co-pay is the amount that you are expected to cover. Make sure that you understand what services require a co-pay and what percentage of the total cost the co-pay is.

There are resources available for investigating temporary and individual health insurance plans. Check with your state's insurance commissioner to make sure that the company is in good standing. Go to www.healthinsuranceinfo.net and check to see what your individual state's rules are about these types of plans and the coverage they must provide. For other resources available to uninsured individuals, see our list at the end of the chapter.

HEALTH INSURANCE

It is not a good time to learn about your health insurance coverage when:

- You wake up with a 102-degree temperature feeling as if someone slammed your head between two encyclopedias and vowing to never, ever eat again.
- Recently back from your trip to Mexico, you notice a strange itching and rash.
- That ankle that you thought you had merely twisted during your company softball game has now turned every color of the rainbow and has doubled in size.

Fill in the following chart with information about your health insurance plan so that you know how, when, where, and for what you are covered.

HEATH INSURANCE WORKSHEET

	Primary care visits	Specialists	Doctors outside of my "network"	Emergencies*	Prescription drugs
Is there a specific doctor, network of doctors, or hospital that I am supposed to go to? A specific pharmacy? If so, how do I know who they are? Do I need "pre-approval"? Do I need referrals?					
Is there a deductible? (An amount I have to pay per year before my plan will begin to cover my expenses.)					
What is the co-pay? (The amount I have to per visit.)					
Is there a limit to the total amount of the co-pay per year?					
Do I pay up front and get reimbursed later? If so, how do I do this?					
Does the doctor or hospital bill my insurance plan later, and if so, what documentation do I need with me?					
# of your ER:					

*Be sure to carry your health insurance card with you everywhere you go, so you have your primary physician's phone number at all times. It is also a good idea to know the number of your local emergency room.

Car Insurance

A lot of twentysomethings have been on their parents' car insurance plan through college. Once you are on your own, look around because you may not be getting the best deal with your parents' plan.

Todd Morgano of Progressive Auto Insurance offers the following tips to first time insurance shoppers:

- **Shop Around.** Because different companies have different operating costs and look at different information about drivers, the same person with the same coverage can get very different prices depending on the company they choose. Morgano cited a Progressive survey conducted in late 2002 which found that the cost of a six-month auto insurance policy for the same driver with comparable coverage varies from company to company by an average of $586. So it is worth doing your homework.
- **Control What You Can.** There are certain things insurance companies typically consider when pricing an insurance policy for you. Some of those things are out of your control, such as your age, gender, and to some extent where you live. But there are other things in your control, such as your driving record, information about your credit history, and the type of vehicle you drive. If you drive safely and don't have any violations, if you consistently pay your bills on time and don't over-apply for credit, and if you choose to purchase less expensive, lower horsepower, less frequently stolen cars, you will increase your chances of paying lower premiums.
- **Choose an Appropriate Level of Coverage.** How much and what kind of insurance is right for you? Talk to your insurance agent or company. Each person's situation is different, and each person will have coverage needs that are appropriate for their situation. For instance, if you have an older car that isn't worth much, you may want to investigate whether

you need comprehensive and collision coverage or whether having only liability coverage would make better sense.

- **Settle on a Deductible That's Comfortable for You.** Generally speaking, the higher your deductible (the amount you pay before an insurance company starts to pay), the lower your premiums. How high or low you should go depends on your risk tolerance and ability to pay the deductible amount.

When choosing a company, there are also some factors to consider:

- **Ease of Purchase.** How easy is the company to work with when buying a policy? Can you compare rates? Can you purchase a policy online? Do they have a Web site and toll-free numbers? Do they have local agents in your area? These are just some of the questions you should ask.
- **Customer Service.** How do they handle claims and how quickly do they handle them? Do they offer authorized repair facilities where the work is guaranteed? Do they track their claims and provide you with updates on the progress of your repairs? Are customer service representatives available 24/7?

WHAT TO DO IF YOU SHOULD HAVE A CAR ACCIDENT?

You may be so upset or traumatized that your first impulse is to pick up the phone and call a parent, a sibling, or your best friend. First, though, you need to remember to:

- Stay calm and make sure that no one (yourself included) is hurt.
- Move yourself and everyone else to a safe place, away from the road.
- If you have flares, set them up on the road. If not, turn your hazard lights on so that your accident does not turn into a major pileup.

COMMON AUTO INSURANCE DEFINITIONS
(Provided by Progressive Auto Insurance)

Liability insurance covers you for damage you do to another's person or property:

- *Bodily Injury (BI)*. Covers you, or a person listed on your policy, if you hit someone and kill or injure them (medical expenses, lost wages, pain and suffering).
- *Property Damage (PD)*. Covers the damage you do, or a person listed on your policy does, to property as the result of an accident (other vehicles, buildings, telephone poles, fences).

These coverages have limits, and most states have minimum coverage limits. They are usually expressed together as BI/PD in a formula that looks like 100/300/100. The first figure is BI per person, the second figure is BI per crash, and the third figure is PD per crash.

Insurance that covers you for damage you do to yourself:

- *Collision*. Covers damage to your auto in a crash (with another car or property, such as light pole, but not an animal).
- *Comprehensive*. Covers damage to car from incident other than collision (fire, flood, hail, wind, animal).
- *Medical (Med) Pay*. Optional. Covers your medical or funeral expenses that result from an accident.
- *Personal Injury Protection (PIP)*. Coverage for medical bills in no-fault states. (In no-fault states, when you get into an accident, you have your own insurance company pay, regardless of who's at fault).
- *Uninsured Motorist*. Covers you or a person on your policy when you have an accident with someone who has no insurance.
- *Underinsured Motorist*. Covers you or a person on your policy when you have an accident with someone who doesn't have enough insurance to cover your damages.

- Once you are sure that everyone is safe, call the police to report the accident.
- It is best not to discuss the car accident with anyone else on the scene. Wait for the police, tell them what happened, and let them figure out whose fault it is.
- The only information you should exchange with the other driver (or drivers) is name, address, phone number, insurance information, and license plate number.
- If there are witnesses hanging around the scene, ask them if you can have their contact information as well.
- As soon as you can, call your insurance company to report the accident. *Then* call your mom, your best friend, or anyone else who will help you feel better.

Renters Insurance

Renters insurance is one of those things that everyone knows that they should have, but many of us don't. Make sure you consider:

- What kind of coverage do you have already? Does your landlord cover your furnishings and belongings if there is a fire or flood that is not your fault?
- Do you have any coverage left over from your parents' homeowner's policy, especially if a lot of the items come from their house? Check to see if you can piggyback off their policy.
- If you do purchase renters insurance, make sure you know what is covered. Your computer may be your most valuable possession, so make sure it is included in your policy.
- Make sure that you are covered for both accidental damage and theft.

- If you are living with roommates, don't assume that just because one of you has coverage you all do.
- Can you get renter's insurance through a company you already do business with? Check to see if you can get a discount.
- If the premium is too high for you, ask about getting a policy with a higher deductible (the amount you have to pay out of pocket before the insurance company pays out). In that case, you'll be paying out of pocket if, for example, your stereo is stolen; but you're still covered if a fire or broken water pipe ruins all of your belongings.

You can get free quotes online at sites such as www.insure.com and www.insurance.com.

Travel Insurance

Traveling to a new or exotic place is an exciting adventure, but don't forget to stay well and stay safe. One common question is "Do I need travel insurance?" Not surprisingly, it depends on the trip and it depends on your health insurance. If you have health insurance, find out whether you are covered and how you are covered if you get sick or injured in another country. If you're attacked by a disgruntled baboon as you start your long anticipated trek up Kilimanjaro, does your insurance cover you if you need to be transported to the nearest city or out of the country altogether? If not, you may need some extra insurance to fill in the gaps in coverage. If you don't have any health insurance, strongly consider getting coverage for your trip. It can really suck to be sick when you are in a different country with a different health system, different language, and, perhaps, a different level of available care.

See our resources at the end of the chapter for further information on purchasing travel insurance.

Life Insurance

You may be lucky enough to be offered life insurance as part of your benefits package at work. If you are like most people though, you probably won't even think about life insurance until you get married or have kids. If you have a lot of debt that would get dumped on someone else in the case of your untimely death, look into it. But most twentysomethings don't have people who are depending on their incomes. Once you do get married and start thinking about kids, however, get yourself some life insurance and write your will. In the meantime, focus on getting health insurance and staying healthy!

Resources

AUTO INSURANCE

www.progressive.com

HEALTH INSURANCE

www.covertheuninsuredweek.org
www.healthinsuranceinfo.net
www.ehealthinsurance.com
www.insure.com
www.carefirst.com (individual plans)

TRAVEL INSURANCE SELLERS

www.insuremytrip.com
www.quotetravelinsurance.com
www.tripinsurancestore.com

CHAPTER 3

Habitat

In college it was pretty much a given that you'd live in the dorms freshman year, then move with friends to a nearby apartment or row house. That housing usually lasted about a year, and you might have furnished it with an old couch you found lying on the side of the road. Maybe you lived with your parents and commuted, which wasn't a big deal then. But now you're supposed to be independent, living the high life in a thriving town, occasionally throwing sophisticated dinner parties, right? Not really. It has become more and more common for graduates to move in with their parents before finding a job and settling into their own place; sociologists are now beginning to reassess the age at which we become adults as a result, referring to the trend as "boomeranging."

As you move from parents to roommates to eventually finding your own place, you will encounter new challenges—as well as benefits—that accompany each phase. We've done our best to provide you with guidelines for a variety of living situations that you may eventually experience.

Livin' with the 'Rents

According to our survey, 61 percent of quarterlifers lived at home for some period of time after college. Moving home can feel like a huge step backward after you have just spent four years gaining your independence on campus, but it is an inevitable result of rising housing costs, increasing debt, and competition for entry-level jobs. And, it does not have to be a bad experience. In fact, even though 61 percent of the quarterlifers who responded said that they would not live with their parents again, 76 percent said that they did get along with their parents. (See Figures 3.1, 3.2, 3.3, 3.4, and 3.5 for various statistics we've compiled about moving back home after college.)

It can, however, be difficult and awkward to adjust to life with your parents again. If you lived on campus during college, you got used to coming and going without anyone checking up

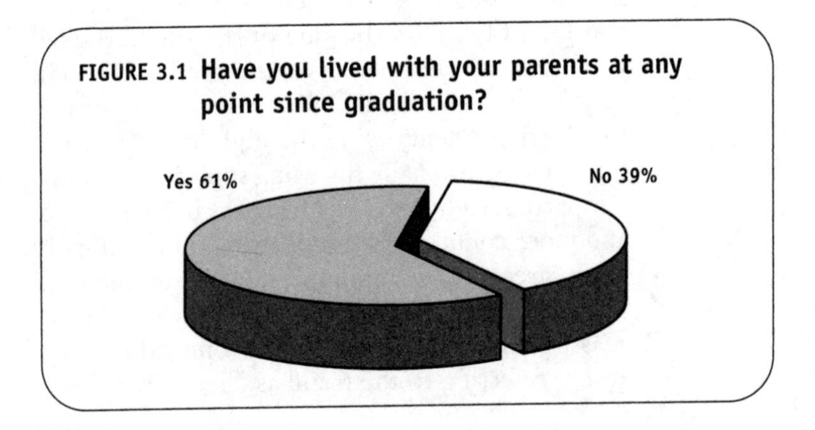

FIGURE 3.1 **Have you lived with your parents at any point since graduation?**

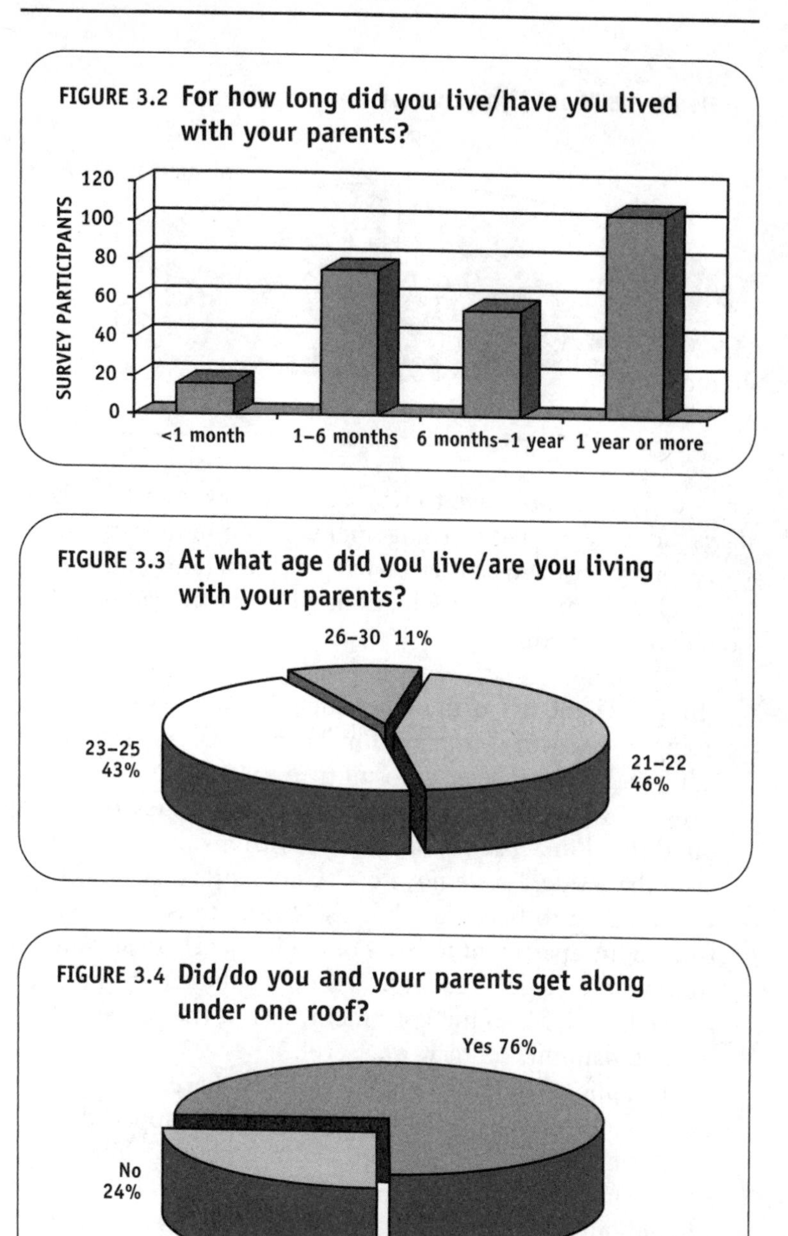

FIGURE 3.2 **For how long did you live/have you lived with your parents?**

FIGURE 3.3 **At what age did you live/are you living with your parents?**

FIGURE 3.4 **Did/do you and your parents get along under one roof?**

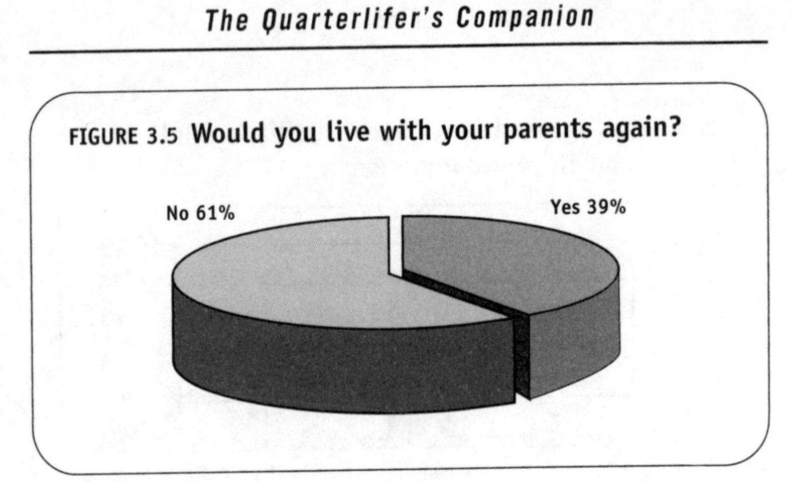

FIGURE 3.5 **Would you live with your parents again?**

on you. You did not have to worry about how your friends or dates judged your living arrangements. "Lumburg" is a typical voice on the message boards—having a tough time adjusting to life back at home, after graduation, when we are supposed to be independent adults:

> "So I'm 22 and live with my parents. And it looks like I'm going to live with them until I'm 25 and finish law school. This really sucks. I have no motivation to date or meet women. I have this constant feeling in the back of my mind that I'm a loser because I live with my parents, and even that aside, I have nowhere to take girls that I meet. I hate going to bars and clubs, so I used to bring them back to my apartment to hang out. That was basically my routine in college—meet girl, go out to dinner, if things go well, go back to my apartment, repeat the process. I liked it, dammit, and it worked well.
>
> "I suppose I could bring girls back here, but that would feel so creepy it's not even funny. I'm supposed to be getting romantic with a girl in my mother's house? And then my father interrogating me about her after? Or what about my mother bursting in to offer us cookies?

Ohhh man, I'd rather just not deal with it at all. This sucks. I really don't have a choice either. I have no money to pay for my own place, and there's no way I'm going to get a job while I'm so busy with school."—Lumburg

While it is not everyone's first choice to move back into their childhood bedroom, there are a lot of sensible reasons to live home for a while. If you are struggling to make student loan payments, if you have an opportunity to take an incredible unpaid or low-paying internship that will propel you into the job of your dreams, or if you are trying to save up for graduate school or for a down payment on your own condo, moving back home is a pragmatic step to take. Try not to beat yourself up about it, but rather appreciate the time you have to spend with your family. And if you think that moving back home seems difficult for you, make sure that you recognize that this change is not easy for their parents either. They have gotten used to living without dependents.

Linda Perlman Gordon and Susan Morris Shaffer, coauthors of *Mom, Can I Move Back in with You?*, note that it is normal in many cultures for adult kids to stay at home until they are married. However, for some families, this is an adjustment period that takes some getting used to. Gordon and Shaffer offer the following guidelines to make everyone a little more comfortable and sane:

- Most importantly, communicate. Talk about the move before it takes place. Make sure you have the same expectations as your parents about rules and responsibilities.
- Set a time limit in advance to begin looking for your own place after a certain number of weeks or months go by at home.
- Remember that courtesies still exist with your parents as adult children; it is still appropriate for them to ask you to

be quiet or neat. At mealtime, call ahead of time to tell them if you will or won't be coming so they know how much food to prepare.

- There has to be room for flexibility; expect some of your preestablished rules to be renegotiated. Just make sure you problem solve *together.*
- Keep in mind that your parents are in a different place emotionally, psychologically, and even financially than they were when you were a teenager.
- It is hard for your parents to see you around the house without a job, and it is not any easier now to see you come in at 3 a.m. from a night out than it was when you were in school.
- Your parent should not be your personal concierge. "Don't fall into the trap of acting like a kid," say Gordon and Shaffer. Some parents go into autopilot with kids no matter what their age. Tell your parents you don't *need* laundry or dinner, that you will do it yourself.
- Don't expect the things that annoyed you in high school to go away.
- If parents are difficult about a boyfriend or girlfriend sleeping over, don't make it a battleground. You won't change them or their values.
- Take personal financial responsibility—this doesn't necessarily mean paying rent. But make sure you are contributing something, such as paying college loans. Let your parents know about the steps you're taking toward financial independence.
- Offer to run errands, drive, or clean for your parents to show them that you can take care of yourself. They want to see you become independent and resilient. The goal is to show "respectful interdependence."

- Tell your parents that what you may need in terms of figuring out your future path is for them to listen rather than give advice. It can be hard to figure out your professional identity when your parents are home talking about their own careers. Tell them you appreciate it; you know they mean well, but you need to figure things out on your own. They can't make decisions for you, but this is a good mentoring opportunity—learn by watching, not by being told.
- This is an opportunity to ask your parents how to fix things rather than have them fix things for you.
- Be respectful of boundaries and sensitive to your hard-working parents. Show empathy that it may be a hard adjustment for them too; otherwise it's a "forced fit." Let your parents know you appreciate them.
- Don't keep problems to yourself, you'll just blow up. You should be able to set boundaries too.
- Face your demons from childhood. This is an opportunity to heal any bad early experiences. Is there anything for which you still blame your parents or feel resentment toward them? Resolve any lingering issues now, put the negative feelings behind you, and begin taking responsibility for your behaviors so you can get on with your life.
- If you and your parents can't seem to get along or communicate well, an objective third party such as therapist can provide some insight.

When it's not healthy to live with parents:

- When they are in need of support because of addictions and disorders such as alcoholism
- When your parents are so overly controlling that they do not even want you traveling to job interviews

A CONTRACT WITH YOUR PARENTS

Think of this as a lease with your parents; sit down and negotiate the terms with them, including chores, length of stay, and renewal conditions of both parties.

I, ____

(your name—tenant)

will live with

____

(parents' names—landlord)

from ____________________ until ____________________

(start date) (end date)

for a maximum of six months, renewable if the following conditions are met (conditions renegotiable on the first of each month).

Landlord must:

Adhere to rules requested by tenant, for example:

- No talking until after being home from work for half an hour.
- No meddling in bedroom.

Tenant must:

- Month 1: Spend _____ hours per week researching careers.
- Month 2: Apply for _____ jobs per week, continuously for six months or until job is found.
- Month 3: If no job is found at this point, tenant must temp or work part-time.
- Tell parents when you'll be home for dinner.
- Keep your room somewhat clean—at least no dishes or old food scattered around your room.
- Chores: ______________________________
- Rent or other monthly contribution: ______________________________
- Miscellaneous: ______________________________

PARENT TRAP ESCAPE PLAN

Think of this one as a contract with yourself.

It's 4 p.m. and you are sitting on your parents' couch watching *Oprah* or reruns of *MacGyver*. You have just finished a bag of chips—a supersized bag. Your mom will be starting dinner in about an hour, and you are wondering which high school friend to call tonight.

My friend, you are falling into a very dangerous place.

You are about to get caught in the "Parent House Trap." We understand that it is ever so much more comfortable to slip back into the comfy, warm familiarity of life at home, with mom and dad taking care of everything. Why keep knocking on corporate America's doors only to have them repeatedly shut in your face when you could just curl up with some book you loved as a kid and then eat a home-cooked meal?

It might sound dreamy. Couldn't you just let yourself slip into that place for a few days?

NO, you can't.

It's time to get off that couch and get a real life of your own!!

Here is our recommended "Parent House Escape Plan," a kind of boot camp for those made flabby by Parent House living.

1. Get up at a normal time, and the same time every morning, just as you would if you were going to work. Don't get used to sleeping in; you can sleep in on the weekends.

2. Schedule one job search outing each day. It must be something that gets you out of the house. It can be an interview, a trip to the library to do research, a trip to Kinkos to copy résumés, anything. It can be a lunch date with an acquaintance who has an interesting job you want to learn more about.

3. Complete one job search task each day. And it can't be "surfing the Web to research the industry." Yeah, nice try! No, you need to create a product: a cover letter sent in with your résumé, a thank you and follow-up letter, or a letter or e-mail requesting an informational interview.

4. Get some type of work. You may not have looked for a part-time job because you are interviewing for jobs, but you can still do some work. You'll feel better about yourself and you'll have some cash:
   a. Sign up with a temporary agency. You can opt to take work that fits around your job search schedule, and temping is a great way to find a permanent job.
   b. Substitute teach.
   c. Have your parents put out the word that you are available for babysitting, house-sitting, or yard work.
5. Do some kind of exercise each day. (What is boot camp without a few push-ups?) You will feel physically and emotionally healthier if you take care of your health and stay fit. Besides, you have to work off all of those chips.
6. Try to connect with a friend each day, someone from school or someone from home. Don't withdraw just because you are not working or are in a crappy job. Stay connected with the important people in your life.

Okay, have you checked off all six items on your list? Now you can watch *Oprah*. If you have time. And at least you won't be in your pajamas.

After earning our first paycheck, most of us are ready to move out of the 'rents, and begin paying the rent. In fact some of us may have moved to a new city directly following graduation and must begin an apartment search even before becoming gainfully employed.

Apartment Hunting

Searching for your first apartment can be an intimidating and exhausting task if you are not properly equipped. Know what you are looking for; prioritize your preferences and needs. Keep in mind that your place of residence affects your daily life—your commute and therefore your energy level; proximity or distance from your friends and social scene; and your financial health.

Finding the right apartment requires some serious sleuthing. If you don't thoroughly investigate, then you could end up in one of the following scenarios:

> "One thing I wish I'd asked at the place I live now—my very first apartment all on my own—is whether there are any smokers above or next to me. The guy above me smokes, and the smoke from his apartment comes down through the bathroom fan into my bathroom. I've taped a plastic bag over it, but I'm trying to get someone to seriously look into how the fan system works."—Libscigrl

> "My landlord recently tried to jack up the rent on a 2-bedroom apartment by about 40%—which is NOT 'what the market will bear' in my neighborhood. We got him down to raising it 12%, and allegedly they're going to put something in writing this week, but that would still have me shelling out over a grand a month in rent and utilities when all is said and done. I have the option to stay there or just move to my own place, much closer to work, where I would save about $150–$350 a month because all utilities are included. My primary concern is economics—I still think the rent at my current place will be ridiculous, and while technically I can afford it, I want to be saving $$$ for an MBA, house, etc., at this point, not throwing it away on rent! I feel a little bad about leaving my roommate needing to find someone else, but she's dead-set on staying there."—GetMeOuttaDC

You may face some tough decisions about what trade-offs you are willing to make. Do you sacrifice proximity to the social scene or being with your friends in order to save money? The more you do your research, the less likely you are to be locked into a lease that you will regret. Make sure you consider:

- **Location.** While no one wants to sit in traffic for an hour or take three different subway lines to get to their office, there are also some downsides to being too close to your office. After a day's work, you want to leave work behind in order to truly relax. Therefore, living footsteps away from your office may not necessarily be a plus, especially if you want to relax at home. Settling on a location in which to reside is more than a means to live; the location of your apartment will affect your social life and the people you hang out with, as well as work and the amount of stress either built up in a commute or left behind in the office.

- **Safety of the Neighborhood and Building Security.** You can request crime reports for your area from the police or public transportation system. If the neighborhood is not the safest but you don't seem to have any options, find out how secure the building is. Is there a 24-hour security guard at the front desk? That is generally safer than a walkup with a phone. Is there a garage for your car?

- **Rent and Utilities.** Generally, it is advisable not to spend more than half (this may vary by area) of your monthly income on rent and utilities. Therefore, if you make *$35,000* a year and bring home *$2,000* a month after taxes, Social Security, and health care, you should not be spending more than *$1,000* on rent. That will leave you enough room to put away some money each month into a pretax 401(k) account through your employer, CDs at the bank, or mutual funds (see Chapter 1). The cost of rent usually includes water, trash removal, and maintenance. In larger buildings, electricity and gas may be included as well, but it is important to ask the landlord whether these utilities are included. If not, they can run you an extra $100 a month, depending on both the size of your apartment and the time of year. In the winter, you may see your gas bills run high because of heat, and in the summer you may see electricity soar because of air conditioning. Of course this also depends on where you live. In case anyone wondered why their parents always bugged them not to leave any lights on at home, you will quickly find yourself becoming less liberal and more stringent with electricity use; you will have a greater appreciation for your parents' concern. If you do live in an apartment building where utilities are included, it may be tempting to leave things on all the time and take as long a shower as you'd like, but do not get in the habit of being wasteful—not only out of concern for resources, but also because you will likely eventually buy a place or move somewhere that demands a greater awareness for utility use.

- **Amenities.** It's a plus to have a laundry room on your floor, a fitness center in the building, and other facilities, but not necessary.
- **Other Residents.** Are your neighbors close in age to you? Do they seem to lead a similar lifestyle? Do you feel comfortable around your fellow residents, perhaps even see the potential for new friends? If you enjoy peace and quiet and notice cigarette butts and beer cans lying around, then it's probably not a good fit.
- **Space.** An efficiency or studio apartment should be enough space for a single person for about five years or less. You may have to sacrifice some amenities you are accustomed to, such as a dishwasher, particularly in older buildings that are convenient to happening city life.
- **Balcony/Patio/Yard.** Like the amenities mentioned above, any outdoor space is a plus but will add to the cost of your rent, so it just matters how important this is to you.
- **Parking.** Do you need space for a car? Does the building offer spaces? Are they covered, or at least reserved?
- **Public Transportation Nearby.** If you don't have a car, make sure you're on a bus or subway line convenient to your job. This can hike the rent, but sometimes it is necessary, and you at least save on gas and car maintenance.

- **Special Needs.** Are pets allowed? Is the building handicap accessible?

INTERPRETING THE LISTINGS—RED FLAGS

Generally, if the apartment listing seems too good to be true, it probably is. If the rent is way below the average in your area, there's a reason why—the place is falling apart, it's in a dangerous area, or you have to walk outside to get to a working bathroom. While the bathroom is probably essential, you may have to make some sacrifices if you really want to save money. Decide what's most important to you—the neighborhood or the space?

CREATIVE LISTINGS

WHEN THEY SAY:	THEY MAY MEAN:
"Beautiful hardwood floors"	There is no carpeting on these old creaky floors.
"10 minute walk to major bus line!"	It's really 20. It's 10 if you run as fast as you can.
"Charm, charm, charm!"	Tiny, old, and cramped.
Two bedroom, 800-square-foot apartment	One of the bedrooms is a closet.
"Gorgeous wooded view"	You will get no natural sunlight in your apartment.
"Quiet neighborhood"	Everything shuts down at 6:00 and there is no nightlife.
"Police-patrolled area"	This area is so dangerous it needs constant police patrolling.

Roommates

One way to save on rent is by having one or several roommates. In many metropolitan areas, there are group or shared houses, where the owner of a home rents the place out to several young professionals. This can be a cost-effective way of renting a good amount of space in a convenient location, while also enjoying the comfortable benefits of a single family home and the social benefits of a dormlike atmosphere.

However, as you surely know from your college years, roommates can also be a source of stress if not properly matched. We hear a lot of good roommate horror stories on the message boards:

> "I had a roommate once, for about 3 days. My job security was quite low at the time, and I needed a place where I could pay month to month without a lease. I visited the apartment twice at night, sorta looked around but didn't really look that closely.
>
> "When I moved in I realized how horribly gross her apartment was. There was a big blender cup in the sink that had been there since my first visit; there was dirt and grime and food stuck to the fridge, the floors, the counters, the carpet, the dishwasher, everything. The dishwasher didn't work. She didn't want me entertaining with friends at all in the living room. The apartment complex was gated, and I was supposed to always come in as a 'guest' and HOPE she would be home to give the okay for me to come in. I wasn't supposed to have mail sent there. I'd been staying with my boyfriend and we were driving each other absolutely nuts, but when I realized my mistake I got the hell out and went back to my boyfriend's."—Libscigrl

> "My last roommate was a little off-balance. He wasn't quite in touch with reality and had a very warped sense of justice. I first noticed it when I didn't keep my room very

clean, and someone ripped off the 'Trash Only' sticker from a trashcan outside and stuck it on the door to my room. Sure, my room wasn't the cleanest (it would insult pig sties to call it that), but this guy was so anal, he would iron his sheets. He would also take his dustbuster and vacuum his vacuum cleaner. I also began to notice little things, for example, my new tape deck started randomly to eat my tapes, and my CD player started to act up. Perfectly fine CDs, even new CDs right out of the package, would skip horribly but play fine in other people's stereos. I looked at my CD player and noticed a large black mark, like from a black permanent marker, on the laser head. I tried to rub it off, but the thing was busted.

"I didn't confront him on any of these things, which in retrospect probably incited him to further perpetrate additional crimes of inconvenience. I found half of a boiled egg in my shampoo bottle, a gooey substance that I can only identify as Thousand Island dressing in my hair gel, and garlic Caesar salad croutons in my saline solution. I started to suspect that something sinister was afoot. After discovering my shoelaces had been superglued together, my prescriptions were swapped into the wrong bottles, all my baseball hats adjusted one notch tighter, and more than the usual amount of socks lost to laundry, I decided to move to another apartment and ultimately another city."—Phil

So, how do you avoid becoming a player in a roommate horror story? You can't just pick your new living situation based solely on the location and how nice the house or apartment is and assume that the roommate situation will take care of itself. In college, you probably lived with close friends so the underlying friendship could help smooth over some of those angry moments when there were dirty dishes in the sink. (Again!) You also knew your friends, how much space they needed, what to do when they were in a bad mood, and what their top pet peeves were. After college, you won't necessarily live with roommates with whom you have a preexisting relationship. You will have to ask the right questions to make sure that you and your roommate are compatible, and set boundaries in advance so you are all aware of your mutual expectations. Sometimes roommates develop into close friendships, which is a great plus, but first make sure that you can live in the same space without making each other late to work, neglecting chores, or completely driving each other insane. Here are some roommate interview guidelines. Whether you are the interviewer or interviewee, make sure you know the answers:

- Do any of your prospective roommates smoke? What will be the smoking policy?
- Do you have a pet? Does anyone else have one?
- Speak ahead of time about bills and how the prospective roommate normally handles the bill-paying responsibilities. Pay attention to this part of the conversation. This may be where you find out that the prospective roommate can't have the phone in his or her name because of a "billing error" and a "misunderstanding" with the phone company. Be careful. You don't want to live with someone who is going to be unable to pay the bills.
- Does the prospective roommate have a boyfriend or girlfriend? If so, how often will they be in your space? This can be either a plus or minus if you are single—you could walk into a make-out session each night after work, or your roommate's significant other could have a friend who is perfect for you!
- Is the prospective roommate's schedule the same as yours? Is there only one bathroom? If so, how will you make your morning schedule work? Make sure you talk about it.
- Does the prospective roommate usually eat in or out? Are you going to end up crowding the kitchen after work?
- Does the prospective roommate lead a nightlife as wild—or

tame—as yours? You don't want to be woken up—or be the one who is disrupting everyone else—at 3 a.m.

- And, of course, how neat is the prospective roommate? If he or she is the interviewee and you can't see the living space, take note of how well put together they are; that's usually a good indication.

SAMPLE ROOMMATE FINDER QUESTIONNAIRE

Make it interesting. Find out what you're really getting into. Don't just ask the typical "are you neat" or "do you smoke" questions. Although these are important and should be included, you should seek out similar interests just as you would with a potential significant other. You may end up living with either one, so the requirements are similar!

Ask about work hours. Also, get a sense of how stressed or self-important they are.

The following questions are meant to be fun, lighthearted icebreakers to get to know a little something about your prospective roommates' lifestyles, but more about their personalities:

1. Thursday night: *Survivor* or *Apprentice*? Or neither?
2. Do you prefer to be warm or cool?
3. What is your No. 1 pet peeve?
4. How do you like to cook your eggs?
5. What is the first section you read in the Sunday morning paper?

And a special bonus question: Do you remember the name of the landlord in *Three's Company*? (Trick question—there were two.)

In addition to conducting your own interview, Harlan Cohen, author of *The Naked Roommate*, suggests getting a roommate referral. Speaking to a former roommate is going to give you a good sense of what your future roommate will be like. "The roommate who was late paying bills, partied every night, brought home strangers, lied, used drugs, and refused to clean the shower drain isn't going to change just because he or she has a new roommate," Cohen warns.

Once you have selected—or been selected as—a roommate, you should set up some guidelines. Cohen suggests discussing the "three basics" before moving in:

1. **Food.** Share or not share?

2. **Money.** When will you send rent? Who pays utilities? (You may also want to list a date each month by which all the bills need to be paid.) What happens if this doesn't work out or someone has to move early? Have a plan for how to handle the unexpected.

3. **Cleanliness.** Who does what and when will it get done? Kitchen, bathroom, common areas? Get a service or rotate who does what. Talk about it before things get dirty.

Make a list of all the chores and how often they need to be done. Some roommates like to set up chore wheels, which hang on the refrigerator, that assign different chores to each roommate every month. If you set up this type of system, just make sure it doesn't end up getting ignored.

You should also set up a night each week—Sundays are usually good—to cook dinner together, to get caught up, and to relieve any tension that may exist. Sometimes the problems between roommates (whether one feels like he or she is doing all the chores or worries about not giving the other enough space) are not discussed, and by setting aside some time together each week, you'll have a better understanding of the stress that each of you is facing.

Cohen stresses that roommates should "make it a rule to talk about problems before they become a habit. When something makes you uncomfortable, you tell the other roommate. Otherwise, one day you will just explode and throw your keyboard at someone's head because there is peanut butter and some other kind of crusty substance coating the buttons—AGAIN!!!"

Cohen's list of warning signs that you and your roommate may not be, well, compatible:

- Your roommate hands out spare keys to significant others without asking you.
- Your roommate borrows your underwear without asking, and then wears it on his or her head—even worse, he or she doesn't wash it before returning it.
- Your roommate invites guests to stay at your place without asking you—even worse, you walk in and find a stranger at home who used the key to get into your place.
- Your roommate wears your clothes without asking, stains them, and then returns them without telling you.
- Your roommate eats your food, doesn't replace it, and then asks you to go shopping because he or she is hungry.
- Your roommate likes to eat, sleep, and hang out naked in all rooms (and refuses to put a towel on the couch, kitchen chair, or desk chair).
- Your roommate's rent check bounces and you get evicted and locked out of your own place.
- Your roommate's idea of a good time is having strangers over every night to have sex, drink, and do drugs—you just prefer a hot cup of cocoa and a movie rental.

Apartment Living

Hopefully, the time you have to yourself or with friends in your new space will be peaceful and welcoming, but there may be things to deal with that you have never dealt with before, aside from difficult roommates—such as maintenance, difficult neighbors, or intrusive landlords. It is important to have an understanding of leases and contracts so that you won't be surprised if your rent increases by $100, or if you are charged a fine for painting one of your walls.

ROOMMATE RULES AND REGULATIONS
Q&A with Harlan Cohen, author of *The Naked Roommate*

How do you get slacker roommates to pay bills on time?
Use eBay—you sell your roommate's clothing, shoes, or bed—actually, you can even sell your roommate (not recommended, but desperate times call for desperate measures).

Make sure your roommate doesn't have a history of being late (again, talk to previous roommates). An unemployed, unmotivated, and unwilling roommate will mean that you have to move out. Avoid it before it becomes a problem. Avoid having utilities in just your name—have them in your roommate's name or in both names. If your roommate has a bad history, get his or her parent to co-sign the lease.

Do you always need to include the roommate when inviting guests over?
No, a roommate doesn't need to always be included. Especially if having a boyfriend or girlfriend over (unless you're into that sort of thing). There are two kinds of roommates: roommates who are friends and roommates who are people who pay rent. You don't have to be friends with your roommate. You just have to pay rent.

Can you change a slob or accept taking responsibility for all chores?
No, no, no. You can't change a slob so don't even try. You'll only get dirty, and you'll get aggravated. Unless your name is Mom or Dad, it's not your job. So don't even try.

What if you have different decorating concepts—how to compromise?
If you can't agree on decorations, you might need an entirely new scheme—like a new roommate. Come on! If you can't compromise on the decorating, you're not going to get along. Find a new roommate.

According to www.Nolo.com, a free legal source on the Web, a landlord typically must give you 24 hours notice before entering your apartment, unless there is an emergency such as a fire or flooding. Should a dispute arise with a landlord regarding a questionable repair, apartment entry, or deposit withholding, try to talk to the landlord about it first. If you are still unsatisfied with the situation, you might want to try a local dispute resolution service or mediation. If that still doesn't get you anywhere and a lot of money is at stake, you may need to look into small claims court. Always keep copies of your written correspondence with the landlord and visit www.Nolo.com for more information on these proceedings.

DECORATING

Since your first couple of apartments are temporary, it's a good idea not to collect too much stuff, so keep a minimalist decorating style. You can still supplement your basic pieces of furniture with fun, inexpensive accents that make your place more livable. Although your apartment may be temporary, you want to come home every night to a comfy, cheerful, welcoming home. You have a lot of expenses when you move into your first apartment. Once you pay the rent and the security deposit, you may feel as if you have no choice but to sleep on cinder blocks and eat off milk crates. There are some fun and affordable ways to acquire some furnishings:

- If you are looking for something nice but can't afford new furniture, check out your local consignment stores for furnishings.
- Head out to the 'burbs on the weekend and look for garage sales.
- Flea markets can be a great place to find rugs, lamps, mirrors, and other furnishings.
- Even if you are super busy, you still have time to browse online at eBay.

- Pay attention when friends and family members move—a lot of people would love to hand off furniture they no longer want, especially if you can come get it.

- If you live near a college campus, hang out on move- day. A lot of usable furniture gets thrown away bec isn't worth the cost of moving or storing it.

- Check out your community's free cycle W people offer perfectly usable items for post a request if you're looking for a s

You may not need (or want) a place *Digest*, but you also don't want to come ho drab, depressing dump. It does not have to your place feel a bit more homey and persona up your surroundings will also lift your spirits.

Other Tips

- **Plants and Pillows.** Particularly consider cacti, they need to be watered often. Even fake plants or flowers look tasteful. Use small pillows of various materials, colo and patterns to liven up a deadbeat sofa. You can also use throws and blankets to make the back of the couch look nicer, if that side is exposed, and keep you warm when staying in and cuddling up to a rental movie.

- **Light.** Lamps are functional and enhance the look and feel of apartments, which don't usually have ceiling lights. Be wary of halogen lamps however, they can start fires. Candles add a nice calming atmosphere to the apartment. You can even get candles scented like cookies or cake to feign the aroma of freshly baked goods. You can find perfectly good candleholders at the dollar store, or even use old glass dishes and bowls. Just remember not to keep them lit when you go out!

- **"Art."** Try framing paintings or photographs from old calendars; anything looks better in a frame. Or, buy a blank canvas and paint it just one or two colors. Ever see those modern art pieces where the top third is orange, the bottom is red, and there might be a black line through the middle, and you think "I could do that"? Well, do it. Since leases usually prevent you from painting your walls, head to the local craft store for a canvas, paint, and a brush. These can be fun bonding projects, too, for roommates or friends.

- **Accent Furniture.** Scout flea markets for side tables and room dividers.

Don't worry about what is acceptable; do whatever fits. Just so long as you're not violating any fire hazard codes.

SAFETY

Andrea Vander Pluym, coauthor of *RESPECT*, was afraid of taking a self-defense class until she finally signed up for one listed in the paper. Impact self-defense changed her life so much that she is now an instructor. She stresses the importance of being prepared no matter what your background or where you live. Just look at the statistics. For women, one in eight will be assaulted. People today are still apprehensive to sign up, but you "shouldn't have to defend taking self-defense, it's like wearing a seatbelt in a car." Self-defense is a good way to "gain control when you lose your sense of security after college."

Andrea offers the following tips for recent grads living in an unfamiliar area:

- Trust your gut when walking through an unfamiliar area. You're not being silly, paranoid, or racist if you think there is something sketchy about someone sitting alone in a car.
- Don't talk on your cell phone in a bad neighborhood, especially at night, because criminals will think you are not paying attention.

- Be aware—if someone is walking quickly behind you, cross the street or duck into a nearby store. Don't worry about what they or anyone else thinks.
- Bus stop walls and kiosks can be used as weapons against you. Avoid situations where you can be trapped or cornered; make sure nothing is behind you.
- If you have just gone shopping and are about to get into your car when someone is coming toward you, wait for them to pass first before putting your bags in the car.
- Try holding eye contact when you feel intimidated by someone approaching you. The person who holds eye contact the longest shows dominance. Don't smile; that may be seen as an invitation. There are different types of gazes, and you can fine-tune yours by practicing in the mirror or with friends.
- Use an assertive voice—this doesn't necessarily mean speaking loudly or in a high pitch. Speak with direction and conviction, don't end on an intonation, and don't smile or giggle. That will undermine your message.

Buying Property

SHOULD YOU BUY?

A lot of our readers in big metro areas are going to look at the title of this section with disbelief and wonder why a book for twentysomethings would have a section on buying a home. We were surprised to learn that there are some places where twentysomethings can actually afford homes, with yards and everything! They don't all live in fourth floor walk-ups that have been converted from utility closets. For what some of us pay in rent, others can afford a mortgage on their own houses or condos.

For those of you who cannot even think about buying your own place, here is your chance to go back to Chapter 1 and reread the section on how to save money.

WHEN TO BUY

It might be painful to write that rent check every month and know that you will never get any of it back. And as prices escalate in hot markets throughout the United States, you may be tempted to rush into the market. Blake Newman of Artists Realty suggests buying because "home ownership is one of the last best tax breaks that exist," not to mention a good investment.

There are a lot of good reasons to buy rather than rent, but first you need to make some important decisions.

- The first thing you have to figure out is whether you are going to stay where you are. Most of us hop around too much to settle down and buy a place, but if you know you will stay somewhere for at least three years, think about buying. You have to pay a lot of transaction fees when you buy a house or condo so you need to be in the same place for a few years to recoup those costs. Newman also notes that "sometimes it is beneficial to rent in a building or neighborhood to make sure you like the area before you buy."

- If you would like to see a return on your investment, then you should buy when the time is right for both you and the property. Newman suggests looking during the winter, when the market isn't as "hot" (literally), and you'll have more room to negotiate. Also, if it's possible, wait until there is a buyers' market: "In a buyers' market, there are more sellers than buyers and you can basically call the shots. There are many properties on the market to choose from. You have lots of time to make a decision. You can force the seller to fix any discrepancies or problems in the home, and you can ask for seller assistance in paying closing costs. However, in a sellers' market, the opposite is true."

HOW MUCH CAN YOU AFFORD?

- The second thing that you should do is go talk to a reputable mortgage lender. Ask around. Talk to someone who has recently purchased a home and ask for the name of their mortgage broker. The bank will tell you how much you can borrow and at what rate. Looking at your finances, the bank will be able to offer some suggestions for how you can finance your purchase and some guidelines as to how much of your income you can comfortably spend on a mortgage. For example, typically lenders do not like you to invest more than one-third of your income on a home, but in some cases you can invest as much as half.
- As you are thinking about how much you can afford, don't forget to factor in property taxes and home insurance and, on the plus side, don't forget to factor in the juicy tax deduction you'll receive for being a homeowner. Again, your mortgage broker can help you with all of this number crunching. There are also some good online calculators on Web sites belonging to companies like Fannie Mae to help you get started.
- Talking to a lender right away will also help you find out if there are any problems with your credit score or discrepancies on your credit report. If a lender discovers a derogatory remark on your credit, be sure to resolve it quickly. Remember our section on your credit score? This is where a problem with your credit can cost you.

SELECTING AN AGENT

Now that you have an estimate of the amount you can spend, you are ready to find a real estate agent. As with finding a mortgage broker, you want to make sure that you find a reputable professional. If you can, go with a friend or family member's recommendation. You want to be sure that your agent is competent when it comes to negotiating the contract details.

Meet with the recommended agent and make sure that he or she understands what you are looking for and doesn't take a lot of time to get back to you. Also, make sure they explain the process clearly. Remember that they ultimately benefit from your satisfaction and should therefore be willing to accommodate your needs and situation.

In addition, Newman notes that "a competent real estate agent will know neighborhoods and conduct thorough market analysis and research so that when you look at properties you will know whether the home is priced at, above, or below market. Some real estate agents are active investors. These agents are always on the lookout for a good buy and are even more keenly knowledgeable of market value. Consequently, they are very attuned to the hurdles, frustrations, and challenges that buyers face."

SELECTING A PROPERTY

Don't buy anything until you've seen at least 5 to 10 places. Think of this as your part-time job. You won't really know whether or not you're getting a good deal until you've done a thorough analysis of the market. There are so many factors that affect the value of a home:

➤ **Location, Location, Location**

Accessibility to work.

Accessibility to public transportation—this can as much as double the price.

Safety/gentrification—it's considered unethical for an agent to give his or her opinion on the safety of a neighborhood, so plan to research this on your own through neighborhood police reports. According to Newman, "Communities that are primarily owned tend to have lower crime rates than communities that are primarily rented."

Accessibility to shops, restaurants, parks, and jogging trails.

- **Square Footage and Number of Rooms.** Newman notes, "If you plan on having a roommate so you can split the expenses, a second full-bath is really nice to have."
- **Updated Appliances and Amenities, Including Laundry.** "If the home was not built for a washer and dryer, then it's very difficult to add this on as an afterthought," notes Newman.
- **Well-Maintained Interior and Exterior.** The more work required, of course, the lower the value. This could be negative or positive depending on your interests. Do you want a "fixer-upper?" Do you like projects? Are you handy? If not, or if you don't have time to deal with projects outside work, then go for something that doesn't need much work. That may mean a smaller place, but less hassle. There are two types of fixer-uppers: distressed property and lacking curb appeal. With the former, there may be "serious structural problems" not worth the cost to fix.

  Natural light "lifts people up and is proven to bolster a person's immune system," according to Newman.

  Look for lead-based paint in houses built before 1978. Flaking may be a sign.

PLACING YOUR BID

Just because you find a place doesn't mean it's yours. If you live in a more competitive market, you may find yourself in a bidding war with other potential buyers. In some cases, sellers are even dropping inspections or selling their homes "as is" because they know that buyers are desperate enough to find a place. If you live in these areas, it's important to move quickly. Your schedule must have the flexibility to drop everything to check a place out as soon as it's available and to write up a contract with your agent.

- In a hot market, "a home that has been on the market for more than a month is probably overpriced, poorly located, or lacks some type of curb appeal that turns off most buyers," according to Newman.

- Depending on the market, you may need to include an escalation clause, which sets the highest price you are willing to buy at to offset any potential competing bids.
- Expect to initially pay a 3 percent earnest money check, which counts toward your down payment of 10 to 20 percent. You can also expect to put down about 3 percent for closing costs, such as inspections and loan application fees.

WHAT NEIGHBORHOOD IS RIGHT FOR YOU?

I go out:

a. Once or twice a week
b. Three to five times a week
c. Every night

I depend on the following mode of transportation for work:

a. Car
b. Subway/buses
c. Bike/feet/scooter

I prefer to live:

a. By myself
b. With a roommate
c. With several roommates

My idea of a good time:

a. Game nights and dinner parties
b. Dinner and a movie out
c. Bars and parties

Give yourself one point for each (a), two for each (b), and three for each (c). The results are as follows:

4–6 Suburbia
7–9 Urban fringe
10–12 City center

Resources

LIVING AT HOME
www.boomerangnation.com
www.movebackin.com

LIVING WITH ROOMMATES
www.helpmeharlan.com
www.roommates.com

CHEAP DECOR
www.freecycle.org

TENANT RIGHTS
www.Nolo.com

NATIONAL APARTMENT LISTINGS
www.Apartments.com
www.craigslist.com
www.Rentnet.com

MORTGAGE CALCULATORS
www.fanniemae.com/homebuyers/calculators

REAL ESTATE DEFINITIONS
www.hud.gov/offices/hsg/sfh/buying/glossary.cfm

CHAPTER 4

Time Management

Believe it or not, there are still 24 hours in the day when you graduate from college. The same 24 hours you had each day in school. The same 24 hours you used to fill with a wide array of activities as a college student. So why does it feel like you could do so many more things while you were a student than now? In school, you took your classes, probably had a job, belonged to clubs, volunteered for causes you believed in, had tons of time with friends, worked out (well sometimes), ran your errands, and still managed to call home on occasion. Now you've graduated and what do you do? You go to work. You go out on weekends and sometimes out for dinner during the week and, and . . . that's it. Where did all the time go? No wonder life after school can feel so empty. All of those things we used to do and the fun that went with them get lost somehow.

Adapting to Your New Schedule

Some QLCers prefer their new schedules, and there are some definite benefits to your new nine-to-five life. Your schedule is a lot more predictable and the nagging feeling that you really should be studying, no matter what it is that you are doing, is gone. When we asked members of the QLC message boards whether managing their time was easier or more difficult, we got a mixed reaction.

Some found it to be easier:

> "I found [the real world schedule] much easier. Because I had no homework, I went in and worked my 9–10 hours/day and that was it. Went home, showered, and went to the bar. The one thing I had to realize though was that missing 'class' now was not acceptable."—natbumpo

> "Now things are more routine. When I was in school, I always felt like I was bouncing around between work, school, home, and my boyfriend's. I feel that things are more structured now, and I have always been good with structure."—Kimmer23

Others said:

> "In some ways it's been easier . . . in other ways it's been harder. I've always been a procrastinator, and now that my job doesn't have deadlines like I did with my schoolwork, that has added to the difficulty of getting things done. In college, it seemed like I had more free time to do little things, like going to the grocery store, or running to the mall. Now I have to plan out those things."
> —Jen312

"When I was a student, I lived at home and always felt a looming pressure to get more schoolwork done; yet I didn't have to worry about bills, grocery shopping, cooking, and cleaning. Now things are more structured, which helps, but there's less personal time and more crap to take care of during that 'off' time. If I only had a 50s style wife to clean my apartment, buy & cook my food, organize my stuff, and iron my clothes, life would just be swell (only kidding!)."—Libscigrl

Even though Libscigrl was just kidding about having a 1950s style wife to take care of the details of her life, these new details really do suck up a lot of time. Do you find yourself wondering, "How do these stupid little errands take up so much time? Do I really have to take a day off, a day I could be sitting on a beach somewhere, to go to the DMV, wait for the cable guy, or get an appointment with my dentist?"

One shocking adjustment that accompanies the transition from school to work is the sudden lack of time for personal activities and errands. You will just have to become savvy about how you use your time so that you can take care of the little details and still have time for the "big picture" items in your life. For example:

- Use your lunch hour as much as possible to avoid running to the grocery store or picking up dry cleaning at the end of the workday when everyone else is there. Pick your bank, dry cleaner, doctor, and pharmacy as close to your office as possible. If you don't have errands to run, schedule lunches with friends both in and out of the office. So many people try to conscientiously work through lunch and never leave their desks. Come in a little early if you need to punch in some extra face time. Getting stuff done little by little throughout the week will leave your evenings and weekends more open and leave you feeling less stressed out on Sunday night.

- Try to find a buddy for things that are hard to motivate yourself to do on your own. If you just dread the idea of going to the Laundromat, find a laundry buddy. You'll get rid of that huge mountain of dirty clothes on your floor and you'll get caught up with a friend. If you are finding it difficult to muster up the motivation to go the gym, find an exercise buddy who will exert positive peer pressure.

- Maybe you are the type of person who is really good at suggesting an idea and getting something started, but you are not so good at keeping things organized. Team up with a friend who is better at organizing, scheduling, and sustaining the idea once you have it going.
- Anything that allows you to multitask is a good thing. A good headset for your phone can help you return all of the calls from your mom or your friends when you have a sink full of dishes or a bunch of laundry to fold.
- Make cooking time a social activity. Are you one of those people who will go to some effort to cook if someone is coming over, but you eat ramen if it's just you? Then invite people over and use your cooking time to catch up with friends as well.

Taking some time to plan will actually save you some time in the long run. We can't be as spontaneous as we were in school, but with a little planning we can maintain some balance in our lives. And while it's important to find time for many of the above-mentioned appointments, San Francisco–based writer Susan Orenstein reminds us not to get overly ambitious with our to-do lists:

- Be realistic with your time to avoid guilt. Give up on the idea that you'll get it all done in one fell swoop—pace yourself, most errands are continuous and will never go away.
- If you prioritize, you'll take care of the most important things. Don't make to-do lists without attaching items to a time frame, and make a fantasy wish list to look at when you have an abundance of free time.

- Carry around a notebook, the "everything book." Transfer your important contact information, appointments, and lists to this book rather than accumulate Post-it notes.

TIMESAVING AND ORGANIZATION TIPS

- **Plan maintenance activities for yourself, your car, and your home ahead of time to avoid unnecessary time and bills later on. Find a doctor and a dentist and schedule your checkups.**
- **Divide up grocery shopping duties and chores with your roommates and try to keep a cleaning schedule. Find a cleaning service you can call in case of "emergency" (i.e., you are all working crazy hours and you are starting to get concerned about the strange smells emanating from the dark corners of your place).**
- **Schedule conference calls with friends to stay in touch.**
- **Set up automatic bill payment, either through direct debit or automatic credit card payment, for all of your bills, your utilities, and the phone.**
- **Set up accounts on airline and travel sites so that you can plan your travel more easily and get frequent flyer points.**
- **Respond to e-mails when you get them—sending off a quick message takes a moment and you won't feel as if you have a big pile of correspondence hanging over your head.**
- **Memorize your important financial numbers, especially your credit card number. If you have your credit card and checking account numbers memorized, you can take care of all kinds of little chores when you are waiting for the bus or standing in line somewhere.**

Work–Life Balance

The previous section discussed how QLCers adapt to their new schedules and how you can better balance your schedule in the "micro" sense by becoming more organized and paying attention to your schedule. But there is also the "big picture" to think about. How do QLCers find the right amount of balance between their work lives and their personal lives?

Achieving balance in your life is not going to be one of the items you check off your "to do" list and then just move on. "Achieving balance is a very dynamic process," says Margarita Rozenfeld, a life coach with her own practice. Even she, a life coach, finds herself getting stressed out juggling her responsibilities as a business owner and founder of a Yes!Circle, a large networking group for entrepreneurs. "It's constantly bringing yourself back" into balance when you find yourself getting stressed out. Once you have taken some steps to figure out what your priorities are, "it becomes about practicing, and forgiving yourself for not being perfect."

Sean Covey, son of Stephen Covey, the author of *The 7 Habits of Highly Successful People*, grew up in a family whose business it was to teach the world how to achieve balance in their lives. He himself has written *The 7 Habits of Highly Effective Teens* and *Fourth Down and Life to Go* and managed to balance his academic life with his very successful collegiate football career. So it was surprising to hear him say in our interview that your life after school isn't going to be balanced and probably shouldn't be.

As Covey explained, "There are seasons of imbalance" in our lives, and life after graduation is one of them. He explained that you will hear a lot of people tell you to achieve balance in your life, but when you first get out of school, "you are in survival mode." You are going to be learning a new job or trying to excel in a graduate program and juggling all of the new responsibilities of being on your own. If you are in a new job, it makes sense that work feels all consuming and that you are completely focused on learning your new job and, more importantly, keeping it.

Covey warns that you won't be able to sustain that imbalance forever, though. Eventually you will feel burnt out and used up and you may start:

- ➤ Resenting your work
- ➤ Not finding enjoyment in anything that you do
- ➤ No longer feeling mentally quick
- ➤ No longer feeling sharp with your skills

At that point, you will need to find ways to "renew yourself" outside of the workplace. One of the seven habits that the Coveys recommend is "Sharpening the Saw," which means spending some time away from the job and doing something rejuvenating for yourself, whether that means going for a hike, working out, or enjoying a nice meal.

While you may think it is frivolous to spend time on yourself if you are feeling pressured about a huge pile of work on your desk, taking an hour to refresh yourself can buy you two hours of extra productivity.

Covey notes that a lot of fun and meaningful opportunities are going to come your way. And although we think that our twenties are a great time to try new things, meet new people, and take advantage of every opportunity, we still need to prioritize: "Figure out what you want to say 'yes' to." That way, you are cramming your schedule full of things that are meaningful to you.

Rozenfeld agrees that knowing your top five priorities is crucial to your well-being and recommends that you share these priorities with the people in your life. Because we can lose sight of the big picture when we are stressing out about the day-to-day, it is our friends and families who can remind us when we are forgetting what is important to us.

The first thing that people have to do is figure out what balance means to them. It will take some trial and error to figure out which strategies work best.

"In my first few years in the workforce after college, I learned that careers are greedy. If left unchecked, a career will devour any amount of time the worker throws at it. Eventually I realized that workplace achievement operates on a completely different time scale than that of college: it isn't a matter of finishing a term paper by the end of the semester, but of making VP within a decade. Once I had the proper perspective, I found it much easier to, for instance, sail out of the office at 5 p.m. (or earlier) when the weather is good, knowing that I would have ample opportunity to demonstrate my commitment to my job over the next, say, 30 or 40 years.

"I have developed specific habits to ensure that work doesn't become all-consuming. In college, I was spontaneous, and never planned my weekend until Friday afternoon. Now I always manage my social calendar at least one week in advance, and ensure that there are no less than one or two nights each week that I have prearranged plans to meet a friend for drinks or dinner at 5:30 or 6:00. This ensures that I do not go an entire week working late every night. Moreover, I have learned to manage my personal relationships much the same way I do my business relationships—if I want to see someone, whether the head of marketing to finish a client presentation or an old college roommate to blow off steam, I contact him or her well in advance, set a specific time and meeting location, and call to confirm just prior to the meeting to make sure it happens."—Brad

BALANCE PYRAMID

Think about the four most important priorities in your life and list them below. They may be family and/or friends, work/professional life, spirituality, volunteer work, physical activity, a significant other:

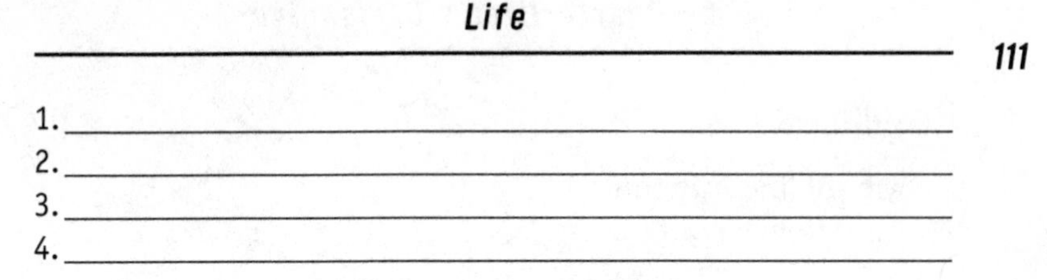

Now fill in the pyramid below to represent how important these segments of your life are from most important (1) to least important (4). Designate what percentage of your time you spend on each segment.

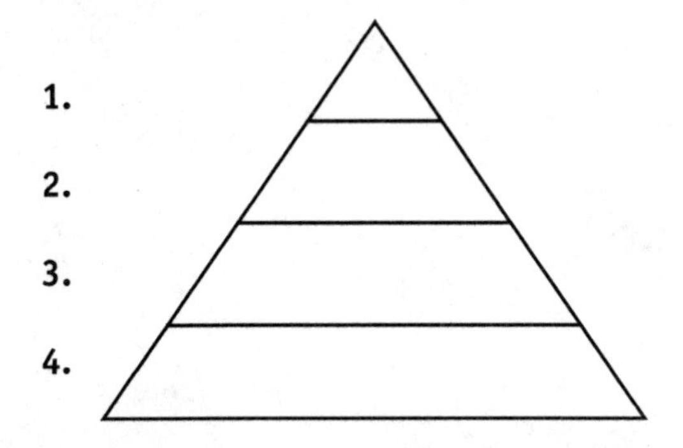

Now think about how you spend your time. Write down in the pyramid below the top four activities of your waking hours from (1) the activity that you spend the most time on to (4) the activity you spend the least time on. Designate what percentage of your time you spend on each activity.

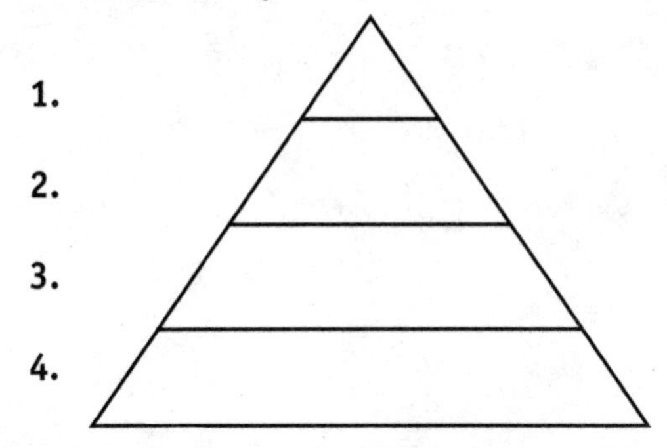

Now compare your two pyramids. How similar do they look? How many categories from Pyramid 1 appear on Pyramid 2? How do your pyramid levels compare?

Resources

www.franklincovey.com
www.ofessence.com

PART 2

Work

CHAPTER 5

Finding a Job

Finding a job can be one of the first really shocking experiences of your quarterlife crisis. Up until the time you leave college there has always been a plan for you to follow: get good grades in high school so that you can get into college. Get good grades in college so that you can get a good job. Except it doesn't happen that smoothly, does it? Do you find yourself yearning for the days of college applications, a predictable process, and published deadlines? Does that wide array of colleges and universities now pale in comparison with the seemingly unlimited number of job categories awaiting you after graduation?

And while plenty of us had part-time and temporary jobs, finding your first "real" job seems . . . so permanent. We thought choosing a major was an important decision, but choosing a job seems so much more significant and life affecting. And that's assuming we can even find a job! As much as we all nervously awaited our college acceptance letters, we all knew *someone* would take us. After all, we would be paying them to keep us busy for the next four years. But we can't be so sure about our chances when it comes to getting someone else to pay us for our qualifications and experience, or lack thereof. The process is so uncertain and impersonal, and we often feel unprepared. (See Figures 5.1, 5.2, and 5.3 for our survey results on the subject of jobs.)

Show Me the Hoops and I'll Be Happy to Jump

A lot of twentysomethings tell us that they wish they had a job search path like investment bankers, management consultants, or doctors—a path that is methodical and straightforward. They want a series of steps and tasks that, if completed well, lead to the job reward at the end. That is what school trained us to do—we studied to get good grades and signed up for the next level once we passed. In the real

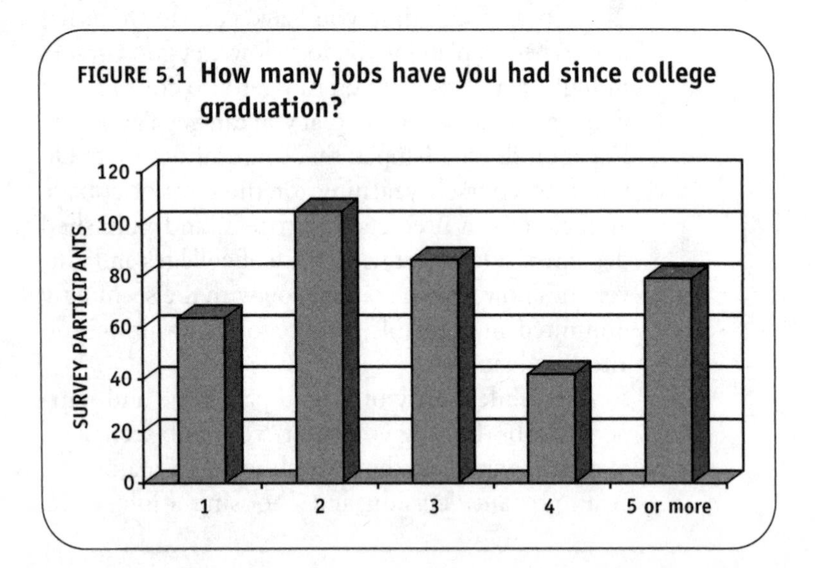

FIGURE 5.1 **How many jobs have you had since college graduation?**

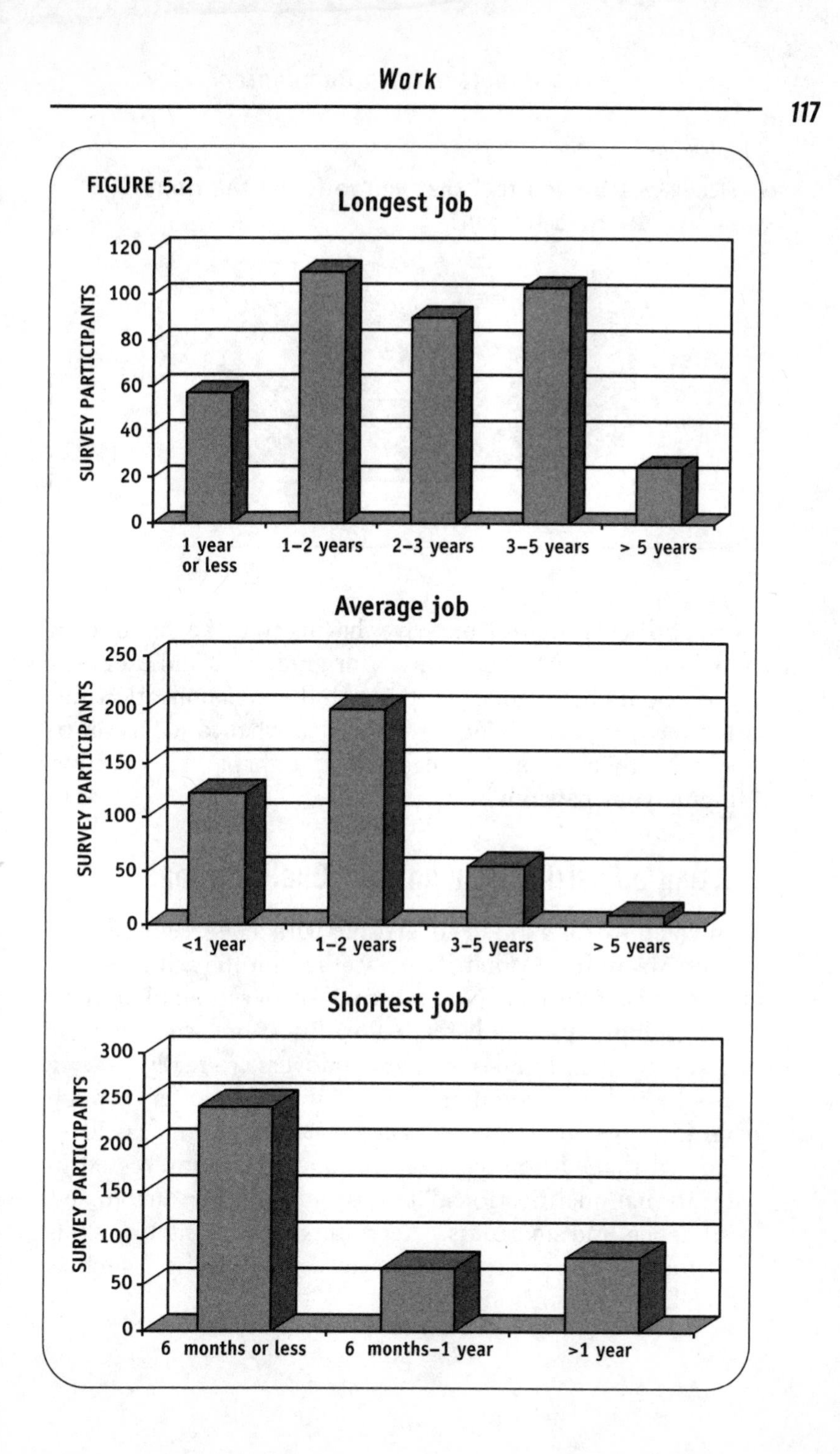
FIGURE 5.2
Longest job
SURVEY PARTICIPANTS
120
100
80
60
40
20
0
1 year or less
1–2 years
2–3 years
3–5 years
> 5 years
Average job
SURVEY PARTICIPANTS
250
200
150
100
50
0
<1 year
1–2 years
3–5 years
> 5 years
Shortest job
SURVEY PARTICIPANTS
300
250
200
150
100
50
0
6 months or less
6 months–1 year
>1 year

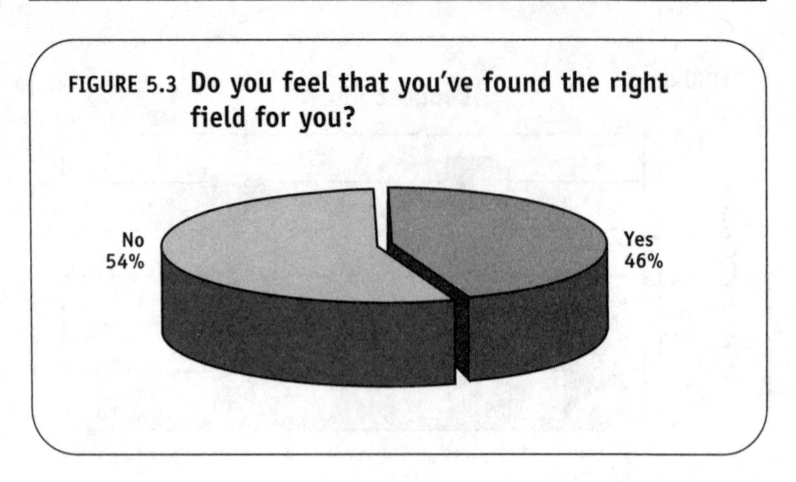

FIGURE 5.3 Do you feel that you've found the right field for you?

world, however, we find ourselves having to make up our own individual paths as we go along. Our guidelines and exercises below should help guide you through the job application and interview process. If you have no idea what kind of job to apply for, then be sure to read our next chapter's section on "finding your passion."

Putting a Positive Spin on Your Qualifications

Can you look for a job in advertising with a degree in philosophy? Absolutely. What if you studied biology, but decide medicine isn't for you? No problem. You have to look beyond the seemingly direct job-related qualifications, such as your field of study, and find out what employers are really looking for—the ability to communicate—that you can offer through your interests and activities. *The Economist,* in January 2004, reported that "Employers are becoming less interested in educational qualifications," but rather look for "articulacy, confidence, and smartness." Recruiters are looking for "skills that formal education does not necessarily bring," such as office lingo and customer service.

QUICK FACT

What if you are one of the many psychology graduates with seemingly limited job opportunities? According to psychologists Eric Landrum and Renee Harrold, the five most important traits that employers want from psychology graduates are:

- **Listening skills**
- **The desire and ability to learn**
- **The willingness to learn new and important skills**
- **The ability to get along with others**
- **The ability to work with others as part of a work team**

THE COLLEGE EXPERIENCE CONVERTER

It's a Catch-22: You need experience to get experience. However, most recent grads minimize the significance of their college academic and extracurricular activities. Although your campus experience may not seem directly related to the skills you'd list on a résumé, you can extract some valuable qualifications to mention in your résumé or during a job interview if you really put your mind to it. For example, did you participate in a sports club or the campus newspaper? If so, did you exhibit leadership skills or develop that coveted team player attitude? Did you learn valuable research tools or presentation skills for a big class project? Did you help organize a club or campus social event?

Extracurricular Activity	Why Did You Like It?	Skills You Used
1. ______		
______		

2.______________________________

____

3.______________________________

____

4.______________________________

____

5.______________________________

____

Looking for a Job in the Digital Age

HEARING BACK—YOU MAY NOT

It can often be surprising and disappointing for twentysomethings fresh out of high school or college and full of ambition and enthusiasm when they do not get so much as a courtesy response from prospective employers. Especially today, with the increased use of online job boards, it is rare to get a courtesy "no" or an explanation as to why you are not qualified to even be considered for an interview.

The Internet offers so many resources for job searching, but a lot of people feel that applying for jobs online just makes the process even more dehumanizing and less personal.

You may already feel like Josh Aiello, author of *60 People to Avoid at the Water Cooler*, who told us, "I never really had any luck looking for a job, unless I knew someone. I yearned for even a negative response—just to know that there is someone out there." Looking for a job can already make you feel as if no one is paying attention to you. Applying for a job online can make you feel even more anonymous. How can you stand out and use online tools to your advantage?

Even though online tools make it so much easier to search for jobs, research industries, and contact prospective employers, "the risk is that people are not customizing their job search and their communication pieces. You get back what you give," warns Rosemary Haefner, senior vice president at online job search service CareerBuilder.com.

Haefner shared the following tips for novice job seekers:

- "We are seeing interesting patterns in networking. There's an attitude that networking is old school," but online job searching does not take the place of all the other job-searching tools at your disposal.
- You have to translate your experiences for them, especially if you don't have a lot of work experience. It is up to you to show the recruiter how your experience as manager of your campus bookstore makes you perfect for a particular job. Don't expect them to connect the dots. That's your job.
- Don't send the same résumé and cover letter in for every job posting! Sure it's easy to hit "send" but there are a lot of online options to help you create multiple résumés so that you can customize appropriately. You also should be customizing your cover letters.
- Use the Web to its advantage. You have access to so much online information about companies, industries, and people. You have no excuse not to do your homework.
- Don't be lulled into a false sense of casualness. You may be e-mailing your résumé and cover letter, but write it just as formally and professionally as if you were printing them out on that really expensive résumé paper.
- For some positions, such as Web developers or journalists, some applicants are showing portfolios of their work. This is an opportunity not easily available before online searching. The problem, though, is that people include personal

photos or a personal Web page that dilutes the professionalism of the application. Even if you are in a creative field, err on the traditional side when it comes to how you present yourself, your résumé, and cover letter.

- Remember, recruiters are trying to reduce the big pile of applications on their desks. They are looking for something that will pull you out of the running, so examine all of the details. It may normally seem cool to have Web addresses such as "luvssexncity@aol.com" or "hvymtlrocks@hotmail," but first of all, you want the recruiters to actually see your name and you don't want to give them any excuse to hit the delete key.

Tips from Patricia Rose, head of career services at the University of Pennsylvania:

- **Don't be passive. You cannot just send your résumés off into cyberspace and expect anything to happen. You have to follow up and be persistent.**
- **Don't wait until you are absolutely miserable in a job before starting to look for the next step. You may end up making another wrong decision out of desperation to get out of your current job.**
- **Every six months, check in with yourself: Am I still learning and growing?**

Once you send off your customized résumé and cover letter into the seeming emptiness of cyberspace, what do you do then?

Should You Call?

It may sound like post-first-date anxiety: "Should I call?" "Or just e-mail?" "How long should I wait to call?" "And then what do I say so I don't sound lame, like I couldn't wait for him or her to call me?" "Do I come up with an excuse to call? 'I was calling in case you tried to call and my voicemail malfunctioned.'"

And, just as in dating, you have to be aggressive without crossing over into the bad place where you get labeled a stalker. As Haefner points out, "It is something that you have to own. Be tactful but persistent—because you want to show them that that is how you are going to be when you work there."

Job Hunting for the Second (or Third) Time

Job-hopping is the "new reality" and that's okay—the stability will happen later. If you are feeling panicked that you have been in three different jobs in the five years since you graduated, don't focus on the number of jobs that you have held, focus on the skills that you have developed. If you are looking for a job and you are worried about how the assortment of recent job experiences looks on your résumé, here are some tips:

- Organize your résumé by showing how your particular set of skills has developed and progressed over time—even if you have been at completely different jobs. Think about how you could apply those skills to the next job—these are what they call "transferable skills."
- If you have held different positions at the same company or in the same industry, stress your knowledge and experience in that industry. If you are switching industries, think about what the similarities are between the industries, or how you can apply your transferable skills from one industry to another.
- The person reading your résumé won't take the time to interpret your transferable skills for you. You have to show how your experience builds a framework for the job you want.

Are you finding yourself on Day 7 of formatting the bulleted points on your résumé? Are you having trouble actually attaching that résumé to an e-mail message and hitting the "send" button? Enlist your friends in the following exercise, designed to help you get the job search party started.

TRUTH OR DARE

This version of Truth or Dare does not involve physical contact or embarrassing secrets. It may, however, involve phone calls. This game is best between friends who are all dissatisfied in their current jobs or have sunk into a bit of a funk and need a kick in the pants. We all know the benefits of a workout buddy, and the same principle applies to starting a job search. It can be a painful process, and the more support you gather around yourself, the more motivated you will feel. Also, just as with an exercise plan, once you start the process, you will gather the momentum and it will feel more comfortable. The hard part is getting started.

You will have to build in the rewards and penalties that are appropriate for your group of friends. For example, if your friend does not finish her dare by the agreed-upon deadline, he or she will have to . . . Also, add your own truths and dares as you all get further in the process.

Truth Questions:

- If you could have any job, and you could magically be conferred with the degrees and experience that you needed to have that job, what would it be and why?
- What personal trait or habit do you have that is holding you back from having the job that you want to have?
- What is the strongest part of your résumé?
- What is the weakest part of your résumé?

Dares:

- I dare you to request an informational interview at an organization you have always wanted to work at. It can be an informational interview with anyone in the organization, even someone who is very junior. You must pick the name of the organization now, and you have one week to complete your task.

- I dare you to contact one person you know who has a job that you would like to have some day. It can be a friend of your parents, or someone you already know through an organization or activity. Conduct a career interview by the end of next week.
- I dare you to answer one help wanted ad this week, either online or in the paper.

Networking

You may not have a lot of experience on your résumé. You may not have a graduate degree. What do you have? You know some people. And those people know some people who might know the powers that be. So get the word out on the street that you are for hire. This is essentially what's known as "networking"—thinking of whom you know and letting them know you're looking for employment.

Networking is something we know we're supposed to do upon graduation, yet it's foreign and intimidating if you've never done it before. You may find that you don't get much response from newspaper or online job listings. Sometimes, companies post job openings merely because they are legally required to do so—although the position may be filled internally. There is however a hidden job market—jobs that are not advertised to the public or do not even exist. Simply put, it's about knowing the right people. Just as you are more likely to rely on a referral from a friend when trying to find a doctor, employers, too, are more likely to pay attention to applicants referred by a current employee, friend, or other contact. If you are bright and talented, have a college degree and communication skills to boot, but can't seem to get past the résumé submission point to an interview, it may be time to start talking to your parents, friends, and their friends.

Courtney Macavinta, award-winning business journalist and founder of Chicks Who Click, a private networking group for women in media, has gotten ahead in the journalism field through networking. She realizes that many recent grads feel uncomfortable about having ulterior motives when initiating conversations. She offered the following tips to give you confidence when expanding your network:

➤ Networking doesn't necessarily entail "name tag" events, but rather can encompass thinking of who you already know who might know someone else who can help. Think about who inspires you, who you want to surround yourself with.

➤ Think about networking as forming relationships; it's all about the six degrees of separation.

➤ Online "networks" such as Friendster can take pressure off the awkwardness of approaching a potential contact face-to-face, and act as good equalizers to facilitate conversation with more experienced professionals. In person, there are more value judgments, and everyone wants to approach the same person as their mentor. It is less intimidating to strike up a conversation on the Internet.

➤ Try to connect to others on a basic level out of general interest; put aside your motives or goals during your first few conversations.

➤ Macavinta distinguishes between "blue" and "silver" chip contacts. The former are higher-ups with influence and fat Rolodexes. The latter, silver chips, are closer to being your peers—former coworkers with whom you might sit down for a beer.

➤ Try to figure out as much as you can on your own, with peers or silver chips first. Don't ask blue chip contacts for favors right away; wait until you have more experience to ask your blue chips for help.

- Do stay in touch with former supervisors. Send them occasional updates to let them know how you're doing and ask about them—they might just think of you for an opening.
- Pay attention to everyone you meet—listen, ask questions about their backgrounds, show interest, try to remember personal details, and connect them with others.
- Don't just call contacts when you need something, make sure that you are available to help them as well when you can. Remember that networking is a two-way street.
- Don't worry about asking for help or taking up time; mentors like having success stories.
- Reach out in a natural way and be yourself, feel worthy to talk to anyone, just do so in a respectful way. Relationships take time; don't expect instant gratification. In other cultures, people never burn bridges with business contacts because business contacts are friends and family members. In China, for example, prospective business partners go to dinner 10 times before making any deals.

NETWORK AD

Once you have put yourself out there and found places to network and people with whom to network, what do you say? Everyone else is going commercial. Why not you? You need your own ad, a way to quickly let hiring execs know who you are, what kind of job you are looking for, and why you would be a great person for that job.

When writing your ad, keep in mind:

- People have short attention spans.
- They would rather be talking about themselves.
- They may get approached by desperate job-searching twenty-somethings all of the time.

So:

- Keep it short and snappy (about the amount of time that it takes for a short elevator ride).
- Connect what you are saying to them in a way that pumps up their egos by showing that you know something about them.
- Make it memorable.

Give it a try—write your five-second ad to market yourself. If you get bored, or in a pinch, this exercise can substitute as a good game of Ad Lib.

Hi! My name is ____________. It is so interesting to hear about your experience at ________________ where I understand that you ______________________________________.

I, too, am interested in ________________ and am currently looking for a job doing ________________. I worked as a __________, doing __________ [or I studied ___________], specializing in ____________ so I am a good fit for a job in ______________________.

Do you have any suggestions or advice you can offer me to get started in this field? How did you get into this field?

What do you like most about your job? What do you like the least?

Is there anyone you know whom you think I should contact? Are there any resources you can recommend for further information?

Thank you for your time.

Say your ad out loud to yourself. And now, for the hard part, say it out loud in front of one of your friends. It might sound really forced and artificial, but that's what impressing people is all about.

Once you have made a contact, *always, without exception,* send a follow-up note. Thank the contact once again for their time and update them on your job search progress. You should be writing so many of these follow-up notes that you will soon be able to write them forward, backward, and sideways.

Why?

- It is the polite thing to do and it will make your mother happy.
- It fans the flames of your new fledgling relationship.
- Unlike with dating, there is no worry that following up so quickly will send the wrong message. It's okay for people to know that you are desperate to find the job of your dreams.
- The recipient will see how professional, courteous, and persistent you are, and think, "I need a professional, courteous, and persistent person on my team!"

FOLLOW-UP NOTE

Dear ____________________:

It was so nice to (meet you, talk to you) at/on ______________. I am glad to hear that (insert comment to slightly suck up and show that you were paying attention) ______________. I found your advice to be really helpful as I continue to pursue a job doing ______________. I hope that you will keep me in mind for any future openings at __________________ or if you hear of any other opportunities doing __________________.

Enclosed are a few copies of my résumé.

Thanks again and I will be in touch.

Job Hunting Resources

Generally, headhunters are not going to do much to help the typical quarterlifer looking for work. There are some headhunters who look for people with very specialized training, but as a twentysomething earning an entry-level salary, you are going to have a hard time getting a headhunter on the phone. (In fact, it is going to be hard to get a headhunter on the phone until they start calling you.)

TIP: And when they do start calling, keep their names, even if you are in a great job that you love because you, or someone you know, may need that name later.

Just because you cannot get a headhunter on the phone does not mean that there isn't help out there for you. Make sure that you take advantage of all of the help that you can get for free. Start with your college or alumni organization. Many university career centers offer help to recent grads or can at least offer you access to online job postings. Your career center can also refer you to reputable career counselors and local area career services. Your alumni network can be a great resource of people who are interested in helping you. Even if they are not hiring, they can offer you information about a particular job or industry and may be able to pass along your résumé to someone who *is* hiring. Check into what resources are offered by local community centers and civic organizations—such as free or cheap résumé and interviewing workshops. Your county or city government may also offer job search tools and career counseling services at a reduced fee.

Twentysomethings are not necessarily in a position to pay for a lot of individualized career counseling—which is one of the reasons that we wrote this book. One critical time period in your job search when it is a good idea to think about paying for a few career counseling sessions is during the "discovery stage," when you are actually trying to figure out what to do with your life. Just being able to brainstorm with someone who knows a lot about all of the varied and available jobs out there will help you direct your search.

If you do opt for the career counseling route when the time is right, follow the same guidelines we provided for selecting a debt counselor in our money chapter: go with a referral if possible, find out if the counselor is certified or licensed, and ask about the length and cost of the program.

When You Score the Interview

"Interviewing is very, very uncomfortable. It's not intuitive," says Haefner. (Well, we never said that this book was going to be one giant pep talk.) It's even uncomfortable for the person conducting the interview; it's just not a natural conversation. And just like anything else, you have to prepare and you have to practice. "The interview is not the finish line," warns Haefner, and she suggests:

- Looking your best. Julie Murphree, an expert and speaker on business etiquette topics, advises "Unless it's a construction site and you're interviewing to be part of the construction crew, show up to the interview in a suit—whether employees wear suits or jeans on a daily basis." Err on the side of conservative: iron your clothes, don't wear any flashy jewelry, put your hair back in a ponytail if it's unruly (but never wear a hat), and follow a strict hygienic routine.
- Turning off your cell phone (this seems obvious but, seriously, a lot of people forget to do it).
- And, most importantly, taking the interview seriously.

Remember that how you conduct yourself on the interview is indicative to the prospective employer of your level of professionalism and how you'd act on the job. That's why it's also important to be on time, be alert, bring plenty of copies of your résumé and references, and do your homework—show that you're punctual, dependable, energetic, and organized.

RELAXATION THROUGH PREPARATION

The best way to relax before an interview is to feel prepared. Brad, an associate at an investment bank, talks about the importance of practice:

> "The most important thing about job hunting is practicing the interview. I find that it takes a few interviews before I get into a groove and start presenting myself in the best possible light. Unfortunately, that can mean that without practice, my first few interviews are a lost cause. It can be difficult to convince yourself of the necessity of practice interviews: they are embarrassing and artificial, and it can be difficult to find someone who is a good interviewer to participate. But it is for these same three reasons that they are so critical—real interviews are also embarrassing and artificial, so practicing gives you an opportunity to feel (or at least seem) comfortable in an awkward setting. Likewise, most actual job interviewers are also not very good, so it helps to practice with someone equally unskilled . . . to get you thinking about techniques for responding well to interviewers who ask poor questions."

Here are some common interview questions and preparation tips:

- Research the company and the industry before the interview. Make sure you know what the company does. What does the company make or what services does it provide? Who are the company's major customers and competitors? Is the company or organization part of another company? Is the company U.S.-based or foreign-owned? You should know the names of anyone you may be meeting during the interview and also brush up on the names of the top executives or leaders of the organization.
- Be prepared to articulate why you want the job and why you want to work for that company. "Determine to be seen in

the interview as a resource person, not a job beggar" and "as part of the solution," recommends Richard Bolles in his perennial bestseller and job hunters' "bible," *What Color Is Your Parachute?*

- Be honest about your qualifications—it's one thing to exaggerate but another to pull a skill out of thin air. If you say you know how to program Web sites using Java and you actually get the job, your employer will be disappointed to learn that you only know how to view Java-based pages, not build them. And if you don't enjoy making cold calls, but find out during the interview that the job is 80 percent cold calling, don't cover up just to get that job—maybe you don't really want it.
- Most interviewers are likely to ask about your strengths; think of honest responses that you can back up with real, and specific, examples. They are also likely to ask about your weaknesses. You may be tempted to talk about a weakness that is really a strength. For example, a lot of people rely on the "I am such a perfectionist" example when talking about their supposed weakness. Be honest about your weakness (you only need to share one)—think of a unique characteristic that really describes you, past situations that exemplify that characteristic, as well as steps you are taking to improve your weakness.
- Know your rights. A prospective employer cannot make a hiring decision based on your race, national origin, religion, gender, disability, pregnancy, or age. If you feel as if the interviewer is asking inappropriate questions about your religion or marital status, reply politely but firmly with an answer that gets the interview back on track. For example, say, "I think that religion is an intensely personal topic and what I want to focus on is how I can make a substantial contribution to this organization." For further information, the U.S. Equal Opportunity Commission has a site for younger workers at www.youth.eeoc.gov.

- Have at least a couple of questions ready for when the interviewer turns it over to you. Show interest in the company mission, the culture, and how your duties would fit into the overall organization. Ask what a typical day's work is for your prospective position. Bolles recommends that you "determine that the interview will be a part of your ongoing research, and not just a sales pitch."

- Prepare for the salary question. You may be asked what kind of salary you are expecting. Use this question as an opportunity to show how much research you have done about the industry. You can go to sites such as www.salary.com to learn what the range of salaries is in your field and in your geographic area. You will impress your interviewer not only by knowing the numbers but also by offering a clear justification for why you deserve your requested salary. For example, you may find out that your job typically pays anywhere between $19,000 and $27,000. You may explain that past internships or extra course work qualify you for the higher end of the range.

- It is appropriate to ask what the salary and benefits are during your interview but don't start trying to negotiate them until after you have the offer. Do make sure that you understand what kind of health insurance coverage you have before taking the offer, as well as vacation time and the possibility of enrolling in a 401(k) plan. Other benefits that can be used as negotiating tools include parking, tuition reimbursement, raises, flextime, and the option to work from home.

- Before you leave, ask when you should expect to hear back, one way or another.

JOB INTERVIEW ETIQUETTE

Interviews are nerve-racking enough without getting caught off guard by a tricky etiquette problem or question. Etiquette Grrl Honore Ervin, coauthor of *Things You Need to Be Told* and *More*

Things You Need to Be Told, offers the following job interview etiquette advice:

- Wait for your interviewer to bring up [small talk]. Starting off an interview with "Say, I see you went to Harvard—I went to Yale—we beat the pants off you in the last Harvard–Yale game, huh?" seems flaky and just a tad pushy. (Well, a lot pushy, actually . . . and rude, in this particular example.) Your interviewer probably will start off with some small talk to set you at ease—perhaps about a common city you've lived in or visited; or your college; or, if nothing else, something as mundane as the weather; or if you would like a cup of coffee or tea.
- At lunch interviews, by all means, never order anything messy (that goes for all business luncheons)—nothing makes a worse impression than spilling marinara sauce down the front of your blouse! Not only is it embarrassing, but an employer who can't trust a future employee to eat neatly probably can't trust her to do her job neatly. Also, don't order anything too expensive—it looks like you're trying to take advantage of a free lunch.
- Never, ever order alcohol at a business lunch. You don't want your future employer to think you're a lush, even if you only order something "light" like wine. Even if everyone else is ordering alcohol, I would avoid it, at least until you have actually secured the job and know what the protocol is. (And even then, limit yourself to one glass—leave the "three-martini lunch" to the power CEOs.)
- Any job interview should be followed up immediately by a thank you note to your interviewer for taking the time to speak with you. Job interviews always require a gracious, handwritten thank you note on your best notepaper. (Nothing silly and childish with pink bun-

nies on it! You're a grown-up! For goodness sake, invest in some decent writing paper!)

- If, after a time, you haven't heard anything from him or her, it's perfectly acceptable to call to find out the status of things, but you must be gracious about it—no "So, have ya made a decision on if I've gotten the job yet? D'you want me to come in for a second interview?" It's better to say something like, "Hello, Ms. Smith. I just wanted to check in and see if you've made a decision yet on the paralegal position I interviewed for last month."
- In order not to appear too overeager, wait several weeks (maybe three or four) before even getting nervous, much less calling.

Mulling the Offer

Once you've made it past the grueling marathon of applications, painful interviews, and résumé rejections, it is tempting to jump at the first job you're offered. Without much experience, you know you can't afford to be too picky. However, you should consider all the details of the offer thoroughly to get a sense of your potential employment situation before accepting it—especially if you happen to be blessed with multiple offers. Here are some things to consider:

- **Salary.** How does the offer compare to the median for entry-level jobs in that field in your geographic area? See our resources for comparison sites.
- **Benefits.** Does your offer include health and dental insurance coverage? (If not, check out our section on insurance.) Does the company offer a 401(k), and if so, does your company match your contribution? When are you vested?
- **Workload.** Just as important, do you know what you will be doing in this office (where you will be spending more waking

hours than anywhere else)? And just how many waking hours will you be spending there each week?

- **Travel.** How much time will you spend on the road? Will you be living out of a suitcase or at a job site for an extended period of time? Companies such as consulting firms often depend on young employees to do a bulk of the traveling.
- **Location.** How long will the commute be?
- **Company.** Does the company have a good reputation? How long has it been around? Is it profitable?
- **Office Culture.** Is the company big or small? Which would you prefer? Is the company very traditional or are there basketball hoops in the break room? What about the department you'll be working in? Will your coworkers be around your age or older?
- **Supervisor.** Does your would-be supervisor seem somewhat easygoing, or at least sane enough to work for?
- **Room for Promotion.** Does the company offer mentorship opportunities? Is there a corporate ladder with clearly defined job descriptions?
- **Miscellaneous Perks.** If you're really torn between two offers . . . does one include free meals?

Be sure to get the terms of your employment, including salary, benefits, and start date, in a written letter of agreement.

Resources

CAREER ADVICE AND JOB LISTINGS
www.careerbuilder.com
www.craigslist.org
www.Jobhuntersbible.com
www.Rileyguide.com

SALARY RESEARCH
www.salary.com

INTERVIEWING GUIDELINES
www.youth.eeoc.gov

BUSINESS ETIQUETTE
60 People to Avoid at the Water Cooler by Josh Aiello
The Etiquette Advantage in Business by Peggy Post and Peter Post
Things You Need to Be Told by The Etiquette Grrls, Lesley Carlin and Honore McDonough Ervin

CHAPTER 6

Surviving Nine-to-Five

Work isn't really about work . . . to get ahead, you need to get along.—Adam Bryant, "Graduation Day? Never!" *Newsweek* review

So let's say that you have finally found a job. You are relieved, you are happy, but you soon learn that your problems do not end with the job search. Just as finding an apartment can lead to problems with roommates or miserable commutes, the work problems may just begin at this point. There is a feeling of excitement initially when recent graduates land their first full-time gigs. They get to work on the first day to find their own cubicles, maybe even an office, business cards, and an e-mail account, and feel that they have arrived.

But after about two months or so they may realize that their opinion is not valued as it once was in school, there is no room for promotion, and the only thing to look forward to every day is lunch and the end of the workday.

QUICK STAT: Ninety-five percent of those who responded to our work survey would like to change something about their jobs. Details about what they would like to change are shown in Figure 6.1.

FIGURE 6.1 What quarterlifers would like to change about their jobs

Graduating from school into the working world can feel like starting from scratch. All of the confidence you gained from being a successful senior is tested by a new set of rules and routines. You may not know how to act or what to say in this new corporate setting.

We attempt to navigate our way through new organizations where we usually don't know anyone and don't have a good sense of who we can and can't trust. And it is a lot more difficult to figure out if we are doing a good job or about to be fired than it is to determine your progress in school. Differences between school and the working world can cause a lot of uncertainty and anxiety associated with the quarterlife crisis. You may remember Courtney from *Quarterlife Crisis*:

> "I was scared a lot because school was very easy—not always academically, but you knew the rules and knew how to get by and not flounder. It was a game, and if you knew how to play the game, you knew you were going to be okay. But this whole career and serious working thing was so remote to me. I didn't understand it, and I didn't know what to do or how I was supposed to act. I tried to give up drinking Coke because I didn't think it was professional—I actually had a conversation with my mom about what I was going to drink at business lunches because I thought I would have to start drinking water and coffee and adult things."

In this chapter, our goal is to provide you with some advice about how to adapt to your new working environment and deal with the differences—both minute and more significant—between school and work. We hope that our advice about the smaller details will give you some confidence and that our guidance about the "big picture" differences will help you achieve greater day-to-day job satisfaction and success in your career.

Welcome to the Working World!

Look at Figure 6.2. Which piece of the pie are you? If you are one of the 14 percent who love their jobs, congrats. For the other 86 percent, welcome to reality. Young professionals aren't dissatisfied with their jobs just because they miss the fun and freedom of school, they are frustrated with the differences between school and work for which they are unprepared. These differences are often a source of stress, disillusion, and general sluggishness.

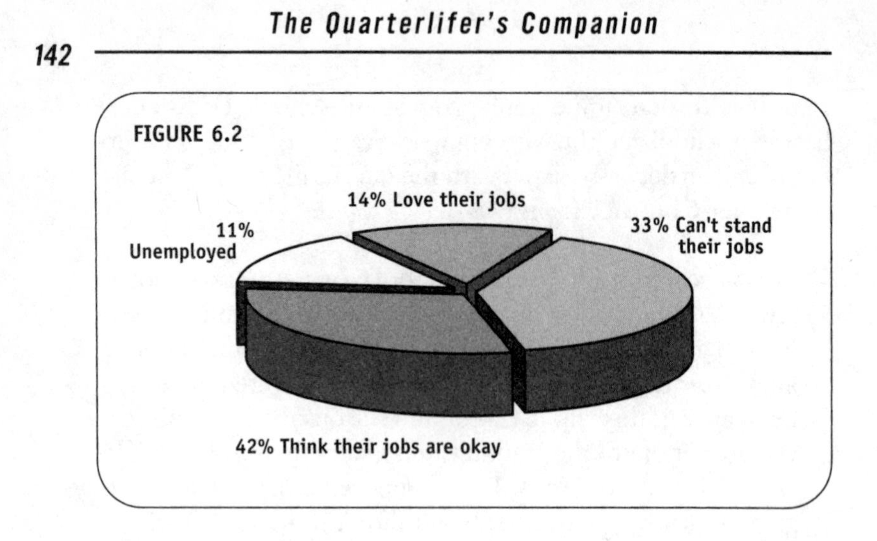

Through our work with twentysomethings, we have learned that there are three major job-related quarterlife symptoms: boredom and frustration with the pace of work, difficulty communicating on the job, and burnout. Just as twentysomethings are not prepared to choose from the multitude of job options out there, neither are they prepared to deal with issues such as filling up eight hours a day, deciphering supervisor feedback, or knowing when to move on.

Boredom

One of the most common complaints we hear from young professionals, most of whom are in entry-level positions, is that they are bored out of their minds. Even if they decide to ask their supervisors for more work, they are assigned menial work that does not fill up too much of the day. Many supervisors are reluctant to assign too much work (and certainly too much work for which they themselves will be held accountable) to recent graduates lacking job experience. Most of these bored twentysomethings automatically turn to the Internet for fun and games to fill up time without realizing that there are constructive ways to both fill up time and further their careers.

QUICK STAT: About half said that they would like to change their workloads.

In our survey, the number of people who said they were bored with their work was 50 percent higher than the number of respondents who said they were stressed out from a heavy workload (see Figure 6.3).

Maybe you relate to some of the comments behind the numbers:

- "I work nine-hour days and have nothing to do! I wish I could just go and sleep somewhere. But I can't, so I sit at my computer and pretend I am doing work while I am really just playing on the Internet. I think I would drive myself to an early death if the Internet didn't exist!"—Klo1335
- "I expect work to be fairly boring; it's work. But it really chafes my bum to think about all the things I could be doing with myself today instead of sitting here, praying that someone will need something typed."—Rosebud621

FIGURE 6.3 **Of those unhappy with their workload . . .**

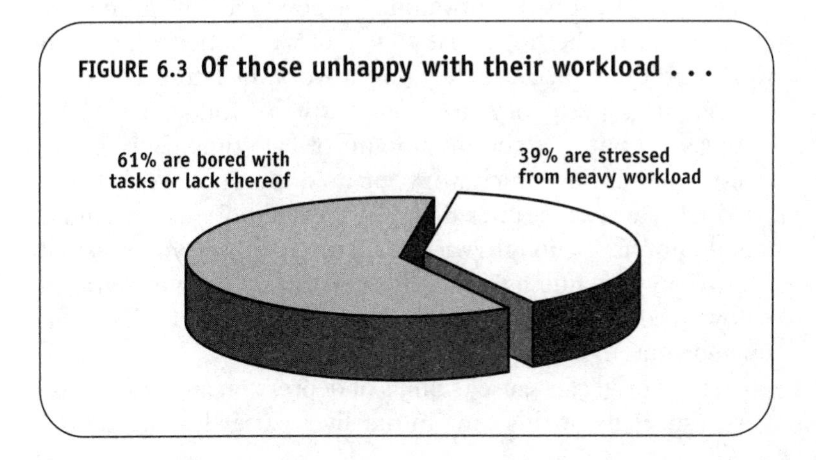

- "I got promoted and was supposed to have more work. So far all I've seen is more money in my paycheck, which is great, but I would like to be fully occupied the 7 1/2 hours I am here each day."—Jen312

Why is everyone so incredibly bored? Some twentysomethings complain that they don't have enough work to fill up their day. Others complain that they are assigned work that consists of boring, menial tasks, especially in comparison with the more analytical, creative projects assigned in school. Even if delegated a great deal of work, that work may still feel like a tedious chore that makes the day drag on endlessly:

> "I do the same thing, day in and day out. Get a box of cataloging cards, go through them checking for errors. Finish box, get a new one, start all over again. VERY tedious. I can't ask for anything different because this was what I was hired to do. Guess some of us are lucky at doing what we really want to and some aren't. (flush) There goes my $100,000 education down the toilet."—Jen312

Compounding the problem of boredom is the ever popular "face time" requirement. Basically, everyone feels pressured to hang around the office, outwaiting the boss, and outwaiting one another, all in the hope that someone will notice what hard workers they are because they stay at work the latest. Depending on the type of organization you work for, you may be required to put in a certain amount of face time each day. It doesn't matter how much work you do or do not have, because you must stay at the office 8, 9, 10, or even more hours. And if you do not have enough work to fill up that time, you must be creative in pretending to work (or you can follow our exercises below to come up with some more constructive activities to fill up your time).

Being bored can cause feelings of depression and worthlessness, especially at this time in our lives. After leaving school filled with enthusiasm and ambition, the letdown of being assigned insignificant workloads can make us feel completely irrelevant.

> "Wow, I honestly thought I was the only one who was bored to tears at work. To be honest, I am quite sick of coming to work and having nothing to do. Many people may like not having something to keep them busy, but I'm about ready to be put into the looney farm because I'm going outta my mind! I like working, I like being kept busy, but none of that is happening. It's getting so bad that I hate coming to work and am considering leaving if the job market betters."—Radgirl

Our twenties are also a dangerous time to be bored at work because we are now forming work habits that are likely to last the rest of our careers, and, like smoking or biting our nails, these will be hard habits to break. All too often we turn to mind-numbing activities, such as surfing the Internet for entertainment gossip or dealing another game of solitaire. We soon learn after our first few months on the job that we can actually be penalized if we finish our work too quickly. You may be left with nothing else to do, and your supervisor may value the appearance of business rather than the benefits of efficiency.

Compounding the problem are the mixed messages that we receive about whether or not it is a good idea to let our bosses know that we do not have enough work:

> "I can never figure out whether to ask for more work because I've heard that companies will see that as a chance to downsize or to reorganize. I am 29 now, and for the 8+ years that I have been out of college, I have very frequently found myself bored with little or nothing to do. I wonder whether some people just get bored because they are more efficient than others."—doctor kaz

In general, it is a good idea to be honest with your supervisor. Hopefully, he or she will appreciate your efficiency and ability to get the job done fast and reward you with a more challenging set of tasks.

ATTENTION SPANNER

Getting bored reading about boredom? Here's what we like to call an "attention spanner." Our top five list of things people do when they are bored at work:

1. Surfing the Internet
2. Paying bills
3. Planning for the weekend
4. Making grocery lists
5. Cleaning out your computer keyboard

As you can see, it is rare that we fill all of our time at work with work-related activities. But no one goes into a job planning on wasting time at work. You will find exercises later in the chapter that will help you find more constructive ways of passing the time. When you pass the time at work with work-related activities rather than personal errands, you feel better about yourself at the end of the day. You feel that you have really earned your paycheck, and you learn more that you can apply to other jobs in the future. And most importantly, the time really flies by.

It may seem funny to talk about not having enough work to do at work. But managers resist placing too much responsibility on a new employee who is inexperienced. Even if you went to a great school or got really great grades, your manager will only care about your experience—or lack thereof.

HOW TIME DOESN'T FLY

In school, you have to turn assignments around quickly. You measure your time from week to week, and you wrap up all of

TIPS FOR BATTLING BOREDOM

- Ask your boss or coworkers for respected background literature or publications in the field (there may even be some material available online, so you can still surf the Internet).
- Do some research on local professional development opportunities. Try community colleges, career-specific institutions, or associations. Most areas have community events that can act as social and networking opportunities as well.
- Set up a meeting with a coworker or supervisor to discuss the status of a project. Let them know that you are interested in becoming more involved.
- Find out if your high school or college has an alumni database, and then try getting in touch with some alumni in your field who could act as mentors.
- If you've made the above attempts to enhance your job and still run out of things to do, chase your wild dreams. Got a book or movie idea? Well start writing already!
- Alexandra Levit, author of *They Don't Teach Corporate in College*, suggests thinking up ways to improve transferable skills such as public speaking and business writing. Try to present to your group within the company; take charge. Work on hobbies such as freelance writing—brushing up on your skills will help you and your company. It's fine to go to the boss and say you need work, but don't say you're bored out of your mind. Tell him or her you'd like to help, but don't admit that you have the whole day. If you say that you can fit in a couple of hours of extra work, it makes you look like a team player with a "can do" attitude.

your work in one semester's time. You mark your progress with yearly "promotions" from one grade to the next. It is not surprising, then, that you feel as if you are standing still in your new job. Projects in the working world may last for months, or even years. Promotions don't automatically come every year, and you can start to get frustrated with your career track. You go from taking a new set of classes, facing new sets of challenges every semester, to doing the same job week after week.

A mentor can really help you adjust to your new "schedule." A mentor may also be able to help you think of ways in which you can develop new skills or learn about different areas of your organization so that you can increase the number and variety of your tasks.

Developing a mentoring relationship can also help you to set realistic goals and expectations about the pace of your career. How do you find a mentor? A mentor can be any person with a career track to which you aspire, whether that is a coworker, friend of the family, or fellow alum. Mentors can provide you with the information and advice specific to your desired career field—an education that is not provided in a school curriculum.

FIVE BEFORE FIVE

It is often hard to remember those things we could be doing at work rather than twiddling our thumbs or surfing the Internet when we've reached that comatose state.

Try to think of five specific things you could do at work in one day to improve your situation. Your Five Before Five don't need to be complicated. Some examples include reading up on industry literature, online computer training or other professional development courses, and discussing the status of a project with a coworker or mentor.

My Five Before Five:

1.____

2.________________________________

3.________________________________

4.________________________________

5.________________________________

Copy your list when you are finished and tape it to your computer or keep it in a drawer. Only once you get through all the items on your list in one day can you get to the guilty pleasures, such as surfing the Internet.

The Long-Term Plan

You should also use this time to think of what you would rather be doing and how to develop your skill set to achieve your goals. Do you know where you would like to be in your career next year? In two years? Five years? We suspect that it is hard for most twentysomethings to think any further than that. In school, we did not think beyond a four-year time frame, while in our careers we are supposed to consider the next 40 years of employment on toward retirement. It is hard for recent graduates to fathom being in a job or even a career field for that period of time. At this stage, when we plan our careers, it makes more sense to plan for a five-year time period, because our interests and desired career path could easily change during that time. Complete the following exercise to get you started on your long-term plan. Try filling out the "10 Year" category for extra credit!

MAPPING OUT YOUR CAREER

Think about the position you'd like to hold next year and several years from now, and the steps needed to reach those goals. For example, let's say you want to be a project manager in three years.

What will it take to get there—any advanced degrees or training, or maybe an excellent performance review at your current position? If you have a change of heart and switch your career field aspirations at some point, try revisiting this exercise and revising your goals and steps needed to reach them.

Date completed: ______________________

In ____________ I want to be doing ____________________.
I need [Skills/Education/Experience] to get there.

1 year ______________________

3 years______________________

5 years______________________

10 years______________________

Date completed: ______________________

In ____________ I want to be doing ____________________.
I need [Skills/Education/Experience] to get there.

1 year ______________________

3 years______________________

5 years______________________

10 years______________________

Once you've completed this exercise, revisit the Five Before Five exercise and see how you can revamp your list to help meet the long-term goals you just established.

(Mis)communication

There is more to learn on the job than the task itself. More than simply performing your job duties, you must master the art of interactions, and you must prove yourself to your employer.

Psychologist Paul Hettich, coauthor of *Connect College to Career* and senior seminar professor at Barat College in Chicago, notes that "You are not accepted when you are hired, you still have to go through initiation and prove yourself."

He goes on to explain that "You can be very successful in college, but you have not been conditioned for processes in the work place." For 16 or 17 years, we've been conditioned for academic learning processes, and now we have to shift our attitudes and expectations. GPA is "not the trick" to success on the job. In fact, according to the National Association of Colleges and Employers (NACE), GPA is ranked seventeenth out of 20 on a list of the top qualifications that employers look for, while communication skills are ranked the most important qualification. Interpersonal skills and teamwork are also in the top five. So clearly, learning the rules of office communication is crucial to your career.

From client and manager salutation dilemmas (Mr.? Or just Bob?) to deciphering feedback, corporate communication is very different from the content learned in any communications course—or even foreign language course—in which recent grads once enrolled. We would like to help you survive and excel at a job criterion that seems to count just as much—if not more—toward evaluations of job performance: the art of office communication.

WE'RE NOT IN SENIOR SEMINAR ANYMORE

By our senior year in college, many of us have had a seminar-style class. Everyone sits around a pretty table and is free to share insights, observations, and ideas. All ideas are valued and everyone is an equal. The professor is more of a moderator, encouraging creative and analytical thinking. Participation is heavily encouraged, and those who talk the most get the best grades. In the working world, sitting around a conference table for the first time, we can be lulled into that false sense of remembered academic security. We think that everyone is interested in what we have to say. We think that if we say something smart and insightful, our ideas will be appreciated. Unfortunately, that is not always the case. And when our input is not appreciated, it can make us feel unsteady, irrelevant, and unappreciated. Maybe you just haven't gotten the hang of how people communicate in the workplace.

As Elizabeth, who works in marketing for a New York City publishing company, explained:

> "I was never hesitant about speaking up in class, and I have been fairly comfortable from day one at my job about speaking up in meetings, especially meetings attended only by members of our company. It took me longer to adjust to bringing up issues outside of meetings—to realize that sometimes it was better to bring something up with one person at a time and sometimes it was better to include as many people as possible in the initial process, so that no one felt that their toes had been stepped on or that they had been excluded."

TIPS ON CORPORATE COMMUNICATION

From Paul Hettich, coauthor, *Connect College to Career*

- ***Listen at First.*** **Listening is just as important to your supervisors, if not more so, than contributing to the conversation. They don't necessarily expect you to have input right away but will appreciate later on that you remembered instructions or advice.**
- ***Find a Cultural Interpreter.*** **As you are learning this new language of "Corporatese," find someone on the job who can help you figure out how to make a suggestion without offending anyone, or can help you decipher feedback you receive.**
- ***Remember, You Can Always Put It in a Memo.*** **If you have an idea or some input on a project but you are still unsure about whether to speak up in a group setting, put your comments in writing.**

LOST IN TRANSLATION: A LESSON IN CORPORATESE

Play the Corporatese Game in Figure 6.4. See if you can match up the five most commonly heard work-related complaints (Column A) with how they get translated (Column B). For extra points, match up the correct "translations" in Column C.

FIGURE 6.4

A WHAT YOU WANT TO SAY	B WHAT THEY HEAR	C WHAT YOU SHOULD SAY IN "CORPORATESE"
1. I have a college degree. Why doesn't anyone trust me to do anything? Why do I have to run everything past my boss?	1. I don't have enough to do.	1. I would like to learn how to do skill X or develop Y experience. Is there a project that I can pitich in on that would help me to do that?
2. I have an idea for making something better. Or more efficient. Or something that will be the next big thing.	2. I think that I am so special. And better than all of you.	2. I am interested in a career here, and I want to feel that I am making a contribution.
3. I am SO bored with this job.	3. I am young and have no idea how it works in the real world.	3. I had an idea that I wanted to run by you to get your input and feedback.
4. I want more responsibility.	4. I want your job.	4. Is there a long-term or less urgent project that I can take the lead on? Something you have been trying to clear off your plate?
5. I want to feel like I am doing something, anything relevant.	5. I am unwilling to pay my dues.	5. Can you suggest some projects that I can seek out that may offer me some new challenges?

ANSWER KEY (A1, B2, C4); (A2, B3, C3); (A3, B1, C5); (A4, B4, C1); (A5, B5, C2)

AMBITION, THE DOUBLE-EDGED SWORD

As we progress through high school, college, and, for some of us, graduate school, our ambitions are encouraged. We are rewarded for trying our hardest and displaying initiative and drive. That is why it can be so confusing, then, for our ambitions to be met with a less-than-warm reception at the workplace. A strong display of ambition can make people suspicious. At school, more than one person can make an A. On the job, you may be competing for just one spot. There is a big difference between losing an A and losing a job: your income is at stake.

TIPS ON CLIMBING THE CORPORATE LADDER

- It's okay to express your ambition, just be careful how you go about it. Indicate an interest in a long-term commitment: "I hope to build my career here."
- Try to put yourself in your supervisor's shoes, as someone with years of experience listening to an employee new to the workforce.
- Remember that people feel ownership toward the "way things are done." From your point of view, you may be suggesting a needed change. But from their point of view, you are criticizing someone else's bright idea.
- Ask those you may be threatened by to help, or even mentor you. They will be flattered and may become vested in your success.
- Don't forget to recognize those who are helping and training you by expressing your appreciation to them and to their supervisors and peers.
- According to Levit, taking initiative can make a good impression, but you must approach the task with the

proper preface and tone. Talk to your boss before going ahead and making a change or adding something, harmless or helpful as it may seem, to the company. Ask for his or her input and opinion, but don't assume that your boss will respond with a favorable opinion. (Don't even assume they haven't thought about it before themselves.) You always want to seem like you're trying to learn and help the company, so use that tone when you approach your boss to get approval before taking initiative.

- Hettich notes that just as you research a topic before claiming expertise in college, do the same at work: try to get facts first. Then show initiative in a passive way. In a group, don't be the first to speak, and when you do, acknowledge that you are not an expert and ask for feedback on an idea—and learn to face the consequences of seeking feedback.
- If your career were a TV show, you would be able to work your butt off for six weeks and end up with the job of your dreams, whether as a rock star or as an apprentice to a billionaire. Our impatience with our own snail-like professional progress is not helped by the growing number of TV hits that show twentysomethings winning huge shortcuts up the professional ladder. Patience and persistence don't make for very exciting TV shows, but if you expect everything to happen on a TV series time frame, you are just going to feel more frustrated.

FEEDBACK (OR LACK THEREOF)—HOW AM I REALLY DOING?

Another jarring difference between the academic world and the real world is the way that we get feedback. In school, the feedback that you get is delivered (somewhat) fast and clear. You take a test or write a paper and, by the end of the term, you get a grade, usually with some accompanying comments. Professors aren't always nice in their criticisms but you know where you stand. And more importantly, you know if you are passing or failing the class.

The way in which our supervisors communicate with us can make us feel uncertain about our performance and anxious about our job security. In a recent conversation with a group of talented twentysomethings, one participant said that every day she felt as if she was not doing a good job and that her supervisors were unhappy with her work. At her company, employees receive their reviews every six months. When she received her review, she learned that her supervisors were thrilled with her work. But those glowing comments came after six months of going home with a knot in her stomach every night.

Even when you ask for constructive criticism, you may find that supervisors are reluctant to give negative feedback. Some supervisors may be worried about discouraging you, and others may not want to say anything negative because they themselves don't want to feel uncomfortable. It was your professors' job to give you feedback and provide guidance, but your supervisors at work have a lot on their plates, and providing you with feedback is just a small part of their jobs.

TIPS FOR FINDING OUT HOW YOU'RE DOING

- **If there is no established performance review system at your company or if you feel that the reviews are too few and far between, ask your supervisor if you can schedule a meeting about your performance.**
- **Ask for feedback on an informal level. For example, when you have finished a project, ask your supervisor if he or she has any specific comments about your work on the project.**

- **Don't forget that your peers can offer you good feedback and suggestions.**
- **Pick the right time to ask for feedback. Make sure that you don't catch your manager when he or she may be swamped with work or trying to meet a deadline.**
- **If you find that your manager is reluctant to offer negative feedback or even a constructive critique, let her or him know that you understand that it may be uncomfortable but that you have a real interest in improving and advancing at the company.**
- **Don't be defensive. Listen to the feedback and think about it. People will hold back on giving you feedback if they feel as if they are in a court of law every time they talk to you.**
- **Hettich suggests looking for nonverbal cues such as voice quality and eye contact if no feedback is communicated regularly. Just don't jump to conclusions based on one day's observation—bosses have bad days too. And don't bug anyone too much, either. Remember that sometimes you only get feedback when you screw up, so silence on the boss's end could be a good sign!**

SELF-EVALUATION

If you have tried to get feedback but still feel as if you have no idea how you are doing, the only thing you can do is to keep trying your best and be your own evaluator. At some point, someone is going to ask you how you think you are doing, so you might as well be prepared. The following exercise will give you a framework for grading your own work. When you finally do receive some structured feedback, you will feel more prepared to speak in specific terms about your accomplishments and your progress as well as acknowledge areas where you need more development.

Please order the following skills from 1–12, 1 being an area where you are most comfortable and 12 being an area where you have the least experience and need the most work.

___ **Supervisor communication:** includes the ability to ask questions and decipher directions and feedback.

___ **Coworker communication:** includes working on teams.

___ **Client communication:** includes answering phones, drafting correspondence, and handling client complaints.

___ **Organization:** includes file and workspace order and scheduling meetings.

___ **Technical skills:** Am I comfortable with all of the programs I should be using at work or do I, for example, need to brush up on Excel or PowerPoint?

___ **Understanding the industry:** Do I understand who the major customers and competitors are? Do I understand which environmental, regulatory, and economic factors have an impact on my industry?

___ **Adaptability:** Am I able to switch course in midstream if my boss tells me to change what I am doing?

___ **Initiative:** Do I seek out new projects and new challenges? Do I suggest ways to improve my current projects?

___ **Presentation skills:** Am I comfortable speaking in front of a group?

___ **Leadership:** Do I communicate clearly with people on my team? Do I feel confident giving direction or delegating tasks?

___ **Multitasking:** Can I handle juggling multiple projects at once?

___ **Punctuality:** includes being on time and getting work done in a timely manner.

___ **Other**

Try to spend the most time on number 12 before your evaluation, then number 11, and so forth. Being more aware of the areas that need improvement will force you to think about them as you perform your daily tasks and interactions. Then, by the time the company's official evaluation rolls around, you will feel more confident about your skill set and your contributions to the company.

Negotiating a Raise

Do you feel lucky that you have a job where you don't have to ask permission to go to the bathroom? Do you think that you should just shut up and be happy to have a job at all? It's great to be content with where you are, but don't be afraid to ask for what you deserve. If you have been working hard, receiving positive feedback, and feel that your salary doesn't match your contribution to the organization, you're not going to lose it all if you decide to ask for a raise. According to Levit, asking for a raise is acceptable after an outstanding performance review. Do make sure that the positive review is documented, and keep in mind that companies may not always give merit increases unless they're scheduled.

The way you ask for a raise is crucial, and the way you go about it can show your boss what a valuable member of the team you are. Tact, diplomacy, good negotiating skills, a sense of good timing, and self-confidence balanced with a touch of humility are all characteristics of a good salary negotiation *and* of a good employee.

Keep in mind the following guidelines from Levit:

- Be certain that you deserve a raise, and that you aren't asking because you *really* want to trade up to that sound system you've been eyeing at Best Buy.
- Be sure that you produced enough work to be worth the expense of keeping you around; ideally you are already doing extra tasks above and beyond your job description.

- Be careful about timing when asking for a raise. Don't ask for a raise on a Friday afternoon, and don't ask right when, say, your boss has just found out that the department may lose its biggest client.
- Send your boss an e-mail that says you would like to discuss your "career goals." The subject line of the e-mail should not be "RE: I want a raise" or you may get a reply that says, "RE: We can't always get what we want." Don't be too in-your-face and confrontational.
- Instead, ease your request into the conversation with such tried and true buzzwords as "compensation commensurate with my accomplishments."

Your boss is going to have some buzzwords too. Be prepared. For example:

Boss: There is no room in the budget for a raise this year.

You: I feel that I have gone above and beyond my job description and really made a contribution to the company. I would also be happy with extra vacation time or some other perk.

Boss: I don't feel that you're quite ready to move to the next level.

You: Could we come up with a six-month plan to increase my responsibilities and then reassess my progress and compensation in six months?

It's like a little one-act play! Rehearse your lines with someone before you try this for real because if you don't, you could end up with a serious case of stage fright, chicken out, and wind up leaving your boss's office with a *lower* salary. We're just kidding, that hardly ever happens. But seriously, ask someone to "play" your boss so you can practice.

Some other things to remember:

- Don't make an ultimatum that you'll quit. Just as in our role-playing example, if your boss turns down your salary request, have a list of alternatives that are acceptable to you:

  Extra vacation days

  An increase in benefits, which could be, for example, matching contributions to your 401(k) plan

  A commitment to invest some money in your training by paying for a course or sending you to a conference

- If your boss says that he or she has no authority to grant your request, suggest a meeting with your boss's boss, but never go over your boss's head without his or her knowledge.

If you are successful, if you somehow manage to get a salary increase, or are somewhat less successful but still manage to score a booklet of sandwich vouchers for the company cafeteria, do not strut out of the meeting and crow to everyone that you just got a raise, because:

- It's not cool.
- Your boss will get upset if everyone else starts asking for a raise and may take yours away.
- It's not exactly going to make you popular.

Which leads us into some advice about office politics.

There Is Such a Thing as Too Much Personality—Office Politics

Josh Aiello, author of *60 People to Avoid at the Water Cooler* and coauthor of *The Field Guide to the Urban Hipster*, says that it's usually not *doing* the job that makes the transition from school into work so hard. Learning how to survive office politics can be a lot harder than any assigned task. Aiello explained: "The jobs themselves are really simple to grasp. It was the culture, the people, the attitudes, and gamesmanship that made it unbearable."

Aiello echoed some of the typical complaints we hear about the politics of work:

> A lot of bosses—they take the assistants for granted. Maybe they are so busy they don't have time to worry about your feelings.
>
> They seemed more concerned about the appearance of work, the appearance of efficiency versus actual efficiency.
>
> [And finally] If only some bosses had a clue, they would realize that there are a lot of bad jobs that you can tolerate if you are treated like a human being.

Aiello suggests the following coping strategies:

- "Taking notes and writing a book!" Okay, not everyone is going to write a book, but being able to step outside of yourself and look at the humor in the situation may help you relax and laugh a bit—even if you are laughing at your own miserable situation.
- "I think that the key is to not take things personally. I was bad about not letting it roll off of my back."
- When Aiello felt as if he were being micromanaged to death ("My boss proofread my e-mails"), he would simply take a walk around the block and cool off. "It's best not to sit in your cube and stew," he warns.
- "I always tried to be on the move. It made it harder for people to find me." If you start by just trying to look busy, you may actually become busy and start to feel busy.

Levit offers the following advice for getting through the personality conflicts that inevitably arise when you work closely with someone eight hours a day, every day, with whom you would otherwise have no interaction.

- Develop a strong "corporate persona"—be mature, confident, and put on a professional face. Project this persona to the work world. Act mature beyond your years, as if you can accomplish anything. Use your corporate persona in every interaction with the company, from the interview to the moment you walk out the door.
- Be a team player willing to learn—that perception is more important than your actual performance.
- Combat negativity and develop a positive self-image—"You are what you think."
- Try to meet your own expectations, not others'. Don't let external circumstances affect your goals.
- Do your best not to work with colleagues you don't get along with; but don't always expect to be able to make that choice either—it is often inevitable. You have even less control over working with a boss you don't get along with.
- Don't feel like you know everything. Accept guidance and advice; remember your place.
- Don't let your emotions get the best of you at work. Determine what sets you off and figure out how to keep yourself from getting upset. Crying repeatedly at work is never a good scenario.

When Miscommunication Becomes Misconduct

What if a coworker makes you uncomfortable by bringing up personal subjects or expressing romantic interest in you; how do you know if that behavior is merely inappropriate or blatantly illegal? According to nolo.com, a provider of free legal resources for the public, sexual harassment is defined as "any unwelcome sexual advance or conduct on the job that creates an intimidating, hostile, or offensive working environment." Truly offensive behavior ranges from "repeated offensive or belittling jokes to a workplace full of offensive pornography to an outright sexual assault." Both men and women, of any sexual orientation, are victims of sexual harassment. Federal and state laws protect employees from sexual harassment just as they do from discrimination, and most employers now have sexual harassment policies in their employee handbooks.

If you feel that you are being sexually harassed at work, the first step is to confront the offender—tell him or her that the behavior is inappropriate and makes you uncomfortable and ask for it to stop. If that doesn't work, try writing a letter—and save a copy for yourself. If at that point you still feel harassed, it may be time to consult the employee handbook and follow your organization's complaint procedure. If your company does not have a sexual harassment policy, talk to someone in the human resources department. Be sure to document all of your correspondence, on the chance your complaint could escalate to a lawsuit. If your conversations with HR or management do not lead to a resolution, you can try your local Equal Employment Opportunity office. Do everything in your power to avoid taking legal action; consult nolo.com or www.eeoc.gov for more detailed information.

Working Friendships

Unlike in school, you're not at work to make friends. You want to get along well enough to work with everyone, but don't necessarily expect to go bar hopping together on the weekends. If you do make good friends, that's a perk. But most often, coworkers are there primarily "to have lunch and help you get through the workday," remarks Levit. "You won't necessarily stay in touch [once you leave]." Levit warns young professionals to "Be cautious about disclosing too much personal information initially. Inevitably, after spending so much time in the same place, it will happen, and it's not a huge deal—especially if you're disclosing positive information rather than anything that might be considered negative or just plain weird."

Although you may not realize it, becoming too "buddy-buddy" with others at your level—gossiping and forming cliques—can be detrimental to any potential movement within the company. Higher-ups may not take you as seriously as a potential leader. And sometimes, if one entry-level employee receives a promotion, his or her entry-level comrades may feel jealous, and then the newly promoted employee becomes the target of gossip. Not all companies have back-stabbing, competitive environments; the culture varies by the nature of the field, size of the company, and other factors such as leadership. Some offices encourage social interactions through regularly scheduled happy hours, while others discourage the development of office relationships. Take some time to understand your organizational culture before becoming the office social butterfly.

Workplace Etiquette

Aside from work relationships, the level of formality with which we communicate with coworkers, supervisors, and clients is different from that outside the office. Etiquette Grrl Honore Ervin, coauthor of *Things You Need to Be Told* and *More Things You Need to Be Told*, recommends the following:

- Always call your boss and clients by Mr. or Mrs. unless you are told otherwise. (Or Miss or Ms., depending on their preference.) As Ervin notes, it's generally the exception today to address your boss formally, but you never know.
- "Don't bring up any non-work-related topics until you get a feel for the office and begin to make friends. And even then, some things are simply TMI (Too Much Information)." Ervin used the example of one woman who forwarded an e-mail to every woman on staff about the dangers of a particular birth control method and what happened to a friend of hers while on it. Nobody wants to know this, especially not the CEO whom you've never met.

- "Never use slang or foul language in work e-mails. And try to avoid sending blank e-mails for which the comment or question is in the subject line. It also depends on whom you're writing to. An e-mail to the Head Honcho or something that's cc'ed to a bunch of people should be more carefully worded than one to a peer. Also, don't forget to spell-check!"

Dressing for Success

Imagine you are the boss and you are running out the door to a really important meeting and it occurs to you that it would be very convenient if you grabbed one of the new hires to carry your bag and set up your digital projector. You quickly scan the cubicles and see a bunch of folks in jeans and slightly suspect collared shirts. And then you spot someone in nice slacks, a pressed shirt, and a blazer hanging over the back of his or her chair. Whom would you grab? So you say, "Hey, what's your face with the blazer. Yeah, you. Let's go."

Sure, we would all like to believe that the smartest or the hardest-working twentysomething wins the chance to carry the bag, go to the meeting, and have all of that extra face time with the big boss. In an ideal world, it shouldn't come down to what you are wearing. But it often does. And you don't want to miss opportunities or be considered less mature or less professional because of your wardrobe.

If your work environment is business casual, it can be a tough call to figure out exactly what middle of the road is and whether to dress up or down. If you dress down, your coworkers may feel more comfortable around you. However, if you err on the side of formality and throw a jacket over your shirt, the more senior employees may notice you and take you more seriously. Like it or not, appearances can affect your movement up or down the corporate ladder.

Speaker, writer, and coach Julie Murphree offers a business fashion and attire seminar, "Dressing for Success While on a Budget." She lists some clear steps to follow below:

- **Dressing for the Job.** Appearance is critical, especially if you're in a competitive environment and nothing separates you from the competition but your outward presentation. I like to say that your appropriate outward appearance is what causes someone to pause long enough to be drawn to who you are on the inside where the real value offerings reside. But you've got to get people to notice you first. After putting the right suit together, upon entering the workplace, always smile, throw your shoulders back, stand up straight, and let the world see who you are! Exude confidence and graciousness, mixed with a dash of sincerity and humility.

- **Business Casual Defined.** Business casual is also known as "employee-friendly fashion," but can lead to confusion. Know your company's casual dress code if written. If your office does not have a dress code, set your own code based on your career objectives. Your goal should be to wear what makes you feel the most comfortable without compromising your credibility. Hence, casual should never be mistaken for careless. As a result, you'll be dressed comfortably, but with class.

  Don't equate casual with sloppy. On business casual day, is your outfit clean, pressed, and well coordinated? Take your day's schedule into account. Even if it is Casual Friday, if you're meeting with suppliers who will be in suits, you should be too.

- **Off Limits.** What's okay in one environment isn't in another. If open-toe shoes are listed as a "no-no" in one corporate manual, then they are off limits in that company. However, in another environment they might be perfectly fine.

- **After Hours.** Again, ask yourself, does what I'm wearing represent who I am (my style) and command the respect I want from my business associates? Semiformal functions usually require a fairly dressy suit, dress, or pants outfit in any length or color. Men can get by with a dark suit and dressier accessories. When in doubt, ask for details when you RSVP.

- **Worth the Splurge.** To me, the best investment is your suit(s). Use a cost-per-wear index to evaluate your investment. A $300 jacket may be expensive at the checkout counter. However, if its cost per wear is less than $2 because you'll wear it three times a week, fork over the money. Your core wardrobe should be in solid colors so that everything else you invest in can be mixed and matched around your core. If you can't wear a clothing piece more than one way, don't even consider buying it. Every piece of clothing must work with the other elements in your wardrobe. [Once you have invested in your new suits, don't forget also to take good care of your new work wardrobe, paying special attention to "dry clean only" tags!]
- **Color Yourself.** More than ever, the office environment has opened its doors to a rainbow of colors. Even men's shirts come in a greater array of creative colors. But do examine your corporate culture. If you can tell by the written dress code and how management dresses that the color palate is a bit more conservative, then limit your color choices in the office. You'll never select a wrong choice with black, charcoal gray, and taupe.
- **Dress Up or Down?** In a word, dress up. But it's good politics never to dress better than your boss. The most important criteria is fit. A well-fitted blazer, for example, is crease-free (if too small, you'll see horizontal creases; if too large, you'll see vertical creases).
- **Fitting in Grooming.** Set the alarm clock 15 minutes earlier than you normally would. Trust me, in the business environment, depending on your aspirations, it's worth becoming a morning person. Remember, you

can sleep in on weekends. Your mornings can still be low-maintenance. Preplan your wardrobe for the week, make sure your clothes are pressed and ready (you don't have to iron them; take them to the dry cleaners). For hair, if you don't want to invest much time with it in the morning, find a cut (consult with a hair stylist) that's quick to style each morning.

Some Final Tips: Keeping the Job Once You Have It

You may do everything right, and you still may end up getting laid off through no fault of your own. The economy may dip or your company may run into some trouble, but there are some things you can do to improve your chances when layoffs begin. Patricia Rose, director of career services at the University of Pennsylvania, recommends that you:

- Take full advantage of every opportunity to meet and learn from people in your organization. Never turn down a project or request from a supervisor because the work is "outside your job duties."
- Be tech savvy and always upgrade your skills to be more efficient and put an edge above the competition, and keep up with the incoming grads!
- Use your analytical skills to come up with original solutions to ongoing problems; share them and you will gain a reputation as someone who can be creative in a crunch.
- Scan the environment and look for the valuable work that needs to be done in your organization and get on those projects.
- It is good to be detail oriented, but not at the expense of getting your work done efficiently. Keep in mind that you are not writing an English paper. Don't agonize endlessly over using the perfect word and miss an important deadline.

Resources

OFFICE POLITICS/COMMUNICATION
www.corporateincollege.com
www.etiquettegrrls.com

HARASSMENT
www.eeoc.gov
www.Nolo.com

DRESSING FOR SUCCESS
www.juliemurphree.com

BOREDOM RELIEF
Self-tests and training:
www.emode.com
www.kaplan.com

JOB ADVICE
www.askannie.com
www.careerbuilder.com
www.wetfeet.com

CHAPTER 7

Moving On to Bigger and Better Things

Job Burnout

QLC FACT:
The average first job lasts less than two years.

If you have followed our advice and worked on exercises to improve communication and quality of life at work but still do not feel satisfied, then the time to move on may have come. If the following quotes seem to echo some of your own daily thoughts, then it may be time to reassess your situation:

"My job is really depressing me once again. I realize that I can't quit my job because I do like the income that comes in. But I seriously have the hardest time coming to work in the morning. There is nothing good or positive about my job. My paycheck is the only reason that I keep coming every day."—klo1335

"[My job] has taken a toll on my health. I have no energy and I hate getting up in the morning. Some days I just don't. It's not that I'm tired. I just can't bear the thought of going to work, so I just lay in bed. Today I left work and just went shopping. I didn't even arrive until 11:30."—paperjam1015

"I'm really sick of my job. I complain about it all the time, I'm not challenged in a way that I would like to be, I feel I'm not gaining anything by being there—the list could go on and on. I was promoted but I'm still doing the same things. There are some job openings for some different things and I'm thinking about going for them. Is it too soon to look elsewhere?"—Jen312

"Once you get to work, it feels like it's sucking the energy right out of you. The only thing that excites me about my job is the amount of time they give me to take OFF and unlimited Internet use; but neither have anything to do with the actual job itself."—coll214

When Is the Right Time to Move On?

Many of us reach a point where we are so unhappy at this place where we spend the majority of our waking hours that we wonder, "Is it worth it? Is this just how working life is? Should I feel as though I am reluctantly dragging myself out the door every morning? Should my cubicle feel like a prison cell? Do those e-mail forwards have any truth to them—that life in prison is in fact more pleasant than life as an office worker?"

We should hope not. We *do* hope that you will assess your situation and consider the options carefully before deciding to move on to your next venture.

You are not going to know after three or even six months if this is the right job for you—you really have to give it a year, suggests Melissa Fireman, founder of Washington Career Services, unless:

- The job is making you feel physically sick.
- You feel completely demoralized by the end of the day.
- You are being harassed or working under unsafe conditions and nothing is being done to help you. (See our harassment guidelines in the previous chapter.)

If, after a year, you are not getting out of the job what you are putting into it, then it is time to look around. Amy Joyce, author of *I Went to College for This?* and "Life at Work" columnist for the *Washington Post* reminds us that, "you should always be looking for the next opportunity." Even if you feel that you need to give your job a full year to make sure that it is not right for you, it does not mean that you cannot be learning about other fields, other opportunities, and other organizations.

As you are deciding whether or not you should leave your job, Joyce says, "You must educate yourself as much as you can." She suggests many of the same strategies that any job seeker should employ. You have to volunteer, network, go to dinners, join groups, and meet as many people in your field as you possibly can. But it is also important to talk to as many people in other fields as you can because a lot of people find a new interest that way.

Joyce also recommends sitting down and creating a list of all of the things you don't like about your current job. It is easy to say, "I hate my job" or "I am bored," but push yourself to be specific.

MOVING ON LITMUS TEST

Look through the following list of tasks and experiences. There is some room at the bottom to fill in your own. Over the course of six to eight weeks, how many items can you check off the list?

- ❑ I made an important contact.
- ❑ I learned a new skill.
- ❑ I read something about my industry.
- ❑ I let someone know that I had some time available and could work on a project.
- ❑ I worked in support of an important project.
- ❑ I assisted with quality control on a project.
- ❑ I was included in a meeting.
- ❑ I was given a new responsibility.
- ❑ I improved my skills in an important area.

Other experiences and opportunities that might be important to you:

- ❑ Laughing with friends at work
- ❑ Invited out for social occasion with the team
- ❑ Participated in some charitable work sponsored by my organization
- ❑ ______________________________
- ❑ ______________________________
- ❑ ______________________________
- ❑ ______________________________
- ❑ ______________________________

If you can only check off a few, or none at all, it may be time for you to think about moving on to another job. Even if you decide not to move on, doing the exercise will help you evaluate what important skills or experiences you are lacking in your current job. Pinpointing these deficits will help give you a solid framework from which you can have a discussion with your boss or mentor, or help to identify a better job opportunity.

STEPS TO TAKE

Look around, first in your own organization. Maybe you are at the right company but in the wrong job. If you are feeling bored and uninspired in the accounting department and look longingly at the creative work being done in marketing, investigate. The following are some questions to consider before making the decision that the only way to improve your current job situation is to look elsewhere for employment:

1. **Is my supervisor aware of how I'm feeling?** Depending on the culture of your office, supervisors may or may not be involved with you on a daily basis to the point that they realize what is going on. And they may or may not want to make an effort to improve your situation. However, if you have gotten to the point that it takes every ounce of effort just to drag your body into work in the morning, then you have only something to gain by expressing your concerns.
2. **Am I unhappy with the job or just unhappy in general?** Sometimes it is hard to decipher the source of our unhappiness; is it our external situation or something going on internally? It is important to figure out whether the problem is that you are depressed or that the job is depressing you—a sort of chicken and egg question. One good way to determine the source of your depression is to try to think of another specific job that you would rather be doing.
3. **Is it the job or someone at the job that's driving me away?** Is it the job itself and related tasks that you can't stand, or the person assigning them to you? Can you do anything to change that situation? Do you want to leave because of negative feelings resulting from an unpleasant or competitive situation at work? Is it possible to move on, forget about that situation and continue with your work?
4. **Is there something else I could see myself doing here? Is there someone at the organization who could act as a mentor?**

Perhaps there are opportunities to explore within the organization. Get to know some of the employees in other departments over lunch and find out if their situation sounds any better to you. If possible, form a mentorship with someone whose position you aspire to be in some day. (See the previous chapter for more information on mentors.)

5. **Is there somewhere else I could see myself working?** After determining whether the source of your unhappiness is internal or external, there are further details to consider. Is it the monotony of tasks that is draining you? Is it the number of tasks, or lack thereof? Or is it your office environment—the people, the size, the culture, even the commute?

After analyzing your answers to these questions, you can then determine the next step. If you try to communicate your concerns to your boss, but he or she seems unreceptive or unsympathetic, then it may in fact be time to look for work elsewhere. If you can't envision a better job, the source may be internal.

WHEN IT IS NOT THE JOB, BUT THE BOSS OR THE CRAZY COWORKER

We hear a lot of stories from quarterlifers whose biggest complaints about work are not about their jobs but are instead about their bosses or coworkers. Don't jump ship because of a seemingly bad working relationship until you try to work it out first. Because this may be the first big problem you have had on the job, the problem may not be as serious as you think it is. One piece of advice that Fireman offers is to "seek out someone in HR whom you can trust. Unless there is something illegal going on, HR usually keeps things confidential. Once you have found someone to talk to you, you can simply ask for some advice—make it clear that you are not just complaining and that you want to fix the problem. Give it a couple of tries before assuming that you cannot make the relationship work."

Considering Another Employer

If you enjoy the work you do but still feel miserable on the job, you must identify what it is about the organization at which you work that you would like to change. Is it:

- **The Size.** Just like choosing a college, the size of an employer must be suited to your personality. Do you feel more comfortable in smaller groups? Or does seeing the same few people every day make you feel claustrophobic? Would you enjoy the variety of people that you could meet at a larger organization, or would it make you feel just like a number to be at a place where the president does not know you by name?
- **The Culture.** Have you always been considered "type A"? If so, a competitive environment may appeal to you. Or, if you prefer a more laid-back environment, then a nonprofit or government agency may be more suitable for you.
- **The People.** Is it more important to make friends or to learn from people with experience? The median age of the office staff could change your daily interactions.
- **The Location.** Is the hour-plus commute to work making you miserable? Would you prefer to be in the suburbs where you can drive and run errands on your lunch break, or the city where there is an excitement in the air and just as many pedestrians as cars?

Playing the Field

Do you feel that your job lacks purpose? Are you feeling inspired to do good for the world? Or, has your job in the nonprofit or public sector left you feeling disillusioned? If your daily tasks have shed some unfavorable light on an industry that you once admired, then it may be more than a change in office culture you desire.

Ask yourself, "What would I like to be able to say that I did when I look back? What would I like to be able to have contributed to business or even to society? Am I moving in a direction now that would allow me to accomplish that goal 20 or 30 years down the road?"

Is it a new job you need or an entirely new career field? If you determine that it is the former, based on our checklists above, then refer to Chapter 5, Finding a Job. But if you are not convinced that you will be any happier doing a similar job at another organization, then you may want to consider switching careers.

Switching Careers

We hope that our guidelines in the last chapter will help to get you through eight hours a day, but keep in mind that there is a reason it's called *work*. Remember, too, that school was not always fun either. It is so easy to romanticize how wonderful and carefree college was, but it was probably a lot of work as well. And in college, you always had some unfinished reading assignment or essay hanging over you on the weekends; at least in the working world you can leave it at the office once you're done for the day. What is important is to try to find a good balance. Work is not always going to be fun, and that is why it is so important to stay active outside of work as a source of fulfillment, as we will discuss later on. But work should not feel like prison either. At the very least, your job should fulfill you with a sense of a paycheck well-earned, if not with the feeling that you are somehow helping to develop yourself, your employer, your customers, or even society.

It may begin as a nagging feeling that you are starting to outgrow your job. Or the realization that you dread going to work each morning may hit you like a ton of bricks. Either way, how do you know that you won't end up in a job that is just as bad, or *worse*? Could it be that the devil you know is better than the devil you don't? Could it be that you just need to give it more time?

Spend some time reflecting: What are the things that you really want to achieve by making a change? Maybe you got laid off from a job you really liked, so the only change you are looking for is finding a place where business is better. But if you are leaving a job that wasn't for you, what have you learned there that makes you think that this change is appropriate? What job would be more fulfilling?

Finding Your Passion

A lot of twentysomethings know that they want to move on to a different job but don't know what that job should be. One of the more common questions we hear is, "I'm trying to figure out my passion but don't even know where to start looking."

Laurel Donnellan, career coach and author of *Passion into Practice: The Path to Remarkable Work*, advises her clients to try and discover their passions early on: "It's better to find your passion in your thirties than in your seventies, even though it is overwhelming. Some people don't think they can make a career out of their passion. Don't give up. It may take you longer than you think." If you don't deal with it in your twenties, it's going to be the same challenge in your thirties, your forties, fifties, and sixties.

There are a number of activities that Donnellan suggests to help people start to find their passion, and frankly, they are all both fun and free:

- Spend a day shopping. (These already sound good, don't they?) Allow yourself to wander and go where you want to go. Pay attention to which stores draw you in. What do they have in common? Can you figure out what attracts you to the stores? Is it what they sell, how they look, the atmosphere, the personality of the staff?
- Go to a bookstore and scour the shelves. Do you find yourself attracted to the same section every time you go into a bookstore? Do you constantly find yourself flipping through colorful cookbooks? Or do you find yourself in the literature aisle? What kinds of magazines do you like to buy?

- Give yourself permission to surf the Internet for a day. What kind of sites do you visit most often? Are you a news and commentary junkie, perhaps revealing a passion for politics?

- Give yourself permission to watch TV for a weekend—whatever you want. Write everything down. Donnellan explains, "I had a client who had an epiphany about her passion while watching TV. She noticed that she loved all of the relationship shows and decided to go into counseling."

While these suggestions sound fun and easy, we know it is not quite that simple to find something you love to do and then get paid for it. "Don't have the impression that you can just do what you love and the money will follow. It really is the hero's journey; it's not the easier way. It's hard to get a law degree, hate the law, and decide to change careers. Mastery takes a long time," Donnellan warns.

After you try some of the initial fun stuff, you are going to have to commit some time to the process. Donnellan outlines some of the steps:

- Don't think that you are committing yourself to one passion or field for the rest of your life. You are going to change. Your lifestyle, passions, and career will change. It can be overwhelming to try to figure out "What am I going to do with my life?" That's just scary and makes us want to crawl into bed and pull the sheets over our heads. Think more along the lines of: "What am I going to do for my next chapter?"

- Sometimes you need to try a bunch of stuff on. It's like going into the Gap and trying on 25 different styles of jeans.

- Settling for a job that stinks is just a bad habit. Donnellan reminds us that, "We're just in a different world—job-hopping is the norm. Enlightened hirers are going to care about your skills and your work ethic." Don't worry about looking too flighty on your résumé, if anything you'll look diversified having varied experiences.

- You may need additional training. It might take you five years. That might mean school, but it could also be an apprenticeship or some time in continuing education courses.
- Once you have figured out what your passion is and what training you may need to complete, you probably still have a day job. Donnellan calls this your "bridgework," and it's what you need to do to get from here to turning your passion into a career. Knowing that you are on a path toward a better job will make your current job, even if it's not your dream job, more bearable. But don't fall into the trap of staying in a job you dislike with a dead-end path and missing out on better opportunities.

POLLING YOUR FRIENDS

We share our opinions about everything with our friends. What should we wear? Who should get fired on *The Apprentice*? And let's face it, we generally complain to our friends about our jobs. Tap into their collective expertise on you—they know your strengths and preferences, and they've seen your ups and downs. Find out how they see you in the working world—and offer to reciprocate.

Before beginning this exercise, promise them that you aren't going to be too defensive or sensitive. Take their opinions in stride and file them away with the rest of your job research. Now, ask:

- What kind of job do you see me in?
- What are my strengths and weaknesses?
- Why do you think I don't like my current job?

Did you learn anything surprising about yourself? Did your friend provide any interesting insight into your career path?

Can I Please Just Go Back to School?

One of the most common ways that twentysomethings attempt to switch careers is by going back to school. Going back to school can seem like the answer to all of your problems, and you may think that graduate school will be like being back in college, where you had a predictable path. And while your classes required a lot of work sometimes, at least that work required a brain. You might make a lot of friends, be challenged by your work, and you may even have a job waiting for you at graduation. But while the thought of going back to school can be a comforting one, you should think very carefully about whether or not you are going for the right reasons.

What will this degree do for you? "For example, if you know that the job you want requires an MBA, that 90 percent of people who hold that job have an MBA, then your decision is pretty clear: Get an MBA," says Patricia Rose, director of career services at the University of Pennsylvania. In general it's a good idea to go to grad school to further your knowledge and qualifications in a particular field that you've already tried and know you enjoy.

But usually the decision is not so simple. Rose explains, "Let's say you want to go into counseling. There is a huge range of degrees you can pursue: You can get your master's in Social Work, you can get a clinical psychology degree, you can get a counseling degree or a certificate in a specific field (such as career counseling), or you can go to medical school and become a psychiatrist."

It's a good idea to try out a graduate field of study in the real world first; do not simply enroll in school as a way to avoid a job search and trying something new, because it's a huge commitment both in terms of time and money. And the job itself will not necessarily be the same in practice as the graduate program curriculum.

If you do decide to go back to school, make sure that you do your homework—check out some programs of interest, and find out:

- What is the job placement rate at graduation?
- Are graduates actually getting jobs in your desired field?
- Are students typically coming from other fields, or are they already in your desired field and going back to school for an additional credential?
- Ask if there are any alumni with whom you could speak about the level and quality of preparation.

Finally, think hard about why you want to go back to school. Make sure that you are not going back in an effort to recapture what you miss from college.

THE LURE OF LAW SCHOOL

We hear from so many twentysomethings who automatically think about going to law school when they are unsure about what they really want to do with their lives. Why the attraction? "It's a guild. As a group, they are well paid and they are respected. We hear people say, 'I want to go to law school to develop my critical thinking skills,' but I don't know that I would want to owe $100K and lose three years of opportunities doing something else because I am uncertain about my career path," Rose warns.

The Entrepreneurial Trap

Perhaps you never will find your dream job; not everyone does. Perhaps there is no one job with every quality that you desire—you may always find something to gripe about. Or, perhaps you were meant to create that job yourself—but be cautious if you decide to take the entrepreneurial route. You hear a lot about successful business ventures but rarely hear about all the failures. Starting a business is a huge risk and requires a lot more than simply a good idea; you have to be someone who doesn't mind instability. And when you care about a job *too* much, when a job you create inevitably becomes an all-consuming passion, you may feel that it eats up all your free time as well. There is also a great deal of paperwork involved with starting a business, and it helps to have the right connections and a lot of luck. Not to completely discourage you from pursuing your entrepreneurial dreams, but you should know it won't be a breeze, and it might be a good idea to hang on to your day job and work nights for yourself while getting the business up and running. There are a lot of resources available to help you, such as the Small Business Association and YES! Circle, a support group for young entrepreneurs, if you wish to learn more about starting a business. (See the Resources at the end of the chapter for more info.)

Switching Careers without Going Back to School

Your twenties are a perfect time to explore all of your career options, but it can be hard to go exploring if you feel trapped in that Catch-22 of needing experience to get experience. What if you want to try a field that is completely different from the one you are currently in? Do you have to take out more student loans and go back to school to get the experience you need? The following alternatives can save you additional college loans, depending on your field:

- Fireman suggests looking at your own organization first. "Let's say that you are a consultant at Pricewaterhouse-Coopers and you decide that you would really like to help run a program at a nonprofit organization. Try to switch into a job like that at your own company first." Your current company will want to hang on to you and may be willing to transfer you to their foundation, where you can learn whether you want to be in a nonprofit setting and culture. If you don't like it, you have a better chance of moving back into your old department and you have maintained your seniority in the organization while still enjoying the freedom to explore.

- Networking is key when trying to break into a field in which you have little experience. Try to find someone in your desired field who knows what a good worker and a quick study you are. They, or someone they know, may be willing to take you on as an apprentice and show you the ropes in your new industry.
- Fireman stresses that you should be realistic. "Maybe you don't need the whole degree to break into a new field. Maybe a few classes or a certificate is enough. Do your research—read job descriptions so you can focus your efforts on exactly what you need to do." Many graduate programs now have city extension centers as well as online options, which are more convenient for working professionals. Once enrolled, make sure that you talk to your instructors and fellow students about your desire to switch careers as a way to make connections and learn more about the field.
- Find a volunteer opportunity that allows you to explore a new field. For example, if you think that you may want to become a teacher, volunteer as a tutor.

Once you have decided what kind of job you want, it can be daunting to look for that position, especially if your current and desired fields are very different. If they are, think about how the skills that you have developed in your current field can be applied to your new field (those "transferable skills" we mentioned in chapter 5). Don't consider your current job description in narrow terms—think about all of the skills that you can bring to a new career. And don't forget that there are some skills that are valued in any field, such as your ability to manage people or projects or your ability to work on a team. Maybe you are very good at generating creative ideas or have great organizational skills. Look outside your current job as well for skills that you have picked up through activities in the community—refer back to our college experience converter exercise in Chapter 5, Finding a Job.

IT'S CAREER ASSIGNMENT DAY!

After a few years of working (maybe even a few months of working), you may be learning what it is you don't want to do. You may even be developing a vague sense of what you do want to do, but it can be hard to zero in on a specific job. One good way to start thinking in specific terms is to start looking for people who have the job you want to have in five years. These people may be in your own organization. Or they may be people you read about in magazines or books. In other networking exercises, we have encouraged you to speak with anyone and everyone remotely connected to your field of interest. This exercise asks you to be much more specific and really hunt for someone who has the job you want to have in five years.

Once you have found your interview subject, ask him or her the following questions:

- What jobs did you have before this job?
- In what way did those jobs help you get this job?
- Do you believe that there are certain academic credentials that you must have to get this job?
- Are there other types of training and/or credentials that would help someone get a job like yours?
- Are there skills that are indispensable for someone in your position? How did you develop those skills?
- What characteristics do you think someone needs to possess to have a job like yours?
- When you interview people who are seeking jobs like yours, what are the common deficits that keep them from being hired (lack of experience? lack of a particular skill? etc.)?

Looking for Work While Working

"Try to do as little job searching at work as possible," warns Joyce. Use your lunch hours for interviews or take a vacation day if you need to. Fortunately, the Internet allows us to do a lot of research about potential job leads after working hours. Expect, and be prepared for, some questions about why you are leaving your current job when interviewing for your next job. These kinds of interview questions may really test your diplomatic skills, so it is very important that you don't come across as negative and difficult. The person interviewing you does not know that your boss takes credit for all your work and has been through five assistants in 18 months. If you complain about your boss, the interviewer is not thinking "Poor guy, how his talent has been squandered these past two years! It's criminal!" Instead, the interviewer is thinking, "What's this guy going to say about me in two years?" Keep it positive. You can put a positive spin on anything. Really.

For example, the interviewer asks, "Why did you leave your last job?"

You are thinking, "I spent 85 percent of my time counting the ceiling tiles in my cubicle. I could literally feel my brain turning to mush."

You say, "I really felt I had developed as much as I could at my last position. I am ready to move on to the next challenge where I look forward to working very hard and progressing in an organization."

Never Burn Bridges

The following example shows that moving on can be a good experience, just be careful not to burn any bridges—exit gracefully and maintain good relationships with your former colleagues. These are contacts that may become important to you in the future, either when you are looking for your next job or even looking for someone to hire yourself.

"I left my first job because I needed more leadership experience for later in my career and my former workplace wasn't providing it . . . I was also lucky enough to get a job I wanted to work at for years. I left on good terms, with my managers practically begging me to stay. I still keep in e-mail contact with my former coworkers."—Tiffy482

"A very old professor of mine at college gave a group of us some advice based on his reflections on the path his career (both in and out of academia) had followed. He advised us not to worry overly about each choice on the path, but (1) to choose work that we found interesting in some respect and (2) to work very hard even at jobs that seemed like dead ends . . . because, in his experience, even dead-end jobs led to new possibilities many years later. It's probably not advice that is applicable for every kind of career, but I've found it helpful to think about my possible career path that way."—Elizabeth, a first-year law student

Moving On—QLCers Share Their Experiences

It is tricky figuring out whether, and when, you should move on. One of the best things that you can do is talk to other people and see if you can learn any lessons from their experiences. The following are some lessons shared by fellow QLCers.

"My first job out of college was great! I moved on because I had been there for years, had gotten the top position I was going to be in, and had the opportunity to try something else in another area of interest."—Wordsmith

"The feeling of complete indifference about my job was the biggest indication that I was ready to leave. I needed change and something to feel excited about . . . [it] turns out that I was going for a career that I now think was all wrong for me, and that explains why I had no strong feelings about it."—inqlc

"My decision to apply to business school was not exactly the best thought-out decision that I ever made—in fact it was somewhat reactionary. I was tired of the job I was in, and not quite sure what I wanted to try next. Many of the other job options that I was interested in required an MBA (at some point), so it seemed like a good thing to do then. I also missed university and academic life. I think that there was even a bit of 'that's what one does' going on in my head."—Genie

Resources

CAREER DEVELOPMENT

I Went to College for This? How to Turn Your Entry-Level Job into a Career You Love by Amy Joyce

FINDING YOUR PASSION

Passion into Practice by Laurel Donnellan or visit www.passionintopractice.com

ENTREPRENEURIAL TOOLS

www.sba.gov
www.yescircle.org

PART 3

Play

A LOT OF THE CHALLENGES THAT WE FACE as recent grads are serious: finding a job, figuring out our finances, deciding whether or not to go to grad school, just learning how to take care of ourselves. But don't let all of these challenges and your new life's "to do" list crowd out all of the fun that you should be having in your twenties, the perfect time to travel the world and explore your hobbies and passions. And, although life after school can prove to be a difficult time to meet new people, you will find that it comes more naturally by exploring your interests through resources available in your community, and by simply giving it time.

CHAPTER 8

Meeting People

One significant component of the quarterlife crisis is the feeling of isolation that settles in as all of your college friends drift away to other towns, cities, and countries. It's hard to have to say goodbye to so many friends. But to top it off, for the first time in your life, you are not automatically surrounded by people your age who are doing the same things you are doing. You cannot assume that you are going to meet a lot of people at work, where you are now spending the majority of your waking hours. The challenge of meeting people and making new friends is one of the more common themes in the QLC community:

> "I think it's been very difficult to make new friends after college, especially since I've relocated to a new city. I've made friends

mostly from work, and then friends of their friends, and also a few of my neighbors. There just aren't as many opportunities to interact with people of your same age range, along with those that have similar interests, in a non-school environment."—Sunshine79

"I think one of the biggest problems with my current job situation is there are NO young people. At first I thought working with a bunch of 40+ people would be a rewarding experience and there would be less drama. But now I have found that it's just depressing. I get up, go to work for 9 hours with people who are as old as my parents, and then head home to my empty apartment. The thing is, I'm an incredibly outgoing person and made several great friends during college. However, I now find myself regressing back to my high school years . . . traveling home on the weekends, going to dinner and a movie with my mom, and just bumming around. It's really pathetic. I always thought when I was in my twenties I would have this fabulous life . . . I'm really praying that I'm only in a post-college rut, and that this won't be my life in a year or two."—Tiredofphilly11

Finding new friends and reconnecting with old friends takes a lot of patience. Try not to be too hard on yourself. Remember, this is probably the first time that you are starting from social scratch, and the relationships you develop are not going to automatically feel like your high school and college friendships. Don't think that you are the only person who is having trouble making new friends. Also, keep in mind that we now have our entire lives ahead of us to make friends, rather than the limited time frame of school. Expect your friendship circles to change as you grow and your interests shift.

"When I first left college, I was in a new city at grad school—it was very tough. Everyone had their own agenda. My college friends were about an hour away, but they were busy too. I later left grad school after one semester and returned to my hometown. At first I was really upset when my friends from high school (who had also moved back home) couldn't get together because they had established their lives. I did give it time and we reconnected. I have met one new friend, actually via the QLC message boards! I am fairly friendly with a few people at work, but not super tight like the friendships I had in high school and college."—Jen312

QLCers have used a lot of different strategies to meet people and make new friends. Take a cue from "Cazort," who recently shared his advice on the QLC message boards:

"I have met a lot of people through common activities and events. I go swing dancing, and it's a very friendly, diverse crowd, and swing dancers tend to be intelligent and creative too! I have met a lot of people that way. Occasionally I will meet people through various events—political gatherings, volunteer activities, speakers, etc. I find that it's hard to look for events in real life—in college, you can find them in one centralized location, or you just see them posted everywhere. In real life, you have to peruse Web sites of local colleges and universities, read the paper, read some alternative/independent papers, talk to your friends, get on mailing lists, get tied into various communities. It takes time, but it pays off."—Cazort

Even for the lucky few who are constantly surrounded by friends, making the effort to branch out pays off. Genie, who moved to New York right after graduation says:

"Living in New York's smallest apartment with roommates right after school ensured that I was never lonely—I had more personal space in the dorms. Luckily, I got on well with my roommates and actually met many friends through them (we had a sort of college friend share program going on). I also worked in a company that employed lots of recent graduates and spent most of my waking hours there, so many of my friends were coworkers.

"Otherwise, I mostly met people through interests I had. I had been involved, at least a bit, in charity work, so when I got to New York, I sought out organizations that catered to working people (Big Apple, Habitat for Humanity) and participated in those. In addition to being a source of new faces, these groups also understood crazy schedules and allowed me to participate when I could. I also had a purpose for being there (other than to meet people), and found that it was easier to start up conversations with random strangers there than at a party or a bar. When my schedule allowed, I also went to late night museum openings, which catered to young professionals (going with a friend made it less scary when you actually wanted to say hello to one of these strangers)."—Genie

Jon Horowitz, editor and founder of *Hatch* magazine, an online magazine for quarterlifers, encourages twentysomethings to take advantage of online communities, but he warns against living in front of your TV or computer. Horowitz explains, "When I was a kid, you were outside all day—and just by being out there and being free, you were meeting people." Even though we aren't kickball age, Horowitz's advice applies to us quarterlifers too. "Everyone is becoming more isolated. The Internet—while it offers some solutions [for meeting people]—can also isolate."

Now that we don't have Mom and Dad yelling at us to turn off the TV and play outside, we have to pull ourselves away from our cubicles, TVs, and computers and just get out there. Everyone is going to have a different way to meet people; start by thinking about what your interests and passions are.

"The best way to meet people is to volunteer," shares Katie, a lifelong volunteer herself. When you meet people with whom you are volunteering, you are automatically in a situation in which:

- You are with people who share your values and interests.
- You are with people who share your value of volunteering and contributing.
- You automatically have something to talk about.

You may not have a lot of experience volunteering. If not, be sure to check out our resources on volunteering in Chapter 11. And think about some other interests you have. Make a list of some things you have always wanted to try.

"Take a language class!" suggests Elizabeth, a first-year law student. "You aren't guaranteed to meet your new best friend, of course, but you meet an interesting cross section of people who probably would never have come within your orbit otherwise. Plus, a language class is an instant equalizer; everyone ends up revealing much more about themselves than they would in most other settings."

If you aren't interested in learning a language, try taking another kind of class. There are so many low-cost options for taking classes that interest you:

- Check your local community colleges and universities for classes that you can audit.
- Find out what classes your local library may be offering.
- Museums and other cultural institutions offer classes and lecture series.
- County extension programs offer low-cost classes and recreational activities.

Perhaps you have had enough school for a while and would like to skip class (now that you can). There are still plenty of great activities where you can meet people who share your interests and, just as important, are looking for ways to meet people themselves:

- Link up with your local alumni group. If your town or city does not have a chapter of your alumni group, start one!

Even if there are just a few of you, of varying ages, you will have a group to watch the game with.

- Look for museums and galleries that throw openings or events geared for younger "patrons" of the arts.
- Check out book clubs at your local library and bookstores.
- Cities and towns have adult leagues for all sorts of team sports. Also, don't pass up playing for your company team just because most of your coworkers are older. You will still be able to meet people on the other teams!

Sure, it is hard to get out there when you could just stay home and call an old, comfortable friend—someone who requires no work, no anxiety, and no effort—but meeting people is like exercise. The first couple of times you work out, it feels uncomfortable and takes a lot of energy. Pretty soon, it becomes a good habit.

If you feel very shy and suffer an anxiety attack at the mere thought of meeting complete strangers, try to put yourself in a comfortable place. Trying to meet someone at a bar can feel very artificial and nerve-wracking. But if you are doing something you like, something that makes you feel confident, you will be less shy, less anxious, and more open to meeting new people.

- If you are religious, try getting involved at your place of worship. Join the young adults group. If you feel shy striking up a conversation in a social setting, join in an activity. One QLCer on our message boards overcame her shyness by teaching a class at her church. She chose a topic that made her feel very comfortable and confident and was able to talk to people she did not know. Just as she did, think about how and where you feel comfortable.
- Try meeting your neighbors or people who live in your building. Now that you don't live in a neighborhood or on a campus anymore, it only adds to your isolation if you walk

home every night to a building or a street where you don't know anyone's name, they don't know yours, and you really have no idea who is living next door to you. If you take the first step, by throwing a little party or inviting some of your neighbors over for a potluck, you will be amazed at how grateful your new neighbors will be. And even if they aren't your age, they may know someone in the neighborhood who is. And knowing your neighbors is also safer for you and convenient when you need your fish fed!

Finding new friends can be like finding a new job, and some of the same advice applies. You may be tired of hearing it, but you need to network. Remember all of those conversations with your mom when she starts to tell you about her friend's daughter who just got a job near you and you should really give her a call sometime—and you are tempted to block her out? Well, you wouldn't ignore a potential contact if you were looking for a job, so don't ignore a potential social contact.

Just as in your job search, you need to let people know that you are looking. If people don't know that you are looking, they aren't necessarily going to volunteer that they know the perfect friend for you. They may try to set you up on a date, but rarely do people think to set others up on a friendship!

Don't limit your potential new friend pool to people your age. One of the biggest complaints we hear on the message boards is that people work in offices with people who are much older. It can be harder to strike up a friendship with someone who is in a different phase of life. (You can't necessarily fall back on the old standby of going out for a drink after work.) But it can be worth it. Horowitz's experience is encouraging: "All of my work colleagues were at least 15 years older than me, but I still got really close to someone who was twice my age." You can learn a lot from people of different backgrounds, as well.

Our final piece of advice is to find people who are going through the same things that you are experiencing. Many friendships have sprung up at www.quarterlifecrisis.com because everyone is going through the same transition.

MEETING PEOPLE

If you aren't lucky enough to work for one of those companies that hires hundreds of recent college grads, you might have trouble finding new friends at work. So where are they?

Write your own "friend wanted" classified (for yourself, not to actually publish in the paper). You aren't going to just trip over a new friend. You are going to have to look for them. Thinking about the kind of people you are hoping to meet will help you know where to look to find them. For example, if you want friends who share your love of art or literature, look into local museum societies or book clubs at the library.

Resources

The following are all online communities that can serve as good places to meet fellow twentysomethings:

www.Craigslist.com
www.Friendeavor.com
www.Friendster.com
www.hatchmagazine.com
www.Myspace.com
www.Orkut.com
www.quarterlifecrisis.com/forums
www.Tribe.com

CHAPTER 9

Maintaining Friendships

Our chapter on meeting people focuses on finding new friends. But most twentysomethings, and especially recent grads, also worry about maintaining the friendships they already have. In this chapter, we discuss some of the common causes of friendship breakdowns in your twenties and what "maintenance" you can do to keep those friendships going.

By the time you left school, you probably felt as if your friends had become a new kind of family who witnessed and supported you through all of the ups and downs of college life. And now that you really need those friends, they may be scattered to the wind or so busy trying to keep their own lives together that they aren't available when you need them. All of the changes in our relationships with friends are a huge contributing factor to our QLCs and the loneliness and loss of support that we feel.

As Jon Horowitz of *Hatch* magazine points out, "You go from being where your friends are to everyone spreading out. It is always a big deal just to make plans. People you saw every day four years ago—now it's a big deal to see each other." This is also a time when our interests and priorities are changing, and these changes can put some stress on even our oldest friendships.

In this chapter, we discuss some of the specific ways that your friendships can change and what you can do to maintain those relationships so that they are healthy and beneficial for both you and your friends. The mounting disconnection with old friends and instability with new ones can be both a cause and effect of the QLC.

We found in our survey that almost all QLCers have friends experiencing a quarterlife crisis, and over half have had fallouts with friends since graduation. (See Figure 9.1.)

Our goal is to help you and your friends help *one another* to get through the QLC and bond over your challenges rather than making them worse. While it is true that some friendships simply have expiration dates—or are put "on hold" until you can relate better to one another—other friendships needlessly fall apart. Some QLCers try so hard to hide their anxieties and paint a pretty picture on the outside that they withdraw from their closest friendships. Others stop making time for friends or don't realize that new rules of friendship apply after we leave behind the easy social environment of college. Adult friendships are simply different in nature than the friendships formed in dorms, over keggers, or by pulling all-nighters together.

It is ironic that the QLC itself—with its accompanying symptoms of depression and anxiety—can cause tension and distance between friendships right when you need your friends more than ever—when you need them to help you get through this period of change and uncertainty.

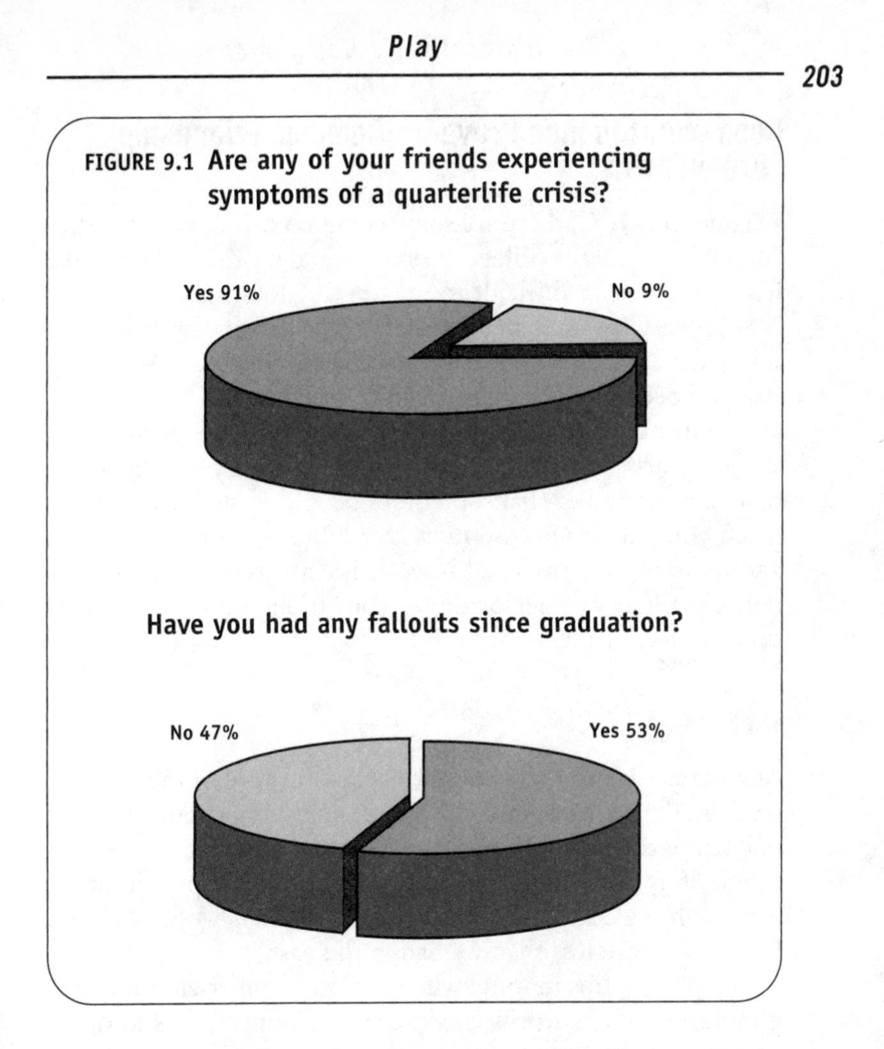

FIGURE 9.1 Are any of your friends experiencing symptoms of a quarterlife crisis?

If you suspect that a friend may be experiencing symptoms of a QLC, be empathetic—and then back off. Although many QLCers are experiencing depression, your friend may not realize how common his or her feelings are and may be afraid to discuss them with you. Even when friends need your help most, their reaction may be to shut you out because they don't think you'd understand. Be sure to let them know that if they ever need someone to listen, you're there. But then, you may just have to give them some space.

Good Maintenance Prevents Common Friendship "Breakdowns"

Beyond the QLC, there are some common causes of friendship "breakdowns" after college. Less time and more distance make friendships more difficult to maintain. Christina Saraceno, a New York City freelance journalist who covers twentysomething life, advises us to "realize that there could be a friendship that you deeply valued all through college and still feel that you value after college but do not maintain simply because space and time drift you apart. Forgive yourself and your friend for that and remember that sometimes people come into your life when you need them the most, for different periods of time, and then are less involved in your life at other times. It says nothing about you personally or your friend or what the relationship was or meant; it's just life."

TIME

At a period in our lives when we become aware of the value of free time, how we spend it is increasingly important. On the one hand, this is a period of freedom and exploration. On the other, it is the initial phase of adulthood responsibilities. Although we have more free time now than we will in the future, we have less than we had in the past.

Keep these tips in mind when you and your friends are juggling each other's work schedule and responsibilities in order to maintain the friendships:

- Be respectful of your friends' mounting responsibilities and increasingly busy schedules, and expect the same from them.
- Do your best not to be late. Leave time for traffic, parking, or subway delays when meeting a friend for dinner or drinks.
- Don't be needy. If you constantly complain that someone doesn't have enough time for you, it will only push them further away.

TIPS FOR FINDING TIME

One good way to make time for friends is to run errands together. Bring a friend along to:

- **Get your car washed**
- **Get haircuts together**
- **Work out at the gym together**
- **Go grocery shopping**
- **Take classes, if you are interested in similar topics**
- **Volunteer**
- **Hone your hobbies together**
- **Veg out together. If you and a friend are going to separately watch your favorite Thursday night show, and then get on the phone to discuss the episode, why not watch together? (Understandably, crummy weather can make it hard to leave our couches.)**

DISTANCE

Although it can take some work to schedule enough get-togethers to stay connected with our new real-world friends, it can be even harder to stay close with old friends, in particular those to whom we are not geographically close.

Let's say you had a group of four close-knit friends who all scattered in different directions in pursuit of different goals. Talking to even four people each month is going to seem difficult as you adjust to a new job, school, city, and schedule.

Saraceno shared her own experience: "The biggest thing that I found after college was that people moved to different cities and maintaining the friendship was a real challenge because you had to decide whether to give it the time it needs. You'd be surprised how quickly you can end up having nothing to say to someone you spoke to every day for four years the minute you go a month without talking—in the beginning you think that would never happen, that in fact you'd have so much to catch up on and talk about. But the only thing you can do is literally make the time if the friendship is important to you."

So how can you prevent the quick deterioration of your closest friendships? It might be hard to make the time and find ways to span the distance, so use technology and get creative.

TIPS FOR OVERCOMING DISTANCE

- **Schedule a conference call. If we can do it for work, we can do it for fun. That way, you can take more time to speak with everyone. Not only does talking to everyone at once save time, it will feel more like old times when you can all chat together. Try scheduling the call after a TV show you all used to watch together or one Saturday morning each month.**
- **"Get a room" online and have your own online chat fest.**
- **Make a commitment to get together once a year. Pick a holiday weekend or a time of year that is easiest for everyone. Knowing that you are all making an effort to get together once a year takes some of the pressure off everybody to stay in constant touch.**

Drifting Apart as Interests and Priorities Change

"I wonder if it's just normal to grow apart. Everyone should take a look at their parents. How many childhood friends do they still have? Is it something that just happens in the twenties? You grow apart? Or only in our generation since everyone is going away to college and moving for jobs, etc. Or is it just a normal human thing to go through in your twenties."—Tartytwenty

"Well, people do move around more than they used to. It used to be that you stayed in the same community from elementary school until you graduate high school. There is time to make lasting connections. I am not sure many people can claim that. Even if you are still in the same city after college. You are no longer down the hall from your dorm pal. Out of sight, out of mind. Working long hours, your friends working long hours, and all those other things just make it harder to have time for pals. On the other hand people change and get married and have kids. . . . Some people do not get married, do not have kids, etc. Priorities change. These things change the nature of your friendships."—Iwannascream2

Because this is a transition period, we are busy exploring new activities, starting new ventures, and managing real-life responsibilities, often for the first time. We are building the foundation of our adult lives: trying to meet as many new people as possible, becoming settled in a new city, not to mention developing our careers—perhaps by going to grad school or taking professional development classes.

While settling into this new and hectic life, it is comforting to maintain the friendships that we have treasured so much up until this point. But this can also be difficult given that we are all moving in different directions. Getting together may become more like a chore—we have to schedule appointments to see our friends rather than simply drop by a dorm room. But it is worth it, because during stressful times it is those people who really know you, your friends, who truly understand your struggles and know how to help.

It may be impossible to maintain closeness with certain friends as an adult; growing apart is inevitable. However, it becomes increasingly meaningful simply that the basis of these friendships exists and that we do not burn bridges or cut ties with friends who can act as a surrogate family as we discover and adapt to life as an adult, which is when we sometimes feel lost and sentimental about our pasts.

Depending on the nature of your friendships, feelings that accompany these life changes can range from guilt because a friend demands more time from you than you can provide, to heartache because the friend is not there for you when you need them.

It is natural for you to expect your friends to be there for you during the hard times, but remember that the less you are available for your friends, the less you can expect from them. Of course there are the friendships that simply fade because you develop separate interests. In these cases, try to nurture friendships to the best of your ability, because even though a friendship may go dormant, one or both of you may need the revival and the support of that relationship in the future.

ROMANTIC "INTERFERENCE"

Your best friend tells you that he or she has found "the one" and you say, "That's great! I'm so happy for you" (as you grit your teeth and die a little death inside).

> "My friend of 20 years (who lives about a mile from me and works in the same building I live in) hasn't sought me out for so much as a casual conversation in close to two months . . . the reason? New guy. And it's a pattern. She'll start seeing somebody, and literally will spend NO time at all with anybody other than him."—wordsmith

This is a time of constantly changing situations—single one day, dating or even committed another. And this causes the rest of our weekend or evening activities to change.

When we are single, we are busy trying to meet new people. We look for places to go and things to do to meet other people, whether they are prospects or more friends to meet prospects through. When dating or committed, we are busy nurturing that relationship. We start planning our schedules around our significant others, but remember to leave enough time to enjoy each other's company as well as get together with friends.

Changing interests and the addition of significant others will affect friendships—sometimes temporarily and, occasionally, permanently. The best you can do initially is to let go of the past: try not to think about how things once were because they may never be the same again. Perhaps you bonded over a situation that you once had in common but which has since changed, such as being single or being in a similar job. Once you or your friend become involved in a romantic relationship, the other one may feel left in the dust. Or you may just find that your interests changed and you don't have much to talk about anymore. Maybe one day you'll find yourself in the same situation again, but until then, MSN.com relationship columnist Dave Singleton suggests being flexible and "adjusting your friendship so that, even if you talk with or see each other less, your friendship morphs into something different but still valuable and worthwhile."

As our lifestyles and priorities shift, so too do the people we share them with. Some of us, as we get older, no longer enjoy spending time at loud, crowded bars, while others are just beginning to experience late-night partying. This can be a source of conflict between friends, particularly when new romantic relationships enter the equation. Elizabeth Dupont Spencer, MSW, coauthor of *The Anxiety Cure*, describes this as the "constant reshuffling" of adult friendships and recommends "putting your energies into more appreciative friendships" if you feel neglected.

ONE-SIDED MAINTENANCE EFFORTS

Aside from a few close friends, real-world friendships in a sense resemble business contacts—we find ourselves keeping track of when we last got together, and who called whom last. And frankly, most friendships will rely on returning favors, whether that's by showing up at a friend's party or inviting friends over for dinner, and that's okay. At some point, however, you may start to feel as if you are the only one making any effort in what's supposedly a two-sided relationship.

> "I had a friend who was miserable at returning my phone calls or initiating time to hang out. So I stopped calling her and left it up to her. I think it was when she realized how much she missed talking that she really started to make a better effort. I told her later that I am busy too but that I always find time to call her and that it's nice that she's doing the same now."—Lorion 11

If you start to feel like a stalker in the friendship, don't obsess, but do take a hint:

- Don't keep score of who called last or who's made more effort to get together. Some people are naturally better meeting planners—and that could be something your friend appreciates about you.
- If you're the one always depending on someone else to make plans, it may be time to get off your butt and send out an invite or two.
- If, however, you've made three or more attempts to get together and your friend has neither accepted an invitation nor returned a phone call, give it a rest. Let them make the next move when they're ready (yes, friendships can be very similar to dating).
- You never know what your friends might be going through, and as mentioned above, let them know you're there if they need to talk.
- If they've found new interests and social circles, then, frankly, there is nothing for you to do but move on.

TIPS ON NEW WAYS TO THINK ABOUT FRIENDSHIPS

Here are some helpful ways to stay afloat (these tips apply to men and women alike):

- Unlike high school and college where you had a group of friends for everything, you may find yourself compartmentalizing them now—one for going out to raging parties, another for intellectual discussions.
- Record even the most minor of get-togethers in your calendar so you can keep track of when you've seen each of your friends last.
- If a friend invites you out but you're feeling lousy and unsociable, say so—you'd be better off at home than being a downer and lousy company. A true friend will understand. He or she may think that taking you out on the town is the cure, so don't be annoyed. Appreciate the offer and politely decline. Just don't make opting out a habit—because staying in every single night for an entire month isn't healthy, and sometimes getting out is what it takes to get you out of a funk, as long as you approach it with a positive attitude.
- Don't feel the need to impress. Be honest; be real. Whatever the circumstances, do not feel that your friends need to know:

  How many other friends you have

  How much you drank the night before

  How busy you are, and certainly never, no matter what,

  How much money you make

  They will be impressed—by the size of your ego.

Unfortunately, most of us don't recognize pretentiousness in ourselves until it's already done some damage, but just knowing that you should avoid those topics will keep you out of trouble. If you're feeling so good about one of those topics that you can't hold it in, say just that, and don't mention any specifics: "I can't believe I got a raise; I'm so excited" or "I met the coolest person the other night; I'm so excited to have her as a friend." Try *feeling* a little humility—and it will show.

REAL-WORLD FRIENDSHIPS

List your five closest real-world friends.

1. ______________________________
2. ______________________________
3. ______________________________
4. ______________________________
5. ______________________________

Can you remember the last time you saw each one? Write down the corresponding dates and activities. For example, "Sam—coffee, last Tuesday" or "Chris—happy hour, August 3."

When would you like to see each next? Establish a deadline for each one and mark it on your calendar. Next time you e-mail, make a point of proposing a specific plan—not just "We should really get together soon." That leaves things too open, and you'll likely get the following response: "Yeah, it's been too long!"

Rather than get stuck in that busy working professional friendship trap, think of something you both like doing and propose a few open dates and times.

NAME	LAST ACTIVITY/DATE	PROPOSED ACTIVITY/DATE/TIME
1.		
2.		
3.		
4.		
5.		

Throwing Parties

A great way to stay in touch with several friends at once is to throw a party. Time to release the Martha in you! No matter how far from being domestic you consider yourself, we've all got the ability to entertain in some form or another. There's no reason why you have to throw a typical, cookie-cutter party—dare to be different. Show your personality through your party. Here are some fun and inexpensive ideas:

- Game night—pull out some cards or board games. Don't have any? One popular game is to tape a piece of paper with a celebrity's name to each other's foreheads, then ask yes or no questions to try to figure out whose name is on your face.
- Choose an obscure holiday and make it the party theme, for example, Flag Day or Secretary's Day.
- Pajama party—single sex or coed, full body coverage and slippers required. It's fun to regress and create a comfortable atmosphere.
- Wine and cheese tasting—make your best attempt to be sophisticated.
- If you don't want all the attention focused on you, throw someone else a birthday party.

And don't just serve Miller Lite; get creative with a concoction that will also provide a fun conversation topic. (See Chapter 12 for cocktail party recipes.)

- Jello jigglers—vodka optional, shaped to the theme of your party.
- Create your own drinks and name them after friends.
- Accessorize drinks with fun straws or cups from the dollar store.

Even making a small effort will pay off. People will remember you for your great party, and you'll end up with invitations to parties from people you don't even know. It's a great way to network and meet new people.

THE NEW SOCIAL WORLD

The further removed from college, the less parties resemble keggers. To cruise these parties with style and avoid embarrassing blunders, Etiquette Grrl Honore Ervin, coauthor of *Things You Need to Be Told*, recommends sticking to her guidelines below:

Never, ever, *ever* bring extra people to a formal party, such as a sit-down dinner, unless your hostess expressly tells you that you can bring guests. (And, of course, you should let her know that you're bringing a friend or a date. But don't show up with a posse of 20 people in tow!)

Happy-hour situations are entirely different and are generally regarded as "the more the merrier." It's fine to have a couple of friends meet you there and introduce them to your work buddies.

While you should always come with something in hand [such as a bottle of wine] to a more formal gathering (e.g., a dinner party or a special bash such as a New Year's Eve party) you don't have to for something like girls-night-in-with-movies-and-pizza unless you want to, or unless it's tradition among your group. ("I'll bring the Ben & Jerry's!")

FRIENDSHIP RINGS

It may seem strange to organize a list of your friends as you might organize your finances or career goals. However, with everything going on in our lives, it can be easy to unintentionally neglect a friend, or forget about someone when you are feeling bored and lonely and want to make plans but the first few friends who come to mind aren't around. Think about your entire universe when listing names in the circles shown on the following page: friends in your area from high school or college; friends from work who you might hang out with outside the office; friends from old jobs; friends from extracurricular activities such as sports teams, religious groups, volunteering, classes; and friends of friends; and friends of their friends; and so on.

- In the center ring, enter your confidantes—the friends most important to you—right up there with family and significant others, friends you could not live without, whom you depend on to get you through the week, and certainly through tough situations.
- In the middle ring, enter your feel-good friends—those friends with whom you often hang out on the weekends, at parties, or other social outings—friends whom you call to make plans but may not spend an hour with on the phone.
- In the outermost ring, enter your acquaintances—those friends of friends whom you're always happy to run into but whose numbers you don't have programmed into your cell phone.

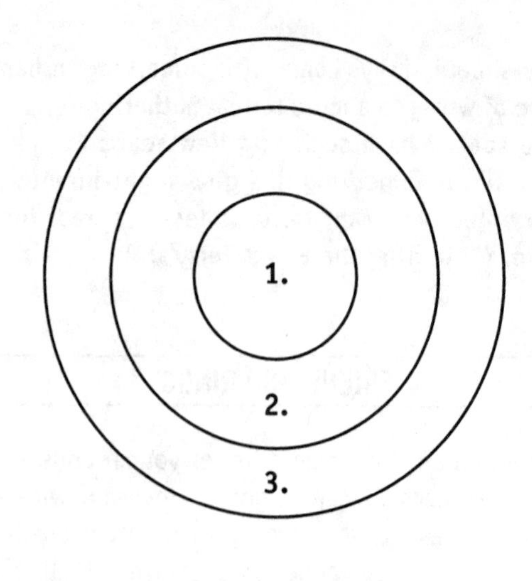

Are there friends from the outside rings whom you'd like to be more "centered" in your life—friends you'd like to get to know better, so you can depend on them for late-night talks? Use the "Real-World Friendships" exercise above to propose some times to get together.

When you find yourself getting down and focusing on all of the ways that your friends aren't there for you anymore, take a moment and think about how they *are* there for you. Your twenties are the first time in your life when maintaining relationships actually takes work, and everyone does it differently. Everyone has different strengths and weaknesses when it comes to how they maintain their friendships. The following exercise will help you focus on your friends' strengths and allow you to reflect on some areas where you could become a better friend.

GLASS HALF FULL

Think about your friends, maybe one you have gotten really annoyed at, and use one or a few of the following phrases to describe him or her and your friendship:

- ❑ Stays in touch with quick and frequent e-mails
- ❑ Always forwards the latest joke or stupid story on the Internet
- ❑ Remembers to send a card or call for my birthday
- ❑ Always gives the most thoughtful gifts
- ❑ Is really good at organizing all of us to get off our lazy butts and do stuff
- ❑ Is a great friend in a crisis
- ❑ Is a good listener
- ❑ Is not in touch a lot, but is completely there for me when we do see each other
- ❑ If I were in trouble, I know I could call this friend at any time for help
- ❑ Makes an effort to visit me even though we live in separate cities
- ❑ Was there for me during a really critical time in my life
- ❑ Other?

Which phrases describe what kind of friend you are? Realizing that everyone has different ways to maintain their friendships will help you adjust and adapt to your changing friendships and not be so quick to discard a friendship that you could really miss.

Resources

STAYING IN TOUCH

www.Birthdayalarm.com
www.Greetings.yahoo.com
www.livejournal.com

PARTY PLANNING

www.Evite.com
www.Etiqettegrrls.com
www.foodtv.com/food/entertaining

CHAPTER 10

Building Lasting Relationships

Many recent graduates tell us that they never went on a real date until after college. Most opted for—or fell naturally into—hooking up at college parties and hanging out in the dorms. Thus, many twentysomethings have yet to master the nuances of checks and dining: who pays, where to meet, what to say, and how to end the night.

Here are some rather humorous first date stories, in retrospect. (They may actually have been a bit painful at the time.)

> "I talked to this girl from match.com for about two weeks and nothing in those conversations made me think she was crazy. She said she had rabbits and talked to them. Heck, I have a cat and I talk to it. Sounded perfectly sane to me. So I show up to her

house right on time, and she opens the door in a towel. Fine, she's not ready; I'm a relaxed person. So she turns on the TV and says she'll be back; her rabbits are over there if I want to talk to them. Thirty minutes later, she comes out. All this time, I didn't say a word to the rabbits. First thing she says was, 'So what did you talk to my rabbits about?' (she used their names, but I can't remember them). I said nothing. She then proceeded to give each of her rabbits a voice and have me talk to them. After about two 20-minute conversations with rabbits, we went out to dinner.

"We went to a nice little restaurant and prepared to order. Shortly after we get our frosty beers, she stands up, goes over to the bar, and brings back a couple of friends of hers. I eat my meal while she and her friends talk, and then I go to pay for the meal and her friends' drinks were on it. They all got up and proceeded to leave, and I stopped them and asked for money for the bill. I said, 'I'll pay for her food and drinks 'cause she's my date, but I don't know you guys.' Which for some reason they weren't happy about.

"Now, most guys would have left long before this time, but I'm pretty easygoing and really had nothing else to do, so we went to a pool hall. After about an hour of pure misery there, I figured enough was enough. I drove her home, and before I came to a stop she said the most remarkable thing, 'I'd invite you in, but I don't think my rabbits like you.' I wasn't going in if she had begged me. And that was the last time I saw the psycho rabbit girl."
—abanky

"First off, I'm not shallow, but I believe first impressions are the best ones. He's wearing sneakers, and the place we went was kinda fancy. We order food, talk, the food comes, we start eating. Now, I had ordered chicken and he ordered fish. I was like, 'Hmm, either this is the most tender chicken I've ever had, or this is fish.' I asked the waitress to bring me the chicken, which is going to take a few minutes to cook. My date keeps looking at his watch and toward the kitchen door for the waiter! I wanted to say, 'Hey buddy are you in a rush to go somewhere?' Not to mention he went to the bathroom TWICE in an hour. He keeps eating his food while I'm waiting for mine—so rude. When mine finally comes out, he's watching me eat, like he's waiting for me to finish up. I was trying to make jokes and he kept taking me literally. Anyway, so the waiter comes back to see how my new meal is and he's like, 'The check would be great.' Then as I'm waiting for my leftovers to be wrapped, he says, 'It was nice to meet you' and we part."—Jen312

"I liked this guy my friend knew. He hadn't been with anyone in a long time and neither had I. I asked him on a date to the movies and he agreed. We spoke a very, very little bit on the ride to the movies. He picked me up. I am pretty sure he was talking about some kids making fun of him because he was gay when he was in high school gym class. The rest of the night was completely silent, and he took me home and that was it. I later found out he was gay. I guess he tried to tell me."—chrisp

"Back in my Internet dating days, I met up with one girl who had been in a sorority in college. Our plan was to meet at this area with a bunch of stores and shops, walk around and talk, and then go get dinner. Dinner never happened. Apparently, I made the mistake of asking her, in a casual and lighthearted way, what she had done to get into her sorority (which she talked about endlessly). She smiled politely and wouldn't answer. Uh, ok, I thought to myself and dropped the subject. We talked for another 15 minutes or so, and I then suggested we walk down the street to the restaurant and get dinner. She freaked out. 'I'm not going to dinner with you. What you said was very rude, asking me about how I got into my sorority.

I'm going home, and besides my toe is hurting, and my grandmother is sick and needs me.' As she was leaving to go to her car, she actually had the nerve to say, 'MAYBE you can try calling me in three days after I cool off!'

"I went home and immediately threw her number in the trash, and that was the end of that. This was a girl who contacted me, by the way.

"Another time I met up with a girl who quite possibly had the most negative personality imaginable. Also an online meet-up, and our first (and only) face-to-face was at some college social event at her school. She spent the entire time talking about how she hated all these other girls and how this one was a slut and this one had an eating disorder and so on and so forth. I was so depressed when I came home from that 'date' that I wanted to cry."—WeirdBrake

"I went out on a date with this guy that my dad set me up with. He knew him from the big brothers program and really thought he was a nice guy, and I had met him briefly before so I agreed.

"The guy called me and asked if I'd like to see a movie. He asked if I liked horror movies, and I said I did. And for the most part I do like scary movies. He said he really wanted to see *Texas Chainsaw Massacre*, so I agreed. The movie was so horribly violent that less than halfway through I thought I was going to have to leave. There were a couple times when I got really grossed or jumped at something scary, and he just laughed at me kind of condescendingly. Afterwards he said how much he liked it and asked what I thought. I was honest and told him how I really felt. So he says, 'Well I was going to suggest we get some dinner but now I'm not in the mood.' He drove me home and I didn't hear from him again (no big loss).

"But seriously, what kind of guy suggests *Texas Chainsaw Massacre* for a date and then gets mad when you don't like it?"—cheshrcarol

While each relationship is unique and impossible to measure against a set of benchmarks (unlike national salary averages and GRE percentiles), there are some general guidelines that you can follow so that you don't appear completely oblivious, can tackle each date with an air of confidence, and hopefully, avoid the scenarios above.

Dating Etiquette Tips

The only formality expected on college dates might have been offering to pump the keg for another plastic cup of beer, or using "points" off the meal plan to pay for a burger. Now, however, we are working adults. We can afford to buy a glass of wine that doesn't come out of a box or a jug. We no longer have the excuse that we're just college students. The days of wearing baseball caps and flannel shirts are over. They have been replaced with jackets and ties, or at least sweater sets and slacks.

Below are some of the more frequently asked dating-related etiquette questions that we hear:

1. How do I make the first move?

"Help Me, Harlan" columnist Harlan Cohen's advice is to: "Say what you're thinking (keep it clean) and say what you're feeling (listen to your voice inside). Be honest, be genuine, and be willing to take risk after risk after risk. The best pick-up line is to say something—anything—'Hi' followed up by, 'What's your name?' 'How's your day going?' 'You have beautiful eyes . . .' What you say doesn't matter as long as it's genuine and not offensive. If he or she is intrigued, it's a start. As many women have told me, the best pick-up line can be just, 'Hello.'"

2. Is it okay to ask someone out online?

Etiquette Grrl Honore Ervin, coauthor of *Things You Need to Be Told*, can't think of any reason not to, now that online chatter seems to have become the most common mode of communication. (She does, however, draw the line at online marriage proposals, although it has been known to happen!)

3. Are past relationships taboo in first-date conversation?

Ervin says that although "past relationships are going to come up at SOME point, on the first few dates, it's a topic best avoided. Your new beau really doesn't want to hear about your last boyfriend who was the Wall Street banker, or who was the stalker, so now you have a few wee mental problems, or whatever. Keep it to yourself until you know each other better." *Washington Post Express* "Baggage Check" columnist and psychologist Andrea Bonior, Ph.D., says only to discuss past relationships for the right reasons—not to feel like hot stuff, or to release some pent up resentment by calling your ex a psycho.

4. To reach or not to reach (for the check)?

Although it is fair to expect that both men and women today are working in their twenties, there is still uneasiness about who should pay on the first date. Many women are unsure about whether or not to "reach" for their wallets, regardless of whether they actually intend to pay. Ervin says, "Women shouldn't bother with the 'fake reach,' because they actually should reach! My goodness, in this day and age, as chivalrous as it is for a boy to pick up the tab for things, you should expect to go dutch, especially in a nascent relationship. Further, if the woman is the one who made the plans, she should pay for everything. (For instance, she invites her beau to the symphony and dinner—she was the one who extended the invitation and planned the date, so she should pay.) However, that said, many guys will actually pay for everything."

Cathy Alter, author of *Virgin Territory*, feels that women should offer to pay for the tip if they are interested in the guy, and offer to treat next time. Just "Don't act entitled."

In other words, it's quite alright for the man to pay—the extent to which that is appreciated depends on the tradition or independence of the woman. However, regardless of the outcome, the woman should make a sincere attempt at good manners by at least offering to pay.

5. When to call—three days, six days, never?

In addition to the awkwardness of ending a date, that sense of ambiguity lingers until the next date—if there is a next date. Is it okay to call? How long should you wait? What if you don't want to call? What if they call? Do you answer or assume an air of business and wait to call back? Or maybe actually keep yourself busy so you have to call back? What if you don't want to call back? Ervin laments, "I wish people would cut out all this 'three-day-rule' baloney. I think calling the next day, simply to say you had a good time, is gracious and not pushy at all. Just don't gush and go on and on . . . you'll probably just sound desperate. And don't call as soon as you get home!"

Cohen believes that there are no hard and fast rules about when to call. He advises that the "only rule is to follow your heart and not call 10 times and hang up without leaving a message. (They probably have caller ID.)" His suggestion? "Call twice—leave a message—and wait a few days until calling again. Then stop."

Alter advises women, "If a guy wants to see you he will. If he hasn't called, wait a week and send a breezy e-mail. If guys are really into you, they may even leave a voicemail seconds after the date, which can make them seem crazy—if so, sleep on it! Maybe you won't feel as passionate the next day." Just as you should not pretend to reach for your wallet, so too should you not pretend to be out while listening to a guy leave a message for you. Alter suggests that you "Actually be busy, so you really are out doing other stuff when you say you are. A little intrigue is good, be a little mysterious." If it's only been a day or two since the first date and you are trying to hold yourself back from calling him, "Call your tough love friend, and listen when he or she tells you not to call."

When you do call, make the message brief. Your main objective is to show you're interested in another date and, of course, to leave the correct phone number.

6. How do you handle the awkward goodbye?

As Alter says, the worst part of the date is the goodbye, because there is a feeling of uncertainty. And although you "sometimes want to jump out of the car when it's still running" to avoid that awkward goodbye when you have absolutely no interest, you can try to "come around wide for a kiss on the cheek" so as not to offend. Just "pretend you're on a witness stand and be as short as possible—answer yes, no, or I don't understand."

Getting Serious: When the Stakes Get Higher or Playing for Keeps

Once you get past the awkwardness of dating and know the person well enough to know that you want to spend even more time with him or her, things can progress to a serious relationship—as long as you both want the same thing out of it.

Match.com relationship columnist Dave Singleton compares dating after college to a corporate merger: "You have to think about integrating friends, families, careers, finances, and possessions. It's good to think about what you want and what the other person wants in advance so you won't be surprised when you start seeing each other seriously, plan to get married, or move in together. We have more expectations now than in college." He points out that it is hard not to think about the long term now that "more of our money goes toward bridal showers than pizzas."

Singleton offers the following advice:

- Go with your instincts. Our willful nature sometimes keeps us from listening to our inner voice.
- Read between the lines. "We're in a socially transactional world now, which has a danger—people often have specific agendas. Look at personal ads; now they are detailed down to the most specific minutia: 'SWM wants 5 foot 6 inch woman with light brown hair, blue eyes, height and weight proportionate, should have a successful career, know how to cook, speak French, and ski, and write novels in her spare time.' We're trained to want exactly what we want when we want it, but the real world doesn't work that way. And it's not exactly romantic either, is it?"
- "Don't try to fit into a Cinderella mold. No one knows what happened to her after the fairytale—was she miserable stuck in the castle while the Prince went riding across the countryside? Probably. But then again, she didn't think past the wedding now, did she? You can chart your own course and create your own fairytale" as long as you think about the long-term picture.

One sign that things are getting serious is that we start using the "boyfriend" or "girlfriend" label. The first time we use the label, even though it is just a label, can be exciting—or scary. Sometimes we are apprehensive about using the label, although we feel ready, because we are worried about the other person's reaction. While the label timing is different in every relationship, San Francisco–based relationship writer Susan Orenstein suggests bringing up the label "in a playful way" rather than making it a serious conversation. The label shouldn't matter, but most people start using the boyfriend/girlfriend tag about three months into a relationship. Cohen believes that if you do not feel ready to have a conversation about the status of your relationship, then you're not ready for the label.

Another milestone in a relationship is spending the night for the first time—whether that means just a sleepover or more—but that can be a dangerous situation if you do not know the person well enough. Bonior suggests meeting some friends or family before staying over for the first time and paying attention to any stories that don't match up. It is true that you can't earn someone's trust without taking emotional risks. Just don't risk physical safety. Make sure you tell someone exactly where you'll be and how to be reached.

If you have met someone through the Internet, treat that person as "someone you've never truly met; you may not even know the state they live in," Bonior warns. Make sure before being alone for the first time that your friends know where you are. It also helps to have met some of his or her friends first, so they can vouch for your date and you can gauge his or her sanity by the company they keep.

Bonior also suggests, before spending the night, to first make sure that you have the same expectations—that one of you doesn't expect to move in together after your first night together. You want the experience to be equally enjoyable; sometimes one person will stay over for convenience, and the other is annoyed because he or she needs some space. Or perhaps you see another side of someone in the morning that isn't as appealing.

Cohen cautions that "hot relationships burn fast. The sooner the sleepover, the greater the risk that it will burn out."

Many couples today move in together before deciding to take the ultimate plunge and get married, and some couples prefer the more traditional route of waiting for marriage to cohabitate, anticipating something new and exciting upon their return from the honeymoon. Orenstein suggests putting a lot of time into this big decision. Rather than moving into one or the other's apartment, which may seem like a way to save money, it is better to find an apartment together, so that you both have the same sense of ownership. Also, many people don't consider that by spending so much time together the fun can be zapped. You don't need to be constantly together 24 hours a day to be close; don't neglect the other important parts of your life. You should still have your own friends and activities.

FROM FRIENDS TO MORE THAN FRIENDS

Although friendships can sometimes morph into beautiful romantic relationships, close-knit quarterlife friendships are harder to come by once you are out of school. Should you risk that friendship? When is it *not* a good idea to transition from friends to more than friends?

Cohen warns against risking your friendship: "When looking for a fling—don't look for a fling with a friend. If you're ready for something committed, long-term, and loving—friends make the very best partners. If your friend is in a relationship—*do not* make a move. Wait until he or she is out of it. It's just going to strain the relationship."

What Do You Think?

It may be tempting sometimes, when friends have significant others of whom you don't approve for one reason or another, to discourage that friend from progressing any further. However you should be careful because your opinion may not matter and may only wreak havoc on your friendship. Singleton notes that sharing your opinion depends on the situation. For example, if you know that your friend's boyfriend or girlfriend is lying or sleeping around, or that your friend's money, health, or safety is at risk, then you are doing a favor and fulfilling your duties as a friend to say something. Sometimes, we know the person isn't right for us and constantly seek approval. If a friend who wants your opinion keeps asking for it, only share your opinion once. If he or she persists and looks to you for acceptance, "Ask why they keep asking. Otherwise you are just playing into their codependency. If people really want to listen, you'll only have to tell them once," advises Singleton.

If you are on the receiving end of a friend's negative and unwelcome opinion of your significant other, Singleton suggests adopting the attitude that "opinions are free." Your friends can have as many as they want, and some may be about your choices, but only what you feel matters. "When you really understand that, you won't be angry. Instead you'll feel slightly annoyed or even bemused. That's when you're on the right track. No one can pressure you without your consent; they can say whatever they want but you're a grown-up."

Bonior, on the other hand, points out that your friends' radar is usually reliable, and that it is important to listen to your friends and hope that they are looking out for your best interests. Occasionally, a friend may have ulterior motives because he or she is jealous. However, if you find yourself censoring your friends' advice because you don't feel that they understand your situation, then you may be afraid of their judgment for a reason.

Cohen agrees: "Your friends don't need to date your significant other—you do. But if everyone in the world sees a problem, trust that there is a problem. It's hard to see the big picture when stuck in the haze of love, but not for your friends. Don't be so quick to think they're jealous or out to ruin you. A lot of the time, they see all the things you can't see. At least listen to [their opinions], then decide if you need to turn a deaf ear."

RELATIONSHIP THERMOMETER

Healthy	Dysfunctional
You don't ever question the relationship; it just feels right.	You are constantly seeking outside justifications for their inappropriate or inconsiderate behaviors.
They call you first with news about work or family, and vice-versa.	You hear through the grapevine about their work, travel, or family illness.

The thought of losing them devastates you.	The thought of losing them means freedom to you.
You feel free to be completely yourself.	You worry that they might think you're weird.
You communicate concerns.	You build resentment every time they piss you off.

Give yourself 20 points for each left-hand column response.

Total score: __________ (Check the thermometer to interpret your score.)

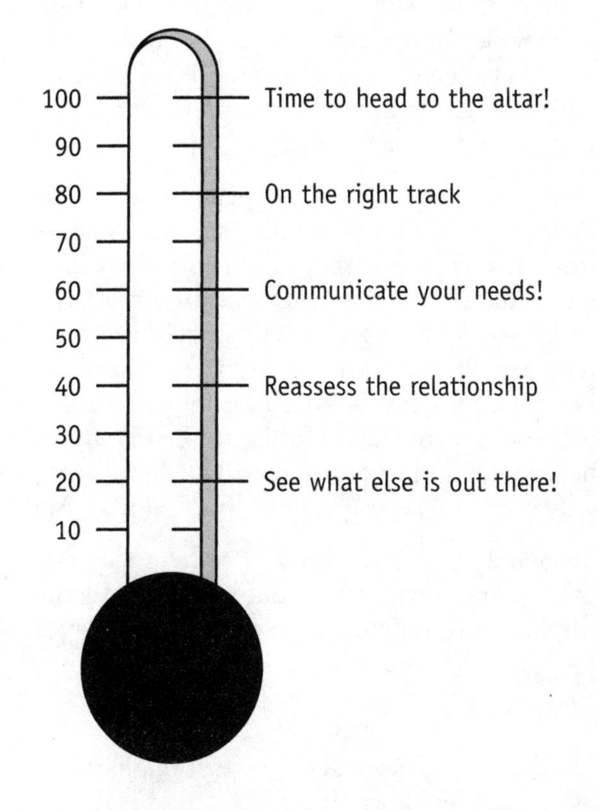

How Do You Know If This One's a Winner?

Orenstein suggests placing emphasis on the little gestures to determine the relationship's sustainability—what your boyfriend or girlfriend does for you on a daily basis, not just on a romantic Hallmark holiday. It's a good sign if he or she remembers the little things about your preferences, such as eating habits. Also, good couples have a lot of eye contact and, of course, trust.

Alter says you should feel celebrated for being you—look for someone who "gets" you, someone who appreciates your individuality and humor.

Bonior points out that in the healthiest relationships, change is embraced. You should not have too much rigidity in your requirements and expectations, and you should be willing to grow and change with each other.

According to Dr. Joyce Brothers in *What Every Woman Ought to Know about Love and Marriage*:

> Under the romantic spell of being in love, couples tend to believe that they think alike and want the same things from marriage. But they don't, and when they discover this, often very shortly after the honeymoon, it comes as a rude shock. They feel as if they have been deceived. And they have been. To a certain extent. During courtship, everyone puts his and her best foot forward. We often misrepresent ourselves, trying to be like the person we believe the other wants rather than being ourselves. It is only natural. We want so much to be loved. And to love.

To avoid this rude shock, Brothers suggests discussing whether or not you agree about big issues relating to money, children, family, religion, and sex before taking the plunge.

WARNING SIGNS

What are some signs to look for that might indicate the relationship's headed downhill?

Bonior warns relationship parties to beware of the "Checklist syndrome"—using status symbols or superficial qualities to justify the relationship rather than actual attributes or how the person makes you feel. If you based the relationship on a checklist, "Your Mr. Right would be right for everyone else."

Singleton lists the following relationship red flags: a waning interest in the things that matter to each other, arguments that never resolve, a general disrespect for one another and lack of trust.

Orenstein advises that your relationship may be in trouble if the other person forgets important details about you, doesn't really listen anymore, never asks about you, and ignores your responsibilities and schedule.

Harlan Cohen's relationship red flags:

- You know that your significant other is cheating, but you still want him or her.
- He or she is verbally or physically abusive, and you make excuses that it's okay. It's *never* okay.
- You know you deserve better.
- You're left with no friends, no support, and no one but him or her.
- You just know in your heart—it's over.

MOST COMMON BREAKUP CAUSES

- **Different values**
- **Distance/change in situation**
- **Change in or lack of romantic feelings/attraction**
- **Not willing or scared to commit**
- **Emotional problems**

Breakup Recovery Tips

Learn to recognize the breakup excuses:

He/she says	It really means
I'm not looking for a relationship right now.	You're not right for me.
I'm getting over a serious relationship.	You are looking for more than a fling, and that scares me.
I'm so busy right now with work.	You are not worth my time.
I think you're a really nice person.	I'm not attracted to you.
I think we'd be great as friends.	I know you can't handle that, but it's the only way to make a clean break.

When you're down in the dumps about the end of a relationship for which you once had such high hopes, it's time to indulge in the little things that make you happy—new books, CDs, or a mini shopping spree at your favorite clothing or gadget store. Hit the gym, and don't spend too much time on the couch. Get out with friends; parties will force you to act cheerful, which may actually make you feel more cheerful. Don't be hard on yourself. Go ahead and sneak in some greasy food or chocolate, even if you're watching your weight.

Orenstein suggests that you "rally your friends' support;" don't be afraid to tell them you need their help. At the same time, embrace being on your own. There will be other relationships, and you'll appreciate the time you have now to enjoy the things that you don't have time for when you are part of a couple. Take advantage of this time to read books and catch up on hobbies. And let yourself experience anger; don't fight your feelings.

Alter suggests keeping in mind the phenomenon of Karma—what goes around comes around. Feel sad for as long as you need to, treat yourself or buy something. Just don't do something really drastic you might regret, like dying your hair or going into debt. Surround yourself with friends who are nurturing and make you feel good, and keep yourself busy. There's no set amount of time for the healing process. Don't lose hope or generalize that all men or women suck; people can sense that negativity. "Don't be a hater," as Alter puts it.

Bonior too emphasizes that you have to allow yourself to be sad: "You need to grieve and embrace your feelings. Don't be afraid of feeling sad; it only grows when it is 'stuffed.' It can become scary when not dealt with. Heal at your own pace." Also, "Do not put pressure on yourself to do an autopsy of the relationship. You may never know why it ended, but you can still move on. You can get 'closure' without figuring out exactly what went wrong." And "worrying about the other one getting over the relationship faster only accentuates the pain." Most importantly, recognize that "it doesn't mean you are a failure or a loser."

Bonior recommends journaling and talking about your feelings. Don't be afraid to look at photos and relive memories. Facing the breakup immediately can be painful, but it's better than crashing your car three months later when you hear the song that reminds you of your ex.

Everyone moves on in their own time and at their own pace. If someone had a serious relationship but is used to being single, he or she may need longer, while someone who is always in a relationship may feel more grounded in these situations.

Just make sure that the "emotional pain doesn't overpower you longer than four to five months," because then you are in danger of sinking into a clinical depression and should seek help, according to Bonior.

WHAT NOT TO DO

If you are the dumpee, you may not want the dumper to see that you're hurt, but you also don't want to parade around with someone new in his or her face just to show you've moved on, either. You'll be figured out and you'll seem immature. Don't become a stalker by calling and hanging up, and don't compare every other person you meet to your ex.

If you are the one initiating the break-up, "Treat your ex with dignity and respect. Just make it clear that they can't call you anymore," says Alter.

Moving On

Bonior reminds us, "Relationships are meant for practice, you are meant to learn from them. Don't view endings as failures. Use the relationship to learn about yourself; you can even learn something from the worst relationships. You are allowed to rediscover who you are and change what you look for in another person."

Alter thinks that women in particular often stay too long in relationships they know are unhealthy. Afterwards, we wish we could have seen the "movie version" of the relationship to get an objective viewpoint. As Alter points out, "Sometimes sitting home on a Saturday night with a book is better than going out, and it's okay. That's big to realize as an adult on your own for the first time."

WHAT ARE YOU REALLY LOOKING FOR?

You might have a working checklist in your mind of those qualities that you look for in a lifetime partner. You might think that person doesn't exist—you might be right. We tend to idealize our mate based on movies we've seen and childhood fantasies. It's important to identify those requirements that are non-negotiable: Is it important for you to find someone of a certain age? A certain religion? Similar educational background?

List the five most important traits you look for in a potential significant other, for example:

Looks
Sense of humor
Intelligence
Kindness
Thoughtfulness
Sensitivity
Appreciation of common interests

What's important to me?

1. ______________________________
2. ______________________________
3. ______________________________
4. ______________________________
5. ______________________________

Now, think about the last time you were at a bar or singles event—what was it *really* that attracted you to someone there?

What I go for:

1. ______________________________
2. ______________________________
3. ______________________________
4. ______________________________
5. ______________________________

Did you notice a discrepancy between your two sets of answers? What traits do you feel are important to look for in someone? And what traits seem important to you when you are looking? Although many of us *feel* that we should look for someone with whom we share similar backgrounds and beliefs to provide for interesting conversations, it is sometimes tempting to ignore all of these qualifications and go for the most magnetic or physically attractive candidate in the room.

YOUR DATING HISTORY—IDENTIFYING RELATIONSHIP PATTERNS

Think about relationships you have had over the last five years. Or, if you have not had relationships, think about people you've dated or been interested in. What was it that you were really attracted to? What ended up being the source of conflict or lack of connection that did not allow the relationship to progress?

1. Name: ____________________ Year of relationship: ___________

   How you met:____

   What you were initially attracted to: _____________________

   Reason for relationship ending: ___________________________

2. Name: ____________________ Year of relationship: ___________

   How you met:____

   What you were initially attracted to: _____________________

   Reason for relationship ending: ___________________________

3. Name: ____________________ Year of relationship: ___________

   How you met:____

   What you were initially attracted to: _____________________

   Reason for relationship ending: ___________________________

You should be able to draw a lesson from each relationship: why it ended and what it was about that person that didn't mesh well with your personality or habits.

DATING RÉSUMÉ

This is exactly as it sounds—not that you will actually FAX this along with a cover letter to your potential date (please, don't!). But think of this as a mental marketing tool when you essentially "sell" yourself at singles events or parties. There is no reason you should not display the same confidence and persuasive demeanor to convince a romantic interest that you would be right for him or her that you would use to convince someone to hire you.

Your Name: ______________________________

Preferred contact information: ______________________

Experience: I have learned the following about myself in relationships [refer to previous exercise]

1. ______________________________
2. ______________________________
3. ______________________________

Interests: I enjoy the following activities (choose from the examples below, or add your own)

Outdoors	Arts and Entertainment	Education	Hobbies
Hiking	Movies	Language classes	Crafts
Biking	Concerts	History lectures	Cooking
Kayaking	Theater	Computer training	Volunteering
Running	Poetry readings	Writing workshops	Dancing
Swimming	Museum exhibits	Personal finance	Reading
Other	Other	Other	Other

Qualities: I would describe myself as (choose from the following list)

Quirky	Thoughtful	Thrifty	Social
Independent	Organized	Laid back	Busy
Free-spirited	Successful	Energetic	Outdoorsy
Introverted	Ambitious	Intelligent	Sensitive
Nurturing	Humorous	Spiritual	Other

Resources

DATING ADVICE

www.helpmeharlan.com
msn.match.com

ETIQUETTE

www.etiquettegrrls.com

PART 4

Self

IT'S ALL ABOUT YOU! Don't forget, while trying to adapt to working life, apartment living, and new rules of social engagement, that this may be the last period of our lives when we are responsible for no one but ourselves. Although we have new responsibilities to worry about and less free time to ourselves, the responsibilities will only continue to increase and the free time decrease as we begin to form our own families. Thus, it is important to make the most of what free time is left now to focus on emotional, spiritual, and physical well-being, before we have to worry about someone else.

CHAPTER 11

Extracurricular Activities

Make these the better years of your life—take advantage of your freedom.

We hear it all the time from our elders—"what are you complaining about, these are supposed to be the best years of your life?" It is true that your QLC can hit hard and fast and leave you wondering what's so great about being in your twenties. While we think that it is important to acknowledge that quarterlife has its share of challenges, we also want to remind you that even if you don't yet feel that these are the best years of your life, there are some ways that you can make them the "better" years of your life! For all of the downsides of being inexperienced, broke, not in the job of your dreams, and feeling lonely sometimes, there are some upsides. It can be a hard time in your life, but you can make it a great time too.

It's a Great Time to See the World

Maybe you got downsized. Or, maybe you have some time before starting a new job or graduate school. It can be hard to find a solid block of time to go see the world, but it's only going to get worse. "Take the chance, now, to travel. Careers and families will happen. It is a lot harder to travel later," encourages Brad Tuttle, associate editor at Arthur Frommer's *Budget Travel* magazine.

That's exactly what Kelly, a political appointee, did when she knew that her job would be coming to an end. She took some time before starting graduate school to take a three-month trip around the world: "Some people thought I was crazy to travel for that long—alone—to places they had barely even heard of. But this transition presented the opportunity and freedom to do something totally different—to take myself out of my comfort zone of job, friends, home, and language." She shares an important lesson, "I learned to take advantage of transitions in life while you can—to take time away from your everyday life. There are so many things that you can't learn in a classroom or on the job." But you don't need two months to get away from it all. Even a weekend road trip can help restore your sanity during stressful times and remind you why it's good to be on your own.

Obviously, any travel, especially a big trip, requires a lot of planning, and you need to know where to go to get some help. "The travel world largely ignores people in their twenties because they don't have much money," Tuttle explains. But there are some companies that specialize in trips for the young, the adventurous, and, well, those of us who are wealth-deficient.

One good resource Tuttle recommends is STA Travel, an international company that can usually be found near college campuses. STA can offer special discounts on airlines but, more importantly, offers tickets that are a lot more flexible than typical airline tickets, so you commitment-phobes don't have to lock yourselves down to a plan.

Don't assume that "student" discounts don't apply to you, especially in Europe. In countries where there is much more of a tradition of traveling, student discounts usually apply to anyone under 25 or 26, whether you are a full-time student or not. For example, the Eurail pass is available to anyone under 26 and offers huge savings on travel through Europe.

Even though most of us don't have a lot of extra money to spend on travel, it doesn't mean that you cannot plan a great adventure. Brad, an associate at a large bank, shares some tips for how he planned some affordable travel:

> "Some of my most satisfying vacations have been to national parks and wildlife refuges. It may not seem so exotic, but there is breathtaking scenery (and affordable accommodations) around Mount St. Helens, New Hampshire's White Mountains, the Okefenokee swamp, and the National Seashore in Key West. Foreign travel can be handled on a budget by targeting locations that are near to major vacation spots, but less immersed in the travel industry. The Dominican Republic has all the surf, sun, and sand of the Bahamas, but at a much lower price. Moreover, the residents are friendlier, having had their patience tested by fewer obnoxious tourists."

CHECK THE EXCHANGE RATE

Check into exchange rates before selecting your destination, suggests Brad Tuttle. Your money will go a lot further in New Zealand, Australia, Brazil, or Mexico than it would in Europe these days.

SAFETY

There is no reason to curtail travel in a post-9/11 world. "The places you shouldn't be going are the same places you shouldn't have been going to before," says Tuttle. "You have to have a more international attitude about things. Don't assume that people are going to be nice to you. Don't be surprised if you feel bad vibes."

One of the great benefits of traveling is learning about other countries, peoples, and cultures. Trying your best to blend in is not only safer, but provides a more authentic traveling experience. Be respectful, especially if you plan to visit religious sites. Make sure that you know what the local religion is and how your dress, gestures, or behavior might offend, especially in Africa and the Middle East. You may not get it right all of the time, but even attempting to do the right thing is going to go a long way in a local person's eyes. You don't want to stick out like a sore thumb. Open-toed sandals, sneakers, and shorts are comfortable but look really American. Being aware of the culture is also an important safety precaution.

Don't take chances you wouldn't take at home. It's amazing that someone who would never even think about hitchhiking at home hitchhikes across a foreign country where he or she may not even know the language. You certainly don't want to be scared all of the time, and you definitely want to be open to new people and new places, but don't leave all of your prudence and caution at home.

BENEFITS

If you feel guilty about taking some time to travel, or feel like it's a hassle, consider some of the benefits:

- Learning about your own or another country can expand your worldview and give you experiences that will help you on the job or in school. Your travel adventures will also provide for good small talk during job interviews or out meeting prospective dates.
- Interacting with people from different cultures will help you learn how to work with coworkers, bosses, and customers who have different backgrounds.

TRAVEL SAFETY TIPS WHEN GOING SOLO

If you are traveling on your own:

- **Tuttle suggests going somewhere with an established tourism infrastructure. Parts of Southeast Asia, South America, and Africa may seem extremely enticing because they are off the beaten path, but these adventures can be extremely challenging on your own. You don't want to get so frustrated on your first big trip that you are turned off to traveling altogether.**
- **The Internet makes it so much easier to stay in touch with family and friends at home and to coordinate plans with fellow travelers. You can find a cyber café almost anywhere in the world. Use the Internet to keep people apprised of your whereabouts so that someone knows where you are and where you are heading.**
- **Avoid getting sick. Before visiting another country, check out the Centers for Disease Control's traveler information site at www.cdc.gov/travel/. Find out if your destination country requires immunizations, or if there are any other precautions you need to take.**
- **Don't forget to make a copy of your passport and keep the copy separate from your passport at all times.**

- You never know whom you will meet on the road, on the train, in the hostel, or visiting a museum. You will make new friends, new contacts, and maybe even meet a romantic interest.

It's a Great Time to Pursue Your Interests

While travel is a wonderful opportunity to learn, explore, and develop your interests, there are also plenty of opportunities at home. The last time you thought about your "extracurriculars," you were probably sweating over your résumé and thinking about all of the things that you did in college that could help you land a job. Now that you have that job, or that spot in grad school, do you feel as if you left some of the best parts of yourself back on campus? What if you had to write an extracurricular résumé, detailing all of your activities and accomplishments outside of work or school? Would you have anything to list?

EXTRACURRICULAR RÉSUMÉ

1. Date ______________________

   Activity ______________________

   Role ______________________

2. Date ______________________

   Activity ______________________

   Role ______________________

3. Date ______________________

   Activity ______________________

   Role ______________________

Maintaining your interests at this stage of your life is an important component of the QLC cure. As we discuss in the section on boredom in Chapter 6, for those who feel uninspired and underutilized in the workplace, engaging in activities that help you feel worthwhile in one area of your life will really help you face your workday. But even for those who love their jobs, letting go of important activities is a cause for regret.

Elizabeth, a law student who just finished a stint with a New York City publisher, loved her job. When asked if she maintained her interest in extracurriculars after college, she explained, "No, and I regret it . . . though I recognize that the reason I didn't was largely because I was really happy with my job and my social life as it was. My job was intellectually challenging, so I didn't feel that I was missing out on that part of my life once I started working. My job also brought its own set of extracurriculars—book parties, readings—which I greatly enjoyed. I do regret that I didn't try to do some freelance writing and that I didn't continue with the volunteer work I had done in college. It takes a lot more commitment to keep up with 'hobbies' outside of school, and I wish I'd made it more of a priority."

With all of the other changes you are experiencing in your life, maintaining and engaging in your hobbies and interests can provide a sense of stability, as well as an outlet where you can express yourself, have fun, and feel confident.

When we asked QLCers whether or not they maintained their hobbies and interests, we received mixed reactions. As you can see in Figures 11.1 and 11.2, our QLCers have a wide variety of interests outside of work. Some choose more solitary hobbies while others do hobbies as a way to meet new people.

Of those who do not engage in hobbies, most blame it on lack of time or money. (See Figure 11.3.) For those of you who miss your extracurricular activities but feel that you don't have time, check out Chapter 4 on time and balance and think about how you can reincorporate these important interests back into your life. And for those of you who are trying to save money, check out our low-cost suggestions at the end of this section.

The stories behind the numbers shed some light on how QLCers are trying to incorporate their interests into their new schedules and lifestyles. While many QLCers said that they did not have the time to maintain their outside interests, others said that their newly structured schedules actually allowed more time for their interests.

> "I actually feel like I have MORE time for extracurricular activities now that I'm not in school. I always had to work while going to school, so now that I only put in eight hours a day I feel like I have an abundance of free

FIGURE 11.1 Quarterlifers' hobbies

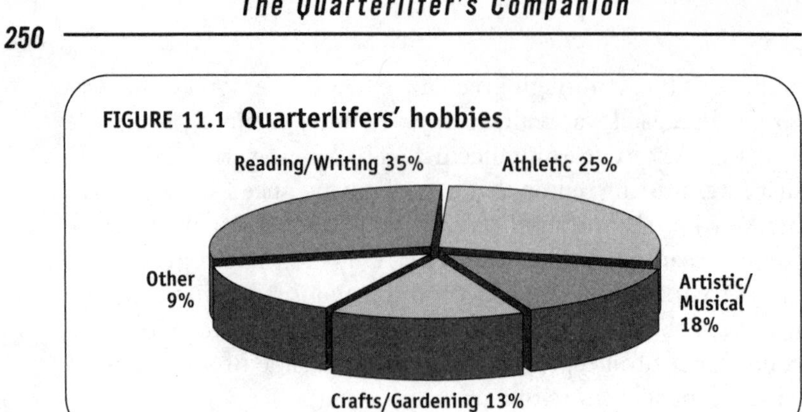

FIGURE 11.2 Engage in hobbies with . . .

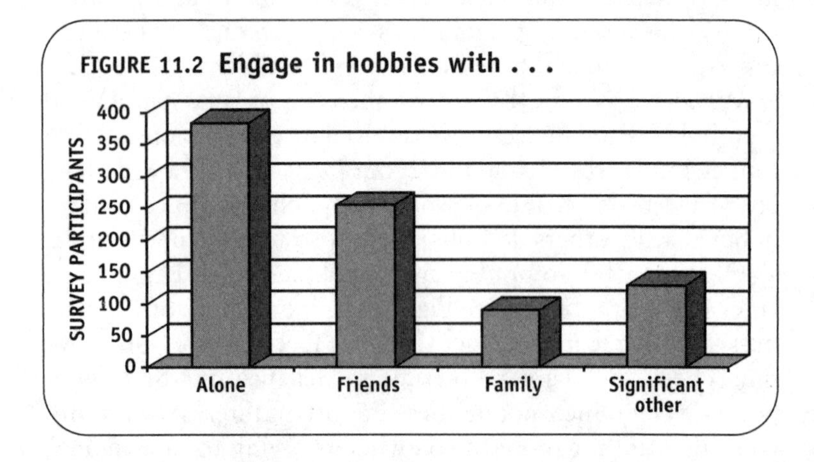

FIGURE 11.3 Why don't you participate in hobbies?

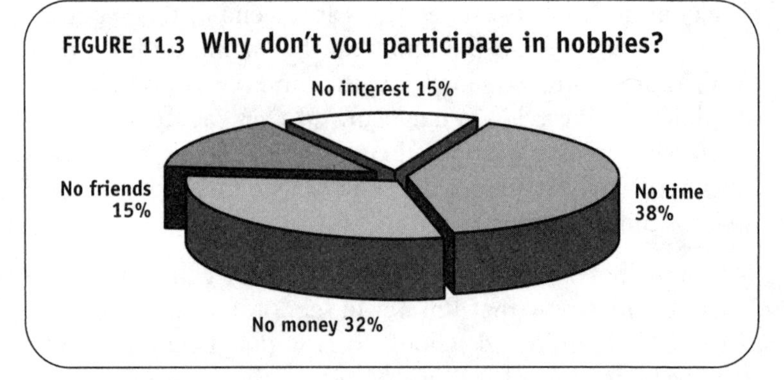

time. (So much free time, in fact, that I'm returning to night school for my Ph.D. in the spring.) Right now I have extra time to attend dance and yoga class, read books, go to movies. My life is a billion times more carefree than it was when I was in school."—Gluegun

Catalytical shows how a variety of activities can be fulfilling and do not need to be completely time-consuming:

"I actually think my activities have increased over time. I've volunteered for community cleanups, I've been a foster home for a no-kill shelter, I've become a junkie for Pilates and yoga (both are great ways to relieve stress and keep your body in shape), and I've participated in walks for various charities with coworkers and friends. I didn't do much in the way of organized activities after high school anyhow, but I definitely make the time for the things I love, even if it's only 20 minutes every few days. I can give up 20 minutes of, say, sleep in order to do something that makes me happy and keeps me sane!"

For other QLCers visiting the message boards, the challenge was not finding the time, but finding the right outlet. Some QLCers had a really hard time finding "real world" substitutes for their college activities.

"I think one of my biggest difficulties out of high school and college was dealing with the loss of group sports. All of my adolescent life I've played group sports: volleyball, softball, soccer . . . so then once I entered college and now after graduation, I don't have anybody to play with. There aren't any more teams. It's so difficult. Now, I've had to switch over to sports like golf and skiing, and although I love them, it's simply not the same."—Heather F

Cheshrcarol had trouble figuring out how she should use her free time:

> "I've been actually having a lot of problems with this lately. When I was in college I had stuff going on practically every day, but most were related to being a journalism major, like working for the campus radio station, the newspaper, and the yearbook. Now that I'm out in the 'real world' and I have a job in publishing, I'm not really sure what I should do with myself when I'm not working."

Others were better able to adapt their interests to available activities. MetFanL shared her experience:

> "After college, I absolutely had to find a way to continue my extracurricular activities. While not in the same format (competitive cheerleading turned into dance and Pilates, etc.), it achieved the same result. I reduced my stress, got some extra exercise and spent my hard-earned money on something I TRULY enjoy rather than something I needed (like a car, food, and those other stupid necessities)."

Sunshine79 found volunteering her time to be less stressful and was able to continue her involvement in her sorority:

> "I too have continued some extracurricular activities, and have picked up even more. Even though I'm tired after coming home from work, at least when I'm done with work, I'm DONE. When I was in school and not in class or an activity, I always felt like I should be studying. I never worked out in college, but I do regularly now and have started taking tennis lessons. I also volunteer at a cat shelter now. My main activities in college centered around my sorority, and I've maintained that by working with the alumnae chapter (though it is MUCH less of a time commitment now)."

Visit our message boards or talk to your friends about how they are adapting their interests to the "real world." You may pick up a helpful strategy or find the encouragement you need to maintain your interest in an activity you really care about.

OUTLETS FOR YOUR INTERESTS

For those of you who think that you don't have enough money right now to pursue your interests, consider the following free or low-cost suggestions:

- If your interests are athletic, there are plenty of community-run free sports leagues. Most outdoor activities such as running and hiking are free, except for the shoes, but those last a while.
- If your interests are artistic, check out your local craft store for free workshops. Also, many museums have young professional societies with lectures, concerts, happy hours, and other events.
- If you like reading, don't forget about the *library*: free books, need we say more? Just don't ignore the due date. If you haven't been in a library since you wrote that 6th grade science report, you may be surprised to learn that you can now renew books and place holds online. Most libraries and bookstores have monthly book groups as well.
- If you're one of those people bored at work, that's your perfect opportunity to work on your writing skills—even through message boards—for the job, *of course*.
- If you want to learn something new, check out your local community center for classes on everything from languages to car mechanics to photography to starting a business.

It's a Great Time to Give Something Back

If you feel as if something has been missing since college, or that you have lost part of yourself, it may be that you have left behind some of the activities that have brought purpose to your life and helped you feel as if you were contributing. So many of us put in a lot of time during our school years volunteering for organizations and causes we cared about. Maybe you volunteered through your fraternity or sorority, or participated in a mentoring program. Maybe you tutored or ran the Web site for a political group. But then, when you left school, you became overwhelmed by your new schedule and left your volunteering behind on campus. It is understandable; school schedules are more flexible, and it is easier to juggle a lot of different commitments throughout the week. Also, you can't walk by a bulletin board or through a campus quad without running into some information about a volunteer opportunity. Once you start working, it can be easy to get caught up in your job and brush aside the other activities that bring value to our lives.

Your quarterlife is the perfect time to start volunteering or, if you have been a volunteer, to keep volunteering. "It's important for everyone to volunteer," encourages Jason Willett of Volunteermatch.com, an online, nonprofit site that matches up volunteers with local organizations. All you have to do is type in your Zip code, pick a category that interests you, and start searching. "Those who do volunteer can tell you how fulfilling it is. It gives us a unique perspective on our community. It can seem important to feel like we are getting ahead in other ways, and it is easy to forget to slow down, take stock, and reach out."

If you are feeling insignificant and bored at work, if you are feeling alone and depressed, reaching out to other people in need and engaging in work that you find meaningful is a sure way to shake off some of your QLC feelings.

If you think that you don't have time to volunteer:

- Volunteering does not have to be an all-consuming daily activity. If you are swamped at work or school, pick a one-day event to begin with, like a school clean-up day or one night at a shelter.

- Find out what volunteer activities are offered at your job. More and more corporations allow employees to volunteer for company-sponsored initiatives during the workday.

- If your company does not have an established community outreach program, why not suggest one? It can be as simple as organizing a one-day blood drive or used-book drive for a local school. You will be showing your initiative and creating something positive in the workplace.

- You can multitask when it comes to volunteering too! If you want to stay true to your fitness routine and volunteer, consider training for a bike-a-thon or run for charity. Or learn a new skill such as home repair by volunteering for Habitat for Humanity.
- Look for "virtual" volunteer opportunities. There are many organizations that can use your help on your schedule. You can offer online support by writing press releases, helping to update a database or Web site, or responding to constituent e-mail.

In addition to all of the altruistic reasons to volunteer, there are some really good practical reasons to volunteer too.

- Volunteering can be a great way to find a job. An enthusiastic volunteer can turn a nonpaying job into a paying job. If you are trying to break into politics, volunteer for a campaign. Work hard and when your candidate wins, he or she may have a staff position that needs filling. Willett said that they noticed a post-9/11 trend at Volunteermatch.com where many people who had been laid off started volunteering because they wanted to help out in some way and were able to turn their nonpaying jobs into paying ones.
- A volunteer environment is also a great place to improve your job skills. If you find that you are petrified to speak in front of a meeting room full of people at work, seek out some similar situations at your volunteer organization. The environment will be less threatening, and you can gain some confidence in developing your skill.
- Volunteering is a risk-free way of trying a new profession. If you are starting to feel burned out at work (see Chapter 7 on burnout) and struggling to figure out what it is that you want to do, volunteering is a great way to try different kinds

of jobs without losing the one you have. Let's say you are a consultant for a big company and you really feel like you should be a teacher; try it out first by joining a mentoring program or volunteering to tutor at your local library. Or you may know what it is that you want to do, but are unsure of the type of environment where you want to do it. Volunteering for a nonprofit can help you figure out if that culture is right for you.

- And finally, volunteering is a great way to meet people and expand your network.

When you volunteer, you know that you are going to feel good at the end of the day. As Willett points out, "You go to a bar, you spend $60, and you can still go home feeling lousy. But if you volunteer, you know that you will have a good experience"—without spending the money!

SO HOW DO YOU GET STARTED?

Now that we have you all fired up about how much good you can do and all of the side benefits you may realize, how can you get started? Keep in mind the following guidelines:

- While it's great to be enthusiastic, don't jump in and make a huge time commitment. Volunteering should not be adding stress to your life. You don't want to promise too much, get burned out, and then end up quitting altogether. Start out with a comfortable commitment for you, even if it's a few hours a month.

- Do something fun! Volunteer organizations want you to enjoy what you are doing. It should not feel like another chore. If you start volunteering for a group and it is not a good fit, you are not doing anyone any favors by sticking around. Try working at a few organizations until you find a place where you are having fun and can invest all of your energy and passion.

DISCOVERING YOUR CHILDHOOD IDENTITY

One way to reconnect with your hobbies and interests is to think about what you enjoyed doing as a kid. As kids, we dived into activities that we enjoyed, not to get ahead in a job, but because they were fun. Spend a few minutes thinking about what kind of kid you were in grade school, middle school, and high school. You may want to focus on just one year during each of the three time periods, or you can consider each time segment as a whole. If you can't remember, ask your parents and siblings to help jog your memory.

This exercise may also help you identify a career passion.

Grade School

When I was in grade school, I loved to . . .
My favorite way to spend my free time was . . .
Some of my favorite organized activities were . . .
I liked to spend time with my friends doing . . .
I liked to read about . . .

Middle School

When I was in middle school, I loved to . . .
My favorite way to spend my free time was . . .
Some of my favorite organized activities were . . .
I liked to spend time with my friends doing . . .
I liked to read about . . .

High School

When I was in high school, I loved to . . .
My favorite way to spend my free time was . . .
Some of my favorite organized activities were . . .
I liked to spend time with my friends doing . . .
I liked to read about . . .

Look back at your answers. There will probably be some activities that you had forgotten about.

Do you see any patterns? For example, did you play a lot of different kinds of sports? Did you spend a lot of time in music or art? Did you like to tinker and build things?

Do you notice that a lot of your activities revolved around a particular place or setting? For example, a theater? A gym? The outdoors? Place of worship?

Did you pursue your favorite activities alone or with other people?

Now that you have recalled some of your favorite childhood memories and detected some patterns, write down two or three activities that you would like to reincorporate into your life:

I remember liking ______________________________

And I liked it because ______________________________

Remembering why you liked the activity will help you figure out how you can transform your childhood hobby into an adult hobby.

For example, if you loved being a Boy Scout or Girl Scout:
. . . because you love the philosophy of Scouting, you can volunteer to be a scoutmaster.
. . . because you love camping, plan a trip with your friends or find a trip through a local club or camping supply store.

If you loved performing in school plays:
. . . because you love to sing, you can join a choir in your community.
. . . because you love theater, get season tickets to a local theater.

Resources

TWENTYSOMETHING TRAVEL

www.budgettravelmagazine.com
www.cdc.gov/travel
www.contiki.com
www.greentortoise.com
www.hiayh.org
www.intrepidtravel.com
www.lonelyplanet.com
www.site59.com

www.statravel.com
www.timeout.com

VOLUNTEERING
www.citycares.org
www.singlevolunteers.org
www.Volunteermatch.com

CHAPTER 12

Staying Healthy

Finding it hard to do anything but veg on the couch after work? Don't have the time or money for anything but fast food? Miss the energy of your college days? You're not alone.

"In college I never had to work out much to maintain a healthy weight. After graduation, I saw my weight creep up slowly. Perhaps due to the fact that I was no longer walking all over campus to get to my next class. Or, perhaps food is comforting when you're in a new living situation. It wasn't until two years after graduation that I had enough of it. I started working out and became a competitive runner. I advise you to get in the habit of working out now before you end up like me and ask yourself when you started buying jeans sized almost twice as large as when you graduated. Yikes!"—GracieTX

No longer can we binge on beer or pull all-nighters. Sitting at a desk all day and having to wake up earlier forces us to change our habits. We start feeling our metabolism slow down. Our guts grow and cellulite appears. A lack of sleep or poor nutrition catches up with our bodies more quickly than in the past. Women find they can no longer leave the house without putting on some makeup. Men might have to start coping with hair loss. Like it or not, we have become higher-maintenance creatures. Now we have to plan out our meals more carefully and, even though we have less free time than ever before, fit in time for fitness.

In addition to the physical benefits, exercise and healthy habits help combat feelings of depression and stress (through the release of endorphins), which makes it even more important to fit workouts into your schedule. Destructive habits such as excessive drinking, smoking, inactivity, and weight gain will only fuel the QLC.

Now is the time to kick those bad habits of late-night pizza and beer to the curb and get your physical and emotional well-being into shape—treat your body with the respect it deserves!

Madeline Dolente, certified fitness and nutrition trainer and star of her own exercise DVD, "Lean, Strong and Defined," suggests combining a program of cardio, strength, and flexibility training to counteract the aging process by burning calories, building back lost muscle mass, and helping to prevent injury. Cardio makes you leaner, while strength training helps to sculpt your body and allows you to burn fat at rest—even sitting at your desk.

To stay consistent and make progress, Dolente emphasizes making your workout a priority, a regular appointment on your schedule that you have to keep. If you are invited out to dinner with a friend, work it around your workout. Dolente says you can even find fitness in the office: climb up the stairs rather than taking the elevator and jump rope or do lunges in the parking lot at lunch. When watching TV at night, Dolente recommends a combination of push-ups and crunches during commercials. Some workout time is better than none. Need some extra motivation? Get friends to go with you for a walk or a bike ride rather than just going out to dinner.

PLANNING A TRAINING SCHEDULE FOR YOURSELF

It's easier to commit yourself to a plan when you have one in writing. Get on a regular schedule using the guidelines below—first, take a look at your schedule and figure out how many workout sessions you can fit in per week. Then, schedule each one into its regular time slot, and do your best to stick with it! Start out slowly if you haven't been exercising at all. Even one or two hours of exercise a week is a great start.

	CARDIO	STRENGTH/ WEIGHT TRAINING	STRETCHING
Number of sessions suggested per week	3–5 1-hour sessions per week	2–3 45-minute sessions per week	15 minutes before/after each cardio session
How many times a week can you fit in?			

Now fit your sessions into a realistic workweek, keeping in mind other commitments and, if you belong to a gym, the class schedule. Here's an example:

I can fit in _3_ cardio sessions, _2_ strength-training sessions, and _3_ stretching sessions per week.

	MON	TUES	WED	THURS	FRI	SAT	SUN
a.m.		st		st	c, s		
p.m.	s, c		c, s				c

c = cardio st = strength training s = stretching

Now try it yourself, using the number of sessions you allotted per week. I can fit in __ cardio sessions, __ strength-training sessions, and __ stretching sessions per week.

	MON	TUES	WED	THURS	FRI	SAT	SUN
a.m.							
p.m.							

c = cardio st = strength training s = stretching

HEALTH BREAKS

Why is it that, given today's strict laws banning smoking at restaurants and bars in the interest of public health, most offices still have smoke breaks? Smokers get to convene outside the office for 15 minutes, three times a day. Does it seem fair that healthy employees are not rewarded? What if you asked for a break to do something healthy?

Start a trend in your office. At midmorning, lunch, and midafternoon, take a walk around the office. Do a few stretches at your desk, such as reaching for your toes and bending your knees and your elbows. If you have privacy, you can even add a little nonimpact strength training to your routine, like side leg lifts, assuming the outfit permits.

Sitting at your desk puts the most stress on your lower back, so it is important to stretch as often as possible at work—ideally, five minutes three times a day, but even once at lunch is better than not stretching at all.

Fitness on the Go

If you have to travel for work, Dolente suggests bringing along some of the following:

- Protein bars
- Trail mix with cranberries or raisins

- Fruit, such as apples and oranges
- Instant oatmeal packets
- Exercise tools, such as tubing and jump rope
- Exercise DVDs to use in your laptop

Madeline also recommends doing push-ups, tricep dips with a chair, crunches, and jumping jacks—all exercises you can do in any hotel room.

Making Workouts Work for You

There are several new, interesting, and creative workout options for both cardio and strength training if you are getting bored with the standard treadmill or bench press.

Gyms today are constantly thinking up new and creative workouts for the busy professionals who are easily bored by the treadmill or step aerobics. Yoga and spinning have become increasingly popular, and fitness classes have morphed into many forms, including cardio kickboxing, body sculpting, salsa, and hip hop dancing. The newest renditions include trampoline workouts and belly dancing.

If you are looking for a little variety in your workout, most gyms have a range of machines, from free weights to Nautilus machines that are adjustable to your dimensions and level of strength. Classes and trainers at the gym have also gotten creative with the use of tools, such as stability balls, medicine balls, bands, and steps.

Although personal training is typically beyond a twentysomething's monthly budget, you often receive a free assessment session when you join a gym. During that introductory session, the trainer can show you some fun and effective exercises. So even if you can't afford to see him or her again any time soon, you can benefit from a more varied workout using their techniques. If you can afford a trainer, visit www.Ace.org to make sure he or she is certified.

If you can't afford or don't like the gym, there are many books, videos, and Web sites available that will show you how to use various tools and equipment at home.

For activities that are also fun and social, try young professional's organizations; sports leagues such as softball, volleyball or soccer; and running, biking, and hiking clubs. There is even a kickball league spreading around the country.

WORKOUT DON'TS

Dolente cites the following mistakes that make working out a waste of time:

- Trying to reach goals without realistically defining them first.
- Looking for the latest fad rather than changing your lifestyle.
- Dedicating yourself to a fitness plan, then giving up after one month. Lack of consistency leads to lack of progress.

Nutrition

You probably adopted at least some unhealthy eating habits in college and assumed that once you entered the real world, you would start eating well-rounded grown-up meals. But it isn't any easier to fit in grocery shopping and cooking now that we are busy working. If you are concerned about your weight, you have every reason to be, aside from fitting into your wardrobe: Obesity is one of the leading natural causes of death in the United States (according to the Centers for Disease Control). Even if you are not that concerned about your weight, this is still the time to commit yourself to healthy eating habits that you can live with for the rest of your life. Don't be overly ambitious by imposing on yourself some drastic new regimen of absolutely no processed flour or sugar. And it is always a good idea to consult with your doctor before initiating a new diet or exercise plan.

Dolente recommends nutrition strategies such as eating several smaller meals a day: "If you put all the wood in a fire, it burns faster. Keep your fire burning all day with five small meals rather than three large ones." Stick to healthy snacks such as apples, cheese sticks, and whole-grain crackers.

Try not to eat out more than once or twice a week, and do your best to pack lunch ahead of time to save money and eat more nutritiously. (See Figure 12.1 for where survey participants tend to eat.) Remember that you are in control of your money and how you spend it—whether it goes to food, gym memberships, or drinking.

FIGURE 12.1 Dining Habits

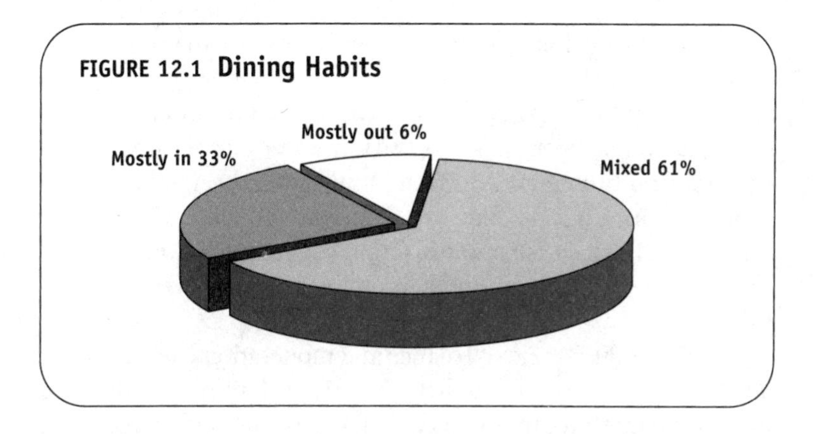

Think about the long-term effects. "In the short term, food tastes good, and it feels good to sit on the couch. When you get sleepy in the afternoon at work, eating protein such as cheese or trail mix will make your evening workout better. Look at food as fuel. If you fill a Rolls Royce with the best versus the cheap stuff, you should treat your body the same way. You shouldn't rely on caffeine for energy," advises Dolente.

According to Sheila R. Cohn, R.D., L.D., Manager of Nutrition Policy for the National Restaurant Association, "It doesn't help [our slowing metabolism] that we're not walking to classes or all over campus, but sitting at our desks all day, and driving to work." She recommends the following strategies, along with regular exercise, to make a clean break from late-night pizzas and beers:

- Get at least eight hours of sleep a night.
- Eat a diet high in fruits and vegetables, whole grains, lean meats, and dairy products.
- Drink alcohol moderately (one to two drinks a day) and limit caffeine intake.

DIETING TIPS

"A calorie is a calorie. When trying to lose or maintain your weight, it's most important to remember the energy equation: energy in equals energy out. This means that in order to maintain your weight, you must eat the same amount of calories you expend. And then if you're trying to lose weight, you'd want to expend more energy than the calories you eat." To find the calorie level that's appropriate, Cohn suggests checking out the Dallas Dietetic Association Web site: www.dallasdietitian.com/calcalc.htm.

"The best diet is one of balance and moderation," notes Cohn. You shouldn't even call it a diet: "You want to think of a diet as a lifestyle, something that you can stick with the rest of your life, not something that you can only do for a month or two. Don't completely deny yourself your favorite foods. There are no 'good' foods or 'bad' foods. Of course, some foods are better than others, but the best diet is one where there are no restrictions."

Cohn recommends a daily multivitamin for everyone, and a daily calcium supplement for women to maintain bone mass. (Exercise and vitamin D also help.)

For dining out, Cohn recommends the following:

- Order dressings and sauces on the side to control the amount.

- When ordering grilled fish or vegetables, ask that the food either be grilled without butter or oil, or prepared "light," with little oil or butter.
- When ordering pasta dishes, look for tomato-based sauces rather than cream-based sauces. Tomato-based sauces are much lower in fat and calories and can count as a vegetable!
- Drink water, diet soda, or unsweetened tea or coffee instead of regular soda or alcoholic beverages. This will save a lot of calories each day.
- Share desserts and appetizers.
- Non-cream-based soups are low in calories and will fill you up, so you eat less.
- Order steamed vegetables as a side dish instead of starch.
- Ask for salsa with a baked potato instead of sour cream, butter, cheese, or bacon. Salsa is very low in calories and a healthy alternative with a lot of spice.
- Stop eating when you are full—listen to the cues your body gives you.
- Order sandwiches with mustard rather than mayonnaise or "special sauce." Mustard adds flavor with virtually no calories.
- Take half of your meal home. The second half can serve as a second meal. (Two meals for the price of one: What a deal!)
- If you want to eat less, order two appetizers or an appetizer and a salad as your meal.
- If you have a choice of side dishes, opt for a baked potato or steamed vegetables rather than French fries. Even if choices are not listed, ask your server to substitute vegetables or a baked potato for French fries.

FIGURE 12.2 **Dining Habits—Cooking Frequency**

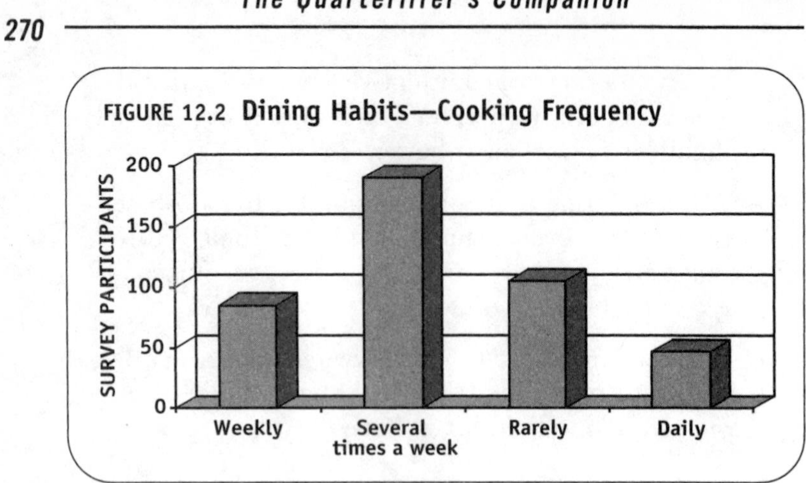

FIGURE 12.3 **Cooking Repetoire**

FIGURE 12.4 **Dining Habits—Why don't you cook?**

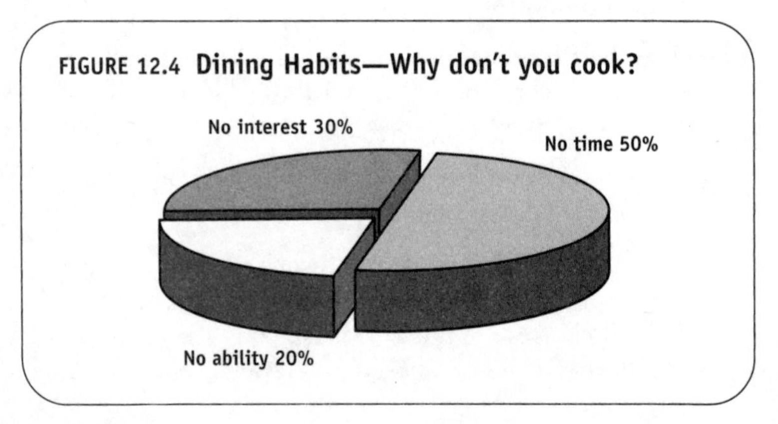

- Look for items on the menu that are baked, grilled, dry-sautéed, broiled, poached, or steamed. These cooking techniques use less fat in the food preparation and are generally lower in calories.
- Don't be afraid to ask for special low-calorie or low-fat preparation of a menu item.
- Choose entrees with fruits and vegetables as key ingredients. Enjoy the flavors they offer. Fruits and vegetables are a good source of dietary fiber as well as many vitamins and minerals.
- Choose foods made with whole grains. Examples include whole-wheat bread and brown rice.
- Enjoy foods that are flavored with fresh herbs rather than fats such as oil and butter. Herbs add a unique flavor to any dish.
- If you are craving dessert, opt for something low-fat, like sorbet, fresh berries, or fruit.
- Remember not to deprive yourself of the foods you love. All foods can fit into a well-balanced diet.

See www.restaurant.org/dineout/nutritionqa.cfm to ask Sheila Cohn your dietary questions.

TO CARB OR NOT TO CARB?

For those of you trying not only to maintain your health but also to regain the body of your youth, you may be confused by all the recent low-carb hype and the shift from low-fat to low-carb foods. Even pizza and bagel joints have somehow been offering low-carb options. Most experts we've spoken to recommend a low-carb diet in moderation. While it's a good idea to cut back on processed carbohydrates (such as white bread), it is not healthy to have bacon instead. Essentially, it all comes down to balance and controlling your caloric intake.

Get Cookin'!

Boston-based food writer Victoria Riccardi emphasizes the importance of taking the time to treat yourself and invest in your health. Eating healthy will make you feel energized, and "There is no better person to cook for than yourself; celebrate yourself through food." When you dine out, you generally eat larger portions with hidden sources of fat and sodium in sauces and dressings. "At home you have more control over your health; you can prepare foods simply but still tastefully." Refined, packaged foods are generally less healthy, being produced for our market that has an affinity for fat and sugar. (See Figures 12.2 through 12.4 for more about the dining habits of participants in our survey.)

Riccardi suggests the following:

- Buy a nice ingredient and cook it simply, bring out the essence—just steam some greens and drizzle with olive oil or lemon juice.
- Keep basic cookbooks such as the classic and annually updated *Joy of Cooking* on the shelf for reference and inspiration.
- Some greens defined:

  Arugula—eaten plain and raw, like an herb in salad

  Chard—eaten cooked, needs braising

  Kale—cook longer, has firm texture
- Try "half scratch" cooking—use packaged items like canned beans to jump start dinner; for example, refried beans on a whole-wheat tortilla with cheese and salsa or rotisserie chicken with salad greens.
- Always incorporate lots of fruit and veggies—seven to nine servings per day are recommended to prevent cancer. (Phytochemicals, which are in plants to protect them against disease, also fight against cancer in our bodies.)

Marty Bryant, a Washington, DC–based advertising executive and food writer, discovered the joy of cooking at the age of eight when her grandmother taught her how to cook. What originally started as a chore turned into a passion. Marty agrees that cooking is a great way to control the fat, calories, and sodium you put into your body while saving money. It is also "a great way to feel empowered by how the simplest of ingredients can help in making a scrumptious meal" and "a gift that you can give to yourself and everyone in your life!"

She offers the following tips:

- "Pay attention to your palettes; support your local farmers' markets, butchers, and vineyards."
- Check the Internet for great recipes, even search engines like Google. (See Resources for some other good sites.)
- While you need to be precise with ingredients and measurements for baking, you can be more interpretive with recipes for cooking.
- If a recipe you're making feeds a lot of people and you only need to feed yourself, you can always divide that recipe in half if you don't think the meal will freeze well.
- Try samples at the grocery store, and ask about the ingredients so you can re-create the dishes you like at home.
- Ask about wines used at tastings and demos so you can really impress guests. Don't be afraid to ask for a good wine in your range at the liquor store. You can find a decent bottle of wine for under $10; just stay away from boxed wine.
- If you are cooking for a date, keep it simple and fun, and always make it for someone else first. You don't want to be "sweating and freaking out" by the time he or she arrives. Make sure your date doesn't have any dietary restrictions, and don't try complicated recipes such as rack of lamb for the first time, but also try to make a meal that is a little nicer than hot dogs or burgers.

➤ If you're afraid of cooking, now's the time to learn. Take baby steps; start by boiling water, and learn to make a couple of standard meals. Grilling is great not only for burgers, but also as a way to prepare veggies such as asparagus and portabello mushrooms, fish in foil, even fruit like peaches. Just brush on some olive oil and add salt and pepper and any other favorite seasonings.

Marty recommends having the following cooking essentials at home.

The basics:

Eggs
Lower fat butter (in sticks)
Olive oil
Milk
Flour

Salt, pepper, and versatile spices such as red crushed pepper and Italian seasoning

Fresh vegetables (including your favorite salad mix—bagged are more expensive but easier, baby carrots, celery, onions, garlic, green/red bell peppers, cucumbers, potatoes)

Frozen vegetables (pick your favorites: chopped spinach, cauliflower, squash, Brussels sprouts)

Fresh fruit (once again pick your favorites: mangoes, bananas, grapes, lemons for cooking)

Canned vegetables (Veg-All or other canned veggie mix of carrots, potatoes, and peas), both canned stewed and whole tomatoes (get lower sodium if you can)

Your favorite tomato sauce

Chicken breasts

Lean ground beef (for freezer)

Low-fat Italian chicken sausage (will need one link per meal)

Canned tuna in water

Frozen tilapia or fresh fish from your local grocer

Canned chicken/vegetable broth (lower sodium)

Pastas (gnocchi or ravioli fresh from your favorite Italian market or grocery store) for your freezer

Prepackaged rice (such as Lipton's or Rice-a-Roni)

Dried pastas (wheat if preferred)

Additional items personalized for your taste buds:

Canned artichokes, olives, or capers

A low-fat, versatile cheese such as feta or parmesan

Fresh herbs such as rosemary or basil

Low-calorie flavoring such as teriyaki sauce or low-sodium soy sauce

Low-fat peanut butter

Cookware, utensils, and storage:

A sharp chef's knife and cutting board

Nonstick and cast iron pans (cast iron pans work best when seasoned; check out your parents' or grandma's cupboard or local garage sales)

Larger pots for pastas and soups

Baking sheet

Aluminum foil

Plastic freezer/storage bags

Plastic freezer/storage containers

Plastic spatula

FOOD STORAGE SAFETY

Storing food can be a timesaver for single professionals on the go—make a big meal Sunday night and store away individual portions for lunch or dinner on later dates. However it's important to store your food safely in order to prevent unhealthy—and unsavory—leftovers. The Partnership for Food Safety Education recommends storing away your perishables immediately in the refrigerator, and if freezing, wrapping tightly in plastic wrap or plastic freezer containers. If using a plastic bag, make sure you get all the air out. The chart below provides refrigerator and freezer storage times for some commonly used foods. (Refer to "Chill: When in Doubt—Throw It Out" at www.fightbac.org/doubt.cfm). What if you find something in the back of the freezer and you can't remember how old it is? Stick to some basic, commonsense guidelines: If you notice any mold or if the general appearance or smell doesn't seem quite right, get rid of it.

	Fridge	Freezer
Fresh steaks or beef	3–5 days	6–12 months
Cooked meat and meat dishes	3–4 days	2–3 months
Fresh chicken or turkey pieces	1–2 days	9 months
Cooked poultry dishes	3–4 days	4–6 months
Cooked poultry with sauce	1–2 days	6 months
Soups and stews	3–4 days	2–3 months
TV Dinners, frozen casseroles (keep frozen until serving)		3–4 months
Lean fish (such as cod, flounder, haddock)	1–2 days	up to 6 months
Fatty fish (such as blue, perch, salmon)	1–2 days	2–3 months

When handling raw meat such as chicken, the Partnership for Food Safety Education recommends "thoroughly washing your hands with soap and water for a full 20 seconds before and after handling raw products. Use plastic or other nonporous cutting boards. Cutting boards should be run through the dishwasher—or washed with soap and hot water—after each use."

Quick and Easy Recipes

BREAKFAST

BASIC FRENCH TOAST

Although thick slices of bread such as Challah are preferred, any bread you have lying around can be used—even white or wheat sandwich bread. For every slice of bread, use 1 egg and a splash of milk. Beat the egg and milk together in a bowl. Dip both sides of each bread slice in the bowl, and place in a heated, buttered skillet until browned on each side. You can also add a dash of cinnamon, nutmeg, or vanilla to the egg mixture. Serve with maple syrup, powdered sugar, or fruit such as strawberries —simple and delicious.

BASIC SCRAMBLED EGGS (courtesy of Marty Bryant)

2 eggs (or egg whites if you're watching your weight)

1 tablespoon or so of your milk of choice

Salt, pepper, and favorite seasonings

Pinch of cayenne

Heat nonstick pan on low to medium heat. Meanwhile, crack eggs into a small bowl, add milk, and whisk with fork until well mixed. Once pan is heated, add egg mixture to pan. Add a dash of salt and pepper and additional seasoning and use your plastic spatula to begin scraping eggs from bottom of pan. Continue until no liquid remains.

Once eggs are almost done, turn heat off and continue to scramble the eggs. Last, when serving and only if you like an added kick, add a pinch of cayenne pepper.

(Another nice touch here if you want to pack in a punch with more veggies: add some fresh spinach leaves, chopped Kalamata olives, and feta to eggs once they're in pan for a Mediterranean twist.)

HOMEMADE EGG AND CHEESE SANDWICH
(courtesy of Marty Bryant)

1 egg

1 slice of your favorite presliced cheese:
American, Swiss, Cheddar, or Provolone

1 slice of cooked deli ham (optional)

1 English muffin
(also can use one tortilla or two slices of toast)

Salt, pepper, and favorite seasonings to taste

Break egg into circular, shallow (microwave safe) bowl, add a pinch of salt and pepper, and place in microwave, heating for approximately 1 minute, 15 seconds.

Meanwhile, toast your bread of choice and if using a tortilla heat in nonstick pan or in microwave until warm. Check on how egg is doing; if needed, continue cooking in 15-second increments until done. Add sliced deli ham and slice of cheese on top of egg in bowl. With spoon, scoop egg out of bowl and onto bread.

Add additional seasoning if you like. If you are on the run, wrap a napkin or paper towel around the sandwich and go!

LUNCH

EASY GREEK SALAD (courtesy of Marty Bryant)

Fill a large plastic bowl with your favorite chopped lettuce. Add a handful of:

Pitted Kalamata olives

Cherry/grape tomatoes

Red/green peppers, chopped

Sliced cucumbers

Handful of feta

Pinch of pepper and favorite seasoning

Favorite dressing or easy balsamic vinaigrette (see below)

This is a great work lunch that I like to pair with one of my favorite canned soups; or for extra protein, I'll add a can of drained tuna in water to the salad. Also, bring dressing separately in a Ziploc bag or bottle. I like to pair salad with either my own balsamic vinaigrette or my favorite store-bought version.

EASY BALSAMIC VINAIGRETTE (courtesy of Marty Bryant)

One part balsamic vinegar to one part olive oil

1 chopped clove of garlic

1 teaspoon of Dijon mustard

Salt and pepper to taste

Combine all ingredients in Ziploc bag. Seal bag and shake. Can be refrigerated for up to four days.

NOTE*:* You can substitute garlic cloves with the pre-chopped/minced garlic in a jar that can be found in your produce center at the grocery store. This type of garlic is much more potent than fresh garlic so use it sparingly with cooking. One fresh garlic clove is equivalent to about a half teaspoon of minced/chopped garlic from jar.

VEGGIE-PACKED PASTA SALAD (courtesy of Marty Bryant)

2 cups of favorite dry pasta (rotini, shells, farfalle)

1 can of black olives roughly chopped

1 large handful of cherry/grape tomatoes sliced in halves

1 can of kidney beans or garbanzo beans, drained and washed

1 handful of chopped red and green bell peppers

6 to 8 baby carrots chopped

Half a red onion chopped

1/4 cup of favorite shredded cheese (mozzarella, parmesan)

3 to 4 tablespoons of favorite low-calorie Italian dressing

Boil water in large pot. Add a dash of kosher salt. Add dried pasta of choice. Cook for directed time.

Meanwhile, place veggies and beans of choice in large plastic container with a lid. Drain pasta and add to veggie-filled container, adding additional salt, pepper, and seasonings (rosemary and oregano are great here). Last, add cheeses and dressing and place lid on container.

Shake until well mixed and place in several different storage containers.

This can be lunch at work with a piece of fruit or can be paired with a piece of fish or chicken for a healthy meal. Be less generous with the dressing, which will allow ingredients to keep their crunch. Pasta should last three to four days.

VEGGIES

STEAMED VEGGIES

A vegetable steamer basket is a great tool to have in the kitchen. Simply fill a pot or sauté pan with about 1 cup of water. Place the steamer basket in the pot, and put vegetables such as broccoli in for about 5 minutes, until bright green and crisp. Remove from heat immediately so the vegetables do not continue to cook. Serve with a squeeze of lemon or dash of lemon pepper.

VEGGIES WITH A TERIYAKI TWIST (courtesy of Marty Bryant)

1 package of frozen vegetable of choice (I love Brussels sprouts, but since many are opposed I'd suggest a veggie medley of broccoli and cauliflower) or, even better, 2 cups of fresh vegetables such as broccoli and cauliflower

Several tablespoons of water

1 clove of garlic chopped

10 baby carrots sliced

Touch of olive oil

1 to 2 tablespoons of low-cal teriyaki sauce

Touch of soy sauce

1 teaspoon of low-fat peanut butter (I use crunchy)

Pinch of crushed red pepper

Into heated nonstick pan (medium heat) pour a touch of olive oil. If using frozen vegetables, place in microwave for several minutes to thaw. If using fresh, add to heated pan immediately. Depending on how moist things look thus far, add water in tablespoons to assist in steaming the vegetables. Cook five to seven minutes.

When liquid is almost gone and vegetables are still only semi-cooked, add chopped garlic and carrots. Add teriyaki sauce and stir. Next, add peanut butter, soy, and a pinch of crushed pepper and stir. Take off heat and let sit for two to three minutes, then serve.

SAUTÉED SPINACH WITH GARLIC (courtesy of Marty Bryant)

4 cups fresh spinach (plus several tablespoons of water) **or**
1 package frozen spinach (thawed and drained a little)

2 garlic cloves chopped

Salt/pepper and seasonings to taste

Olive oil

Heat nonstick pan on medium heat, adding a touch of olive oil. Add spinach (if using fresh, add touch of water) and cover with lid or large piece of aluminum foil for two to three minutes. Add chopped garlic and seasonings and simmer until done.

NOTE: Much of the moisture should be gone. Simmering is when you bring to a boil, reduce heat, and cover.

DINNER ENTREES

QUICK TILAPIA IN FOIL (courtesy of Marty Bryant)

1 to 2 slices fresh fish, lightly coated with olive oil, freshly squeezed lemon, salt/pepper, and seasonings

1 to 2 fresh tomatoes, chopped, **or**
14.5 ounce can diced tomatoes (low sodium)

1/2 onion, chopped

1 to 2 cloves of garlic, chopped

1/4 cup of white wine or veggie/chicken broth

Touch of olive oil

Salt/pepper and seasonings to taste

Preheat oven to 375 degrees. Into heated nonstick pan pour a touch of olive oil. Add onions, garlic, and tomatoes and let cook two to three minutes. Add 1/4 cup of wine or broth and seasonings and let simmer. Meanwhile, cut several large pieces of aluminum foil for fish.

Next, line baking sheet with aluminum foil. Take sections of aluminum foil and place one piece of fish on each. Once tomato mixture is fully heated and has somewhat less liquid, add on top of fish in spoonfuls. Seal fish in aluminum foil by folding over top and bottom sections of foil and fold in on sides. With sealed fish on sheet, place in oven and cook for 20 to 25 minutes until done. Fish should be moist and firm.

Serve with fresh lemon slices atop fish.

GNOCCHI WITH ITALIAN CHICKEN SAUSAGE, ARTICHOKES, AND SPINACH IN TOMATO SAUCE (courtesy of Marty Bryant)

1 to 2 cups of favorite frozen gnocchi

1 to 2 links of favorite Italian chicken sausage, sliced

1 to 2 cups of fresh spinach

1 can of canned artichokes, drained, washed, and roughly chopped

1/2 26-ounce jar of favorite tomato sauce

1 clove of garlic

Freshly grated parmesan cheese to taste

Fill a large pot almost to the top with water. Add a pinch of salt and bring to a boil. Meanwhile, heat nonstick pan with touch of olive oil, add sliced sausage and garlic, and stir. Add artichokes and spinach and cook for three to five minutes. Last, add favorite tomato sauce and simmer.

Place frozen gnocchi in boiling water, cooking as directed. Drain pasta and serve with sauce. This meal is also great for lunch, so if you have extras, place in storage containers.

ROASTED CHICKEN

1 whole chicken, rinsed and patted dry

Salt and pepper

Several fresh rosemary sprigs

1 lemon, cut into wedges

1 white onion, cut into large chunks

Preheat oven to 350 degrees. Rub salt and pepper on the chicken. Stuff the cavity with rosemary, lemon, and onion. Place prepared chicken in a baking dish and into the oven and cook for about 2 hours, maybe longer depending on the size of the bird. Make sure the middle is no longer pink and cooked all the way through.

BEN'S BASIC BURGERS

1 pound of ground beef

1 finely chopped onion

1/2 tablespoon salt

1/2 tablespoon ground black pepper

2 to 3 tablespoons chopped favorite herbs, such as parsley or cilantro

2 tablespoons Worcestershire sauce

Mix all ingredients together, form patties, and grill! Delicious served with sautéed mushrooms or guacamole.

EASY TURKEY CHILI (FROM TRADER JOE'S)

1 tablespoon oil

1 package (about 1 pound) ground turkey

1 jar chunky salsa

1 can marinated bean salad

Shredded cheddar cheese, sour cream, chopped green onions (optional)

Brown the ground turkey in a large pot with oil. Add the salsa and bean salad, stir until combined. Bring to a boil, then reduce heat, cover, and simmer for 20 minutes. Sprinkle with cheese, sour cream, or onions. Also recommend serving with rice, pasta, or chips.

ESTHER'S CHICKEN SOUP (also serves as a cold remedy)

1 4-pound chicken, cut into 8 pieces

4 quarts cold water

1 big onion or several small onions

3 carrots

2 stalks celery

Half a bunch of parsley

2 teaspoons chicken bouillon

Salt and pepper, to taste

8 ounces egg noodles (optional)

Scald chicken or take the skin off. Clean well under cold running water. Place in a pot with the water and bring to a boil. Add ingredients up to and including celery. Cover, bring to a boil, and simmer for 1 hour and 10 minutes. Occasionally skim the top for fat. Add the parsley, chicken bouillon, salt, and pepper and return to a boil. *Optional:* Add 8 oz. egg noodles and simmer 20 minutes longer.

Makes 12–15 servings.

FROM KEG PARTIES TO COCKTAIL PARTIES

SIMPLE CHEESE PLATTER (courtesy of Marty Bryant)

5 to 6 blocks of various types of cheeses ranging in size and color from your local gourmet grocery store (brie, cheddar, chevre, stilton, and gouda, for example)

2 boxes of your favorite crackers

1 cup of assorted olives (preferably Kalamatas or other stuffed variations)

Dash of mixed Italian seasoning dried or fresh for garnish

2 to 3 cheese knives

1 large platter for serving

Unwrap various cheeses and arrange on platter, do the same with crackers. Sprinkle olives and herbs over arranged platter and serve.

MOZZARELLA, TOMATO, AND BASIL MINI SKEWERS
(courtesy of Marty Bryant)

1 to 2 cartons of cherry/grape tomatoes

1 1/2 cups fresh basil

1 to 2 packages of fresh mozzarella balls

1 package of toothpicks

2 to 3 tablespoons balsamic vinaigrette (recipe above)

1 large platter for serving

Wash both tomatoes and basil and pat dry. Break basil leaves off stems and set aside. Take toothpicks and begin layering mozzarella, basil, and tomato on each toothpick. Repeat until you have filled the appetizer tray and or have a suitable amount for your group.

Last, drizzle balsamic mixture over the mini skewers and serve.

HUMMUS, PITA, AND PEPPERONCINI PEPPERS
(courtesy of Marty Bryant)

1 package of store-bought hummus

1 package of pita, cut into wedges
(and heated in oven at 300 degrees for 7 to 8 minutes)

1 lemon cut into wedges

1 jar of pepperoncini peppers, drained

Dash of both paprika and cayenne

Dash of dried Italian seasoning for garnish

1 platter for serving with bowl in center for hummus

Place store-bought hummus in bowl, garnishing with both paprika and cayenne. Arrange pita wedges around bowl and do the same with pepperoncini peppers. Squeeze one wedge of lemon on hummus and arrange remaining wedges on platter. Last, sprinkle Italian seasoning and paprika over both pita and hummus for garnish.

EASY, FRESH GUACAMOLE

2 ripe avocados

1 onion

1 tomato

1/3 cup cilantro

Juice of 1 line

Salt and pepper

To make sure avocados are ripened, try squeezing. They should give a little, but they should not be too soft. Cut in half lengthwise around the pit, scoop out the flesh, and mash in a bowl. Chop the next three ingredients and mix together with the avocados. Squeeze in lime juice and add salt and pepper to taste. You may also add garlic powder or red pepper flakes for an extra kick.

MY SHOPPING LIST

If you categorize your shopping list, it will be easier to remember what to get once you are at the grocery store.

Staples
(milk, flour, butter, etc.)

Canned goods
(tuna, beans, soups, etc.)

Frozen veggies

Grains, bread, and pasta

Poultry

Spices, seasonings, sauces, and spreads

Red meat

Specialty/gourmet/ethnic items

Fish

Additional items for recipes I'm making this week

Beverages

Other

Resources

FITNESS

www.ace.org
www.madfitness.com

SPORTS LEAGUES

www.bikeleague.org
www.rrca.org
www.worldkickball.org
Check local listings for softball, soccer, and volleyball

NUTRITION

www.healthierus.gov/dietaryguidelines
www.Ediets.com
www.foodsafety.gov
www.restaurant.org/dineout/nutritionqa.cfm

RECIPE WEB SITES

www.allrecipes.com
www.cookinglight.com
www.foodtv.com

CHAPTER 13

Psyche: New Life, New Feelings

The transition to adulthood is not only a time of changing situations, but also one of major internal evolution. As we become full-fledged adults, our values change, our bodies change, and sometimes, our emotional well-being changes.

In college, your goal might have been to save the world—perhaps you frowned upon materialism and pledged to devote yourself to a lifetime of nonprofit work. Or maybe you were preparing for an investment-banking career that would allow you to retire by the age of 40. Once you enter the real world, you might see that plans and ideals you had formed based on theory are quite different—and possibly disillusioning—in practice. Perhaps you discover it's not possible to work for a nonprofit while paying off college loans and also paying rent in a thriving city. Or maybe you do end up in investment banking but do not see retirement anywhere in sight and feel burned out already by the 12-hour days.

Before joining the workforce, political issues such as tax reform or Social Security overhaul were simply subjects of interesting debates. Now, in the workforce, we see the funds taken out of our paychecks and wonder how or if they will eventually help us. We discover that a salary is not the only thing capable of making us happy—or miserable—on the job. We begin to realize, as we spend at least eight hours a day confined to our indoor space, that we had a lot more free time than we thought we had in college. We begin to understand the frustrations our parents may have faced, trying to juggle finances, car and house maintenance, meetings, promotions or layoffs, and still have dinner on the table (or, in our case, dinner on the couch) and beds freshly made.

VALUE-METER: THEN AND NOW—HOW HAVE YOU CHANGED?

Please rate your value of each issue now as compared to when you were in school. (1 being not important at all, 5 being very important to me.) How has your experience in the real world changed your values on political issues?

	SCHOOL					NOW				
World Peace	1	2	3	4	5	1	2	3	4	5
Social Security	1	2	3	4	5	1	2	3	4	5
Taxes	1	2	3	4	5	1	2	3	4	5
Environment	1	2	3	4	5	1	2	3	4	5
Homelessness/Hunger	1	2	3	4	5	1	2	3	4	5
Health Care	1	2	3	4	5	1	2	3	4	5
Other:____________	1	2	3	4	5	1	2	3	4	5

The changes in your values might confuse you and lead to internal conflicts, the physical changes can lead to decreased energy, and the drastic lifestyle changes might lead to stress and anxiety. In general, we may feel an unwillingness to let go of the past when things seemed to be so much easier and clear-cut. We knew how to succeed then: We were aware of how we were ranked by our grades in school. And we knew what came next. We knew—or had decided rather—what was right and wrong. Things were very black and white. We weren't, perhaps, worried so much about our future financial security or health; we felt invincible, as if we'd never experience those problems we heard so much about. We figured it would all work out for us when it was our time to enter the real world.

In addition, as Elizabeth Dupont Spencer, MSW, coauthor of *The Anxiety Cure*, points out, we begin to make choices in our twenties that will affect the rest of our lives. We begin to think about what it would be like to juggle our careers and finances while trying to raise a family.

These collective changes in ourselves and our surroundings cause an even deeper shift in our feelings and, consequently, in our behavior. Maybe you are growing less patient; maybe your attention span seems to be decreasing. Maybe you feel a sense of loneliness you never felt before, or hopelessness and helplessness about the future.

Many twentysomethings who are experiencing depression for the first time don't realize it's a common scenario, and therefore can't identify or deal with their feelings and don't seek help. According to the National Depressive and Manic-Depressive Association (NDMDA), "The vast majority of patients with chronic major depression are misdiagnosed . . . or are given no treatment at all. Only about 1 in 10 of those suffering from depression receive adequate treatment."

The most important thing to realize is that all these feelings and changes are normal. Once you can recognize and admit to feelings of confusion and sadness, you should try talking about them with friends or family, or anonymously on the Web site message boards. If the feelings persist after exploring their source with others who are in or have been through your situation, you can follow the guidelines below to form a plan of attack.

When Things Don't Go as Planned—What to Do When You're Down in the Dumps

First, it is important to recognize the new feelings you are experiencing and to try to take some steps to help yourself:

- Surround yourself as much as possible with positive people, even if you think you'd rather be alone.
- Sometimes we mistake symptoms of depression for hostility. When someone is depressed he or she tends to appear negative and drive others away. But if we let our loved ones and close friends know what's going on, they will understand that we are not purposely being critical, brash, or even nasty, but rather channeling deep feelings of sorrow that we cannot always control on our own.
- While you shouldn't deprive yourself of those things that make you feel better when you're feeling down, you should avoid destructive vices such as drugs and alcohol. Alcohol and many drugs are downers, and consuming downers while depressed will only make things seem that much worse. Uppers may give you a temporary lift, but coming back to reality will feel particularly harsh.
- Spencer says that things that help physically—sleep, exercise, sunshine, high protein, and low carbs—also help mentally. She recommends getting out of the late-night college sleep cycle. When you stay up late, you eat more and you're tired, and you can't live like that when you're working. High levels of caffeine are also bad, even one or two cups of coffee a day can be detrimental, depending on your natural tendency for panic attacks. And try to avoid caffeine in the evening, because it has a greater effect on you now than it did when you were in college.
- It's okay to indulge occasionally in *nondestructive* comfort foods and entertainment. For example, if you are counting calories but a slice of cheesecake would really make you feel

better after a crummy day at work, then go for it. And even if you are on a really tight budget but the latest Eminem CD would lift your spirits, then go ahead and splurge. In the long run, a 300-calorie slice of cheesecake or $13 CD will not prevent you from reaching your goals. But they could make you feel better right now.

THE FACTS ON DEPRESSION

- Although not everyone is open about their depression, it is more common than you might think. Twenty million Americans aged 18 and above are impacted by depression each year (National Institute of Mental Health, 1998).
- According to the 1994 National Comorbidity Survey on depression, the onset of major depressive episodes occurs most often in your mid-twenties (age 24 for men, age 25 for women). The NDMDA found that "many people experience their first episode of depression in their late teens or early adulthood."
- The National Institute of Mental Health found that "with treatment, up to 80 percent of those with depression show an improvement in their symptoms generally within four to six weeks of beginning medication, psychotherapy, attending support groups, or a combination of these treatments."
- Depression can affect your job, your finances, and your relationships. Depression makes forming new connections very difficult. "Lack of energy, loss of initiative, and decreased self-confidence challenge people with depression to develop new relationships" (NDMDA).
- Depression is one of the 10 most costly illnesses in the United States (NDMDA).
- "An estimated 200 million days of work are lost each year because of untreated symptoms of depression," according to the Society for Human Resource Management.

Because feelings of depression may unintentionally begin to interfere with interactions at work or in social settings, at some point we must seek professional help. If you think that professional help is too expensive, consider what your depression is costing you—being unproductive and losing work, and even people you care about.

Remember, there is nothing shameful about seeking help. Although the stigma is beginning to disappear, it is still not a common topic of conversation. Therefore, you may feel like the only one being treated for depression, when, in fact, several of your friends or colleagues may already be receiving help.

Spencer suggests talking to family members, in particular older siblings who have been in your situation, to see if they think your level of stress or anxiety is normal. You could also try talking to friends or spiritual leaders in the community. If these contacts don't help, you can seek professional help from not only a therapist, but also from a primary care physician or gynecologist (for women). Any doctor can prescribe antidepressants. In fact, primary care physicians prescribe one-third of all antidepressants. At some point, however, you should see a therapist to monitor your progress and explore the possibility of cognitive, or behavioral, therapy.

We are not suggesting that if you are upset because of a breakup or other upsetting event you immediately run to the doctor and ask that he or she prescribe Prozac for you. It is important to distinguish between situational depression and clinical depression. Stress is a normal, healthy, external process, important for growth, just as exercise is required to build muscle. However, when your body internalizes stress, either as a state of worry (anxiety) or sadness (depression), the stress becomes unmanageable.

A psychiatrist once said that, much like the loss of eyesight, which should be repaired through eyeglasses or contact lenses, clinical depression, too, is a deficiency that should be treated through cognitive therapy or antidepressants. The first step when feeling depressed is to visit a psychologist who can diagnose your problem as either short-term, situational depression, which can be treated through several therapy sessions, or more serious, clinical depression, which may require medication.

- If you are unsure if you are clinically depressed or anxious, you can get a free evaluation using online checklists and screenings on sites such as www.mentalhealthscreening.org. (See the Resources at the end of the chapter for additional listings.)
- Once diagnosed by a professional, talk to your insurance company first to find out if anyone convenient is on your plan, how much would be covered, what types of professionals are covered (only psychiatrists and psychologists? family therapists and social workers as well?), and whether or not you need to get a referral first. The prevalence of depression in twentysomethings is yet another reason to secure good health insurance coverage. (See Chapter 2 for more information on your health plan.)
- If your health insurance plan doesn't cover mental health care, you can try to find free counseling services through local hospitals, community centers, and places of worship. There may also be resources available through your workplace, such as Employee Assistance Programs.
- Once you have begun therapy, Spencer recommends the three-session rule: if you're not getting better after three sessions, then it's not the right fit. This will save you not only time but also money in the long run.
- You can also try support groups, depending on your symptoms. Spencer points out that sometimes anxiety support groups lead to too much focus on other people's problems, which can be contagious and lead to more anxiety, rather than on your own progress. Spencer recommends an established support group such as Recovery Inc., which employs trained leaders and a structured way to talk about feelings. You can also find groups in your area through organizations such as the Anxiety Disorders Association of America (see the Resources section).

- Consider participating in a confidential clinical trial to try antianxiety or antidepressant medications. Typically, participation in these trials pays $35 to $55, including weekly sessions with well-qualified professionals. All the drugs are FDA approved and some are already on the market. The only drawback to these studies is that you can occasionally end up with a placebo, which you won't know until the end of the study. However, the experience could still be valuable because of the interaction you will have with doctors, and you will have a better idea of whether or not to pursue medication therapy.

Different types of treatment work for different people. You may go through a period of experimentation at the beginning of your treatment when you try different types of antidepressants or different types of cognitive therapy. Some examples of antidepressants include Prozac, Zoloft, Celexa, Lexapro, and Effexor. Each has its own side effects and each may interact differently with your body's chemical makeup. Be patient; there is a solution for you. And once you find that solution you will be amazed at the difference in your daily thoughts and behaviors. Your past depression will seem so distant that you will feel like a different person.

IS IT DEPRESSION OR JUST THE DUMPS?

Symptoms of anxiety and depression can manifest themselves in a number of ways. This exercise is not intended as a replacement for true diagnostic tools in a doctor's office, but simply as an opportunity for you to assess your negative feelings and take some steps to combat them.

Have you noticed an increase in the following symptoms, and if so, how long have those symptoms persisted? If you can only check off a few and haven't noticed any major changes, you may just be going through a funk or a case of the blues. But if you have experienced many of the following symptoms, and they have persisted several weeks or more, you may want to consider seeking professional help by following our guidelines below.

- ➤ Changes to appetite or sleeping patterns
- ➤ Thoughts of death and suicide
- ➤ Constant sadness
- ➤ Frequent and uncontrollable crying
- ➤ Diminished pleasure in daily activities you once enjoyed
- ➤ Fatigue, loss of energy
- ➤ Feelings of worthlessness, self-blame, and intense guilt
- ➤ Diminished concentration
- ➤ Indecisiveness
- ➤ Irritability
- ➤ Anger, agitation
- ➤ Worry, anxiety
- ➤ Extreme pessimism
- ➤ General indifference
- ➤ Social withdrawal

SOME STEPS TO TAKE

1. According to our *depression or dumps* exercise, are you dealing with the "dumps" or do you have reason to suspect that you may be suffering from clinical depression? In both cases, speak with a close friend or family member, but if you suspect that you are clinically depressed or if you are still having trouble shaking the blues, move on to No. 2.

2. Find out if your insurance plan covers therapy. If so, make an appointment with a psychiatrist or psychologist convenient to your office or home. If not, see your primary care physician.

3. Discuss the options with your therapist or physician. What medication is right for you? Should you supplement the prescription with cognitive therapy?

4. Try your doctor's recommendation and stick with him or her for three sessions. If the treatment plan seems to be helping, continue. If not, return to step 3 with a new doctor. Your doctor may recommend joining a support group or a drug trial as part of your recovery process.

Once you are feeling better, get out on the town! Never turn down a social invitation—whether it's to a happy hour, dinner party, movie, whatever. When you are feeling good about yourself and your situation, that's the best time to meet new people. We tend to be drawn to people with positive energy. It may seem like a shame that when you need people most is when they don't want to be around you. But that is why it is so essential to have a few close friends to lean on during "down" time, and then to get out there and make the most of your time when you are back on track.

Daily Thoughts

We can also change our feelings by changing our daily thoughts and developing a more positive spin on things. Spencer suggests feeling empowered rather than stressed out by your choices: Think of how amazing it is to have all these rich, diverse opportunities. And don't worry about making the "right" decision, because "it's not about making the perfect choice, it's about making the choice that's perfect for you."

Spencer suggests listing your negative thoughts and anxieties. How true are they? What would be more realistic? For example, you think that your boss is going to fire you. Do you have any evidence to back this up? Have you been doing a good job? Perhaps that worry is a result of only getting feedback when your performance is negative. A more realistic thought would be "My boss does not praise my good work." All you can do is get through the situation, make the best of it, or change it—don't feel trapped. Not every situation will work out for the best, and sometimes it's just time to move on.

JOT DOWN YOUR JITTERS

Whenever you are in a bind and experiencing anxiety over a current situation or approaching event, it can help a great deal simply to write down the source of your fear and the most realistic outcomes. The next time you come back to jot down a jitter, look back at the past event in retrospect. Was it worth the anxiety? Did your worst fears come true? What was the outcome?

1. **Date:**__________ I am nervous about ______________ (event)

   I am worried that I will seem/act/do ____________________

   ____

   Or that I will do____

   ____

   Retrospect:

   I should/should not (circle one) have been nervous about event No. 1.

   My worries did/did not (circle one) come true.

   I succeeded/failed (circle one) by doing __________________

   ____

2. **Date:**__________ I am nervous about ______________ (event)

   I am worried that I will seem/act/do ____________________

   ____

   Or that I will do____

   ____

   Retrospect:

   I should/should not (circle one) have been nervous about event No. 2.

   My worries did/did not (circle one) come true.

   I succeeded/failed (circle one) by doing __________________

   ____

3. **Date:**__________ I am nervous about ______________ (event)

I am worried that I will seem/act/do ____________________

____

Or that I will do______________________________________

____

Retrospect:

I should/should not (circle one) have been nervous about event No. 3.

My worries did/did not (circle one) come true.

I succeeded/failed (circle one) by doing ____________________

____

The point of this exercise is that our thoughts and anxieties are not beyond our control; we can change them. We can take control of our day-to-day anxieties. Negative thinking only leads to more anxiety and negative thinking, a vicious cycle that's tough to escape.

Spiritual Healing

Some twentysomethings turn to spirituality to help them through this stressful transition period. Margaret Feinberg, author of *Twentysomething: Surviving and Thriving in the Real World*, says,

> There are many benefits from becoming more spiritually active. You can learn about your heritage, and some religions are bottomless when it comes to personal development, knowledge, and growth. You can also connect with people who are your age, struggling and wrestling through many of the same issues. Faith can give you solid ground in the midst of so many changing circumstances. It also puts you on the same page with people who at first glance couldn't seem more different—which can be so

enriching. In addition, faith gives us the opportunity to wrestle through tough questions including "Why do good things happen to bad people?" It gives us the opportunity to encounter and embrace something greater than ourselves. And a good faith system serves as the reminder that it's not about you. In a postmodern world, a faith-based belief system provides solid ground to stand on as you develop and grow.

Feinberg offers the following advice to help you rediscover the right faith for you as an adult:

- The twentysomething years are when our faith becomes our own. For some that means wandering away and rejecting everything that was learned growing up. But for many, it's more of a discovery process—deciding whether attending temple or church is going to become a part of our lives.
- Reflect on the faith of your parents—what parts of their belief system do you accept or reject? What are the strengths of their belief system? What are the weaknesses? If you grew up in a home that didn't provide any exposure to a particular faith, then it's a good time to begin looking.
- Look at the history of a particular religion. Read the critics. Study on your own.
- It helps to have people around you to encourage and challenge you, and to share what you're learning as well as learn from them.
- If it's tough to make it to a service every week, look for a gathering that meets on a different day of the week or for an abbreviated time period.

Everyone gets different things out of spirituality. Some people find friends. Some people find comfort. Others find a certain satisfaction and joy through the ritual. (See Figures 13.1, 13.2, and 13.3 for our survey results on religion and the QLCer.)

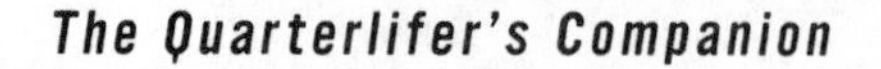

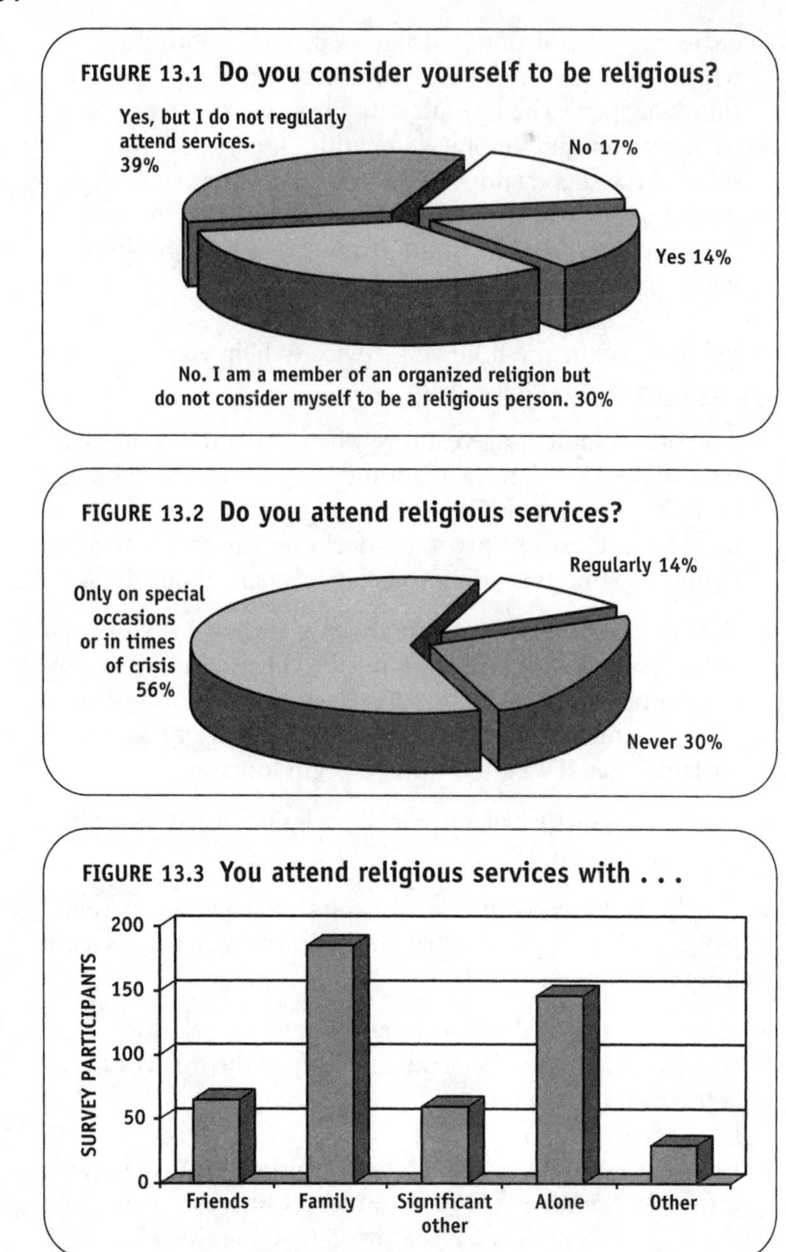
FIGURE 13.1 Do you consider yourself to be religious?
Yes, but I do not regularly attend services. 39%
No 17%
Yes 14%
No. I am a member of an organized religion but do not consider myself to be a religious person. 30%
FIGURE 13.2 Do you attend religious services?
Regularly 14%
Only on special occasions or in times of crisis 56%
Never 30%
FIGURE 13.3 You attend religious services with . . .
SURVEY PARTICIPANTS
200
150
100
50
0
Friends
Family
Significant other
Alone
Other

Resources

SUPPORT GROUPS

www.recovery-inc.com
www.ndmda.org

DRUG TRIALS

www.adaa.org
www.clinicaltrials.gov

DEPRESSION SCREENINGS

www.depression-screening.org
www.mentalhealthscreening.org
www.psychcentral.com

SPIRITUALITY

www.margaretfeinberg.com

CHAPTER 14

Conclusion

We hope that the advice and exercises presented to you in this workbook will provide you with an experienced perspective to help you survive stressful situations and make important decisions. Our intent is that this workbook will help you both on your own and in groups, but we think this book is just a start to the QLC solution.

We have begun and plan to continue providing much-needed support to our community of QLCers, both online and in person through workshops and seminars. Everything we do at www.quarterlifecrisis.com is based on your feedback, so we encourage you to visit the Web site and tell us exactly how we can help you.

It may also help to revisit the exercises a few years down the road when you are in another phase of the QLC to compare yourself to where you once were.

You will feel good about how much you have accomplished, and you will learn from your decisions and behavioral patterns.

People often ask, "What's next, the one-third life crisis?" It is our hope that the QLC, which is more significant than ever, will actually replace the midlife crisis for our generation. It is taking us much longer to begin to get all the things that our parents complained about at midlife—the responsibilities of the house, the cars, and the kids—that once we finally do achieve all that, we'll feel so relieved to be settled down that we won't want to change anything. We're not saying that everything will be fine and dandy once you figure out your role in society. Sure, you'll have your own set of problems then. However, we hope

CONTRACT WITH SELF

This exercise brings together all those aspects of our lives we've covered so far: careers, relationships, finances, and self.

We want this book to be a reference for you when you run into trouble. It can help to keep track of your progress every few months—review the things you've written down about yourself, your aspirations, and your values and make a note of how things have changed.

We recognize that each phase of life presents its own difficulties, and we are not in any way suggesting that simply completing our exercises will make your life free from any worries or complaints. But what our exercises can do is get you thinking about the areas of your life—or yourself—that you would like to improve.

Begin by checking off the chapters you've completed. Which ones represent areas of your life that need work? Prioritize the top three areas you'd like to work on this year, from most important to least important. For example, let's say that in this year you'd like to get a new job, get in shape, and meet new people. Check off those areas as needing more improvement and decide which you'd like to tackle first. Then fill in the contract to yourself that appears on the next page, and when you've got some time on your hands, don't forget to refer to the form!

that doing all of this exploration and experimentation now will avoid uncertainty about your choices later on. At the very least, we hope you pick up some coping mechanisms now for dealing with major life decisions and stressful situations in the future.

People also ask, "How do you know when your QLC is over?" And we simply reply with the truth, which is that the QLC is a unique experience for each individual. It can occur at any time between the ages of 21 and 35, and it can range from a few months to several years. Maybe you'll be done with the QLC when you can feel content staying at home alone on a Saturday night watching a video. Maybe you'll feel like an adult when you make a down payment on your first house. Maybe

I will complete all chapters and exercises by:__________(date).

I will focus on improving the following areas of my life that I feel need the most work:

1. ______________________________
2. ______________________________
3. ______________________________

I will make some attempt to improve at least these three areas of my life by:__________(date).

TOPIC	EXERCISES COMPLETED	I WOULD LIKE TO IMPROVE
Money	________	________
Insurance	________	________
Habitat	________	________
Time	________	________
Finding a job	________	________
Getting through nine-to-five	________	________
Moving on	________	________
Meeting new people	________	________
Maintaining friendships	________	________
Building relationships	________	________
Extracurricular activities	________	________
Health	________	________
Psyche	________	________

you'll go through more than one QLC. But mostly you know your QLC is over when you feel at peace with your decisions, learn to embrace life's overwhelming daily responsibilities, and don't feel the need to justify who you are or what you are doing with your life.

While we offer specific advice relevant to each life topic, there are some basic themes that apply to the twentysomething transition as a whole:

- Learn to accept and embrace change—whether you are jumping from job to job, relationship to relationship, or apartment to apartment, remember that this is the norm and think about how much you've learned from each experience rather than panicking about never settling down. It will happen, but if you try to get there without sampling various options, you will later regret that you did not explore more when you had the opportunity.
- Talk about your apprehensions and don't pretend that you have it all figured out. Remember that no one expects you to have all the answers without having any experience. Don't be afraid to ask for help or advice from your peers and mentors.
- Don't listen to anyone who tells you that your twenties should be completely easy and carefree. Yes, this is a time of freedom and independence, but it is also a time of constant change, confusion, and instability. If you don't deal with this transition properly, it can trigger feelings of anxiety and depression. And that has become an all-too-common reality. You're not a loser if you faced some challenges during the transition to adulthood—you're just like everyone else experiencing a QLC.

We would like to thank once again the experts who contributed their time and wisdom to our readers, and the QLCers who help us understand their needs by sharing their stories and experiences.

We look forward to hearing from you at www.quarterlifecrisis.com.

BIBLIOGRAPHY

We would like to give special thanks to all of the authors and experts who we have interviewed over the past few years for lending their sage advice to our twentysomething readers: Josh Aiello, Cathy Alter, Marty Bryant, Andrea G. Bonior, Ph.D., Harlan Cohen, Sean Covey, Madeline Dolente, Laurel Donnellan, Honore Ervin, Melissa Fireman, Donna Fisher, Tom Gardner, Paul Hettich, Jon Horowitz, Amy Joyce, John Lee, Alexandra Levit, Courtney Macavinta, Tom Morgano, Julie Murphree, Blake Newman, Susan Orenstein, Victoria Riccardi, Patricia Rose, Margarita Rozenfeld, Christina Saraceno, Stuart Schearer, Dave Singleton, Elizabeth DuPont Spencer, Brad Tuttle, Andrea Vander Pluym, Jason Wilmett, and the experts at Young money.com. We have included some of their publications below, along with resources we used or recommend for quarterlifers.

Aiello, Josh. *60 People to Avoid at the Water Cooler.* New York: Broadway, 2004.

Aiello, Josh, and Matthew Shultz. *A Field Guide to the Urban Hipster.* New York: Broadway, 2003.

Alter, Cathy. *Virgin Territory: Stories from the Road to Womanhood.* New York: Three Rivers Press, 2004.

Arnett, Jeffrey J. "Learning to Stand Alone: The Contemporary American Transition to Adulthood in Cultural and Historical Context." *Human Development* 41 (1998): 295–315.

Bach, David. *Smart Women Finish Rich.* New York: Broadway, 1998.

Baxter Magolda, Marcia B. "Helping Students Make Their Way to Adulthood: Good Company for the Journey." *About Campus* (January–February 2002): 2–9.

Bittman, Mark. *How to Cook Everything: Simple Recipes for Great Food.* New York: Wiley, 1998.

Bolles, Richard Nelson, and Mark Emery Bolles. *What Color Is Your Parachute? 2005: A Practical Manual for Job-Hunters and Career-Changers.* Berkeley, CA: Ten Speed Press, 2004.

Bridges, William. *Transitions: Making Sense of Life's Changes.* New York: Perseus Books Group, 1980.

Brothers, Dr. Joyce. *What Every Woman Ought to Know about Love and Marriage.* New York: Ballantine, 1985.

Bryant, Adam. "Graduation Day? Never!" review of *Most Likely to Succeed at Work* by Wilma Davidson and Jack Dougherty. *Newsweek* (November 17, 2003).

Bureau of Labor Statistics, U.S. Department of Labor. National Longitudinal Survey of Youth 1979 cohort, 1979–2000 (rounds 1–19) [computer file]. Produced and distributed by the Center for Human Resource Research, The Ohio State University, Columbus, OH, 2002.

Chicago National Opinion Research Center. "Coming of Age in 21st-Century America: Public Attitudes Towards the Importance and Timing of Transition to Adulthood." 2003.

Cohen, Harlan. *The Naked Roommate: And 107 Other Issues You Might Run Into in College.* Naperville: Sourcebooks, 2005.

Cohn, Sheila R.D. "Want to Watch Calories When Dining Out? Tips for Eating Smart." Restaurant.org, 2005.

Conlin, Michelle. "Middle Class and Maxed Out." *Business Week* (September 15, 2003).

Coplin, Bill. "Lost in the Life of the Mind." *Chronicle of Higher Education* 51 (2) (September 3, 2004): B5.

Coplin, William D., and Bill Coplin. *10 Things Employers Want You to Learn in College: The Know-How You Need to Succeed.* Berkeley, CA: Ten Speed Press, 2003.

Covey, Sean. *Fourth Down and Life to Go: How to Turn Life's Setbacks into Triumphs.* New York: Barnes & Noble Books, 1990.

Covey, Stephen R. *The 7 Habits of Highly Effective People.* New York: Fireside, 1989.

Crenshaw, Albert B. "Cash Flow—New Graduates Need to Get Health Insurance." *Washington Post* (May 12, 2002): H4.

Donnellan, Laurel. *Passion into Practice: The Path to Remarkable Work.* Brooklyn, NY: Lulu Press, 2004.

DuPont, Robert L., Elizabeth DuPont Spencer, Caroline M. DuPont. *The Anxiety Cure: An Eight-Step Program for Getting Well.* New York: Wiley, 1998.

Erikson, Erik H. *Childhood and Society*. New York: W.W. Norton & Company, 1993.

Etiquette Grrls (The), Leslie Carlin and Honore McDonough Ervin. *Things You Need to Be Told*. New York: Berkley Publishing Group, 2001.

———. *More Things You Need to Be Told: A Guide to Good Taste and Proper Comportment in a Tacky, Rude World*. New York: Berkley Publishing Group, 2003.

Feinberg, Margaret. *Twentysomething: Surviving and Thriving in the Real World*. Nashville, TN: W Publishing Group, 2004.

Furman, Elina. *Boomerang Nation: How to Survive Living with Your Parents . . . the Second Time Around*. New York: Fireside, 2005.

Furstenberg, Jr., Frank F., et al. "Between Adolescence and Adulthood: Expectations about the Timing of Adulthood." Network on Transitions to Adulthood and Public Policy Research Network Working Paper No. 1 (July 29, 2003): 4.

Gardner, David, and Tom Gardner. *The Motley Fool Investment Guide: How the Fool Beats Wall Street's Wise Men and How You Can Too*. New York: Simon and Schuster, 1996.

———. *The Motley Fool's You Have More Than You Think: The Foolish Guide to Personal Finance*. New York: Fireside, 1998.

Gordon, Linda Perlman, and Susan Morris Shaffer. *Mom, Can I Move Back In with You?: A Survival Guide for Parents of Twenty-somethings*. New York: Jeremy P. Tarcher, 2004.

Greider, Linda. "Hard Times Drive Adult Kids Home." *The Nation* (December 2001): 3.

Hettich, Paul I., and Camille Helkowski. *Connect College to Career*. Belmont, CA: Thompson-Wadsworth, 2005.

Hirschfield, et al. The National Depressive and Manic-Depressive Association Consensus Statement on the Undertreatment of Depression. *JAMA* 277(4) (January 22–29, 1997): 333–340.

Jayson, Sharon. "It's Time to Grow Up—Later: The Gap between Adolescence and Adulthood Gets Longer." *USA Today* (September 30, 2004): D1.

Joyce, Amy. *I Went to College for This? How to Turn Your Entry-Level Job into a Career You Love*. New York: McGraw-Hill, 2002.

———. "Coping When Illness Isn't Obvious: For Depressed Employees, Good Insurance and an Understanding Boss Are Vital." *Washington Post* (July 21, 2002): H6.

Kessler, Ronald, et al. "Sex and Depression in the National Comorbidity Survey I: Lifetime Prevalence, Chronicity and Recurrence." *Journal of Affective Disorders* 29 (1993): 85–96.

Kim, Jane J. "More College Graduates Postpone Their 'Dream Jobs' to Pay Loans." *Wall Street Journal Online* (September 2, 2003).

Kiyosaki, Robert T., and Sharon L. Lechter. *Rich Dad, Poor Dad.* New York: Warner Business Books, 2000.

Lagnado, Lucette. "Full Price: A Young Woman, an Appendectomy, and a $19,000 Debt—Ms. Nix Confronts Harsh Fact of Health-Care Economics: Uninsured Are Billed More—Moving In with Mom at Age 25." *The Wall Street Journal* (March 17, 2003): A1.

Landrum, R. Eric, and Renee Harrold. "What Employers Want from Psychology Graduates." *Teaching of Psychology* 30(2), 2003.

Levit, Alexandra. *They Don't Teach Corporate in College: A Twenty-Something's Guide to the Business World.* Franklin Lakes, NJ: Career Press, 2004.

Lynn, Matthew. "The Quarter-Life Crisis Strikes in the UK, US." www.Bloomberg.com, July 5, 2004.

Macavinta, Courtney, et al. *Respect: A Girl's Guide to Getting Respect & Dealing When Your Line Is Crossed.* Minneapolis, MN: Free Spirit Publishing, 2005.

Mann, Lisa Barrett. "Grads, Playing without a Net." *Washington Post* (April 27, 2004): HE01.

Mott, Gregory. "Elusive Adulthood." *Washington Post* (August 3, 2004): F3.

Post, Peggy, and Peter Post. *The Etiquette Advantage in Business.* New York: HarperResource, 1999.

Ray, Rachel. *30-Minute Meals.* New York: Lake Isle Press, 1999.

Robbins, Alexandra, and Abby Wilner. *Quarterlife Crisis: The Unique Challenges of Life in Your Twenties.* New York: Penguin Putnam, 2001.

Rombauer, Irma S., and Marion Rombauer Becker. *Joy of Cooking.* New York: Scribner, 1985.

Rubenstein, Carin. "What Turns You On?" *My Generation* (July–August 2002): 55–58.

Sahadi, Jeanne. "Job Outlook Brightens for Class of '04." www.cnn-money.com, May 6, 2004.

Sher, Barbara. *I Could Do Anything, If I Only I Knew What It Was: How to Discover What You Really Want and How to Get It.* New York: Dell, 1995.

Singleton, Dave. *The Mandates: 25 Real Rules for Successful Gay Dating*. New York: Three Rivers Press, 2004.

"Social Mobility: What's It Worth?" *The Economist* (January 15, 2004).

Stevens, Laura. "A Promising Outlook for Graduating Seniors." www.collegejournal.com, October 2004.

Tannenhauser, Carol. "Why Won't Kids Grow Up?" *MORE* (July–August 2000).

"Tenants' Privacy Rights FAQ and Landlord-Tenant Dispute Resolution." www.Nolo.com.

U.S. Department of Education, National Center for Education Statistics, Baccalaureate and Beyond: 1997–2000 (B&B:97-00), Data Analysis System, Washington, DC, 2001.

Weiss, Julie. "Bringing Up Adultolescents." *Newsweek* (March 25, 2002): 38–40.

Winter, Greg. "College Loans Rise, Swamping Dreams." *New York Times* (January 28, 2003).

Winters, Rebecca. "Relationships 101: Is a Classroom the Place to Learn about Love? Some College and High School Students Are Finding Out." *Time* (November 24, 2003).

INDEX

ABOUT THE AUTHORS

Abby Wilner has appeared on *Today*, *The Oprah Winfrey Show*, and on MSNBC and CNN. A higher education consultant with JBL Associates, Wilner also lectures and runs the Web site www.quarterlifecrisis.com.

Catherine Stocker is the director of marketing and business development for quarterlifecrisis.com. Stocker is a former marketing and management consultant who now runs Quarterlife Crisis seminars and workshops.